EXPLORING
WORSHIP

A Practical Guide to
Praise and Worship

EXPLORING
WORSHIP

A Practical Guide to Praise and Worship

by
Bob Sorge

Trinity Media Press
Buffalo, New York
Son-Rise Publications and Distribution Co.
New Wilmington, PA 16142

Exploring Worship: A Practical Guide to Praise and Worship
Copyright © 1987 by Bob Sorge.
All rights reserved.
Printed in the United States of America.
Library of Congress Catalog Card Number: 86-063973
International Standard Book Number: 0-936369-04-3
Co-published by Trinity Media Press
 Buffalo, New York 14209

SON-RISE
Publications & Distribution Co.
Rte. 3, P.O. Box 202   New Wilmington, PA 16142

DEDICATION

To Patrick Prior, my cherished friend, who has continually encouraged and supported me in the ministry of worship.

CONTENTS

Section Two: The Leading of Praise and Worship

FOREWORD

In the choosings of God I have been a pioneer for my generation in the field of praise and worship and have ministered on this theme in conferences and conventions throughout the world. I am thrilled to see younger men catching this vision and picking up the mantle to be proclaimers of this glorious truth to the generation that is coming behind me.

Bob Sorge is one such man. He has served as the music director for a major Bible college and as assistant to a pastor who emphasizes expressive worship, and he is now a pastor in his own right. He is an accomplished musician and a dedicated worshiper who has combined his talents in writing *Exploring Worship*.

This book is enjoyable and is full of quality material. How I wish I could have had this book available to me many years ago when I began to teach this theme.

If followed, the principles expounded here will keep a congregation from extremes, and the practical teachings will keep that congregation fresh and progressive in its worship. I am totally unaware of a more comprehensive treatment of this subject in any book, including those of mine. It should be read by all who want to participate in congregational worship, and it should be required study for all who aspire to lead congregational worship.

Judson Cornwall, Th.D.

Phoenix, AZ
November 1986

PREFACE

As I contemplated writing this book, I asked myself why another book on worship needed to be written. After all, many good books certainly are available today that cover a wide range of interests in praise and worship, including the function and administration of music in the church. Actually, more reading is available on the practical, administrative applications of church music than is available on devotional aspects of praise and worship.

Direction for this book began to emerge as I looked at the emphases of the books already in circulation. I realized that with very few exceptions, almost every work that addresses the subjects of music, praise, and worship tends toward one of two poles: either it focuses on the practical administration of music in the local church, or it highlights devotional and inspirational aspects of praise and worship. The practical books tend to be music-oriented, with little devotional emphasis on praise and worship; the inspirational books tend to be praise and worship-oriented, with little practical application of how to implement musically the concepts discussed.

Most devotional books on praise and worship are written by pastors, teachers, or church leaders who are not music ministers, and consequently they leave the practical implementation of their ideas to church musicians. Most practical books on church music, on the other hand, are written by music ministers or people involved in music leadership, but these do not always reflect the devotional concerns of a pastor or teacher. Given my experience as both a pastor and music minister, I began to be challenged with the prospect of combining both flavors into one work.

I also noticed that much of what is written about worship is directed toward liturgical contexts, or what has been termed the "mainline" denominations. The Baptists, for instance, have produced a wealth of material in the area of church music administration. But comparatively little has been written to address specifically the pentecostal and charismatic traditions. And for those of us who confess a fuller experience in the Holy Spirit (the baptism in the Holy Spirit, together with the "charismata" of the Spirit), worship plays a more visible and vital role in our corporate church life. In an era when pentecostalism is spreading around the globe more quickly than any other church emphasis, we need more than ever a solid theology of worship in the pentecostal and charismatic traditions.

The church has fallen prey to sincere folks who have placed too strong an emphasis on the practical functions of music in the church but who have not learned sensitivity to the Holy Spirit by spending time at the feet of Jesus. Many church leaders, on the other hand, struggle with the problem of having a vision and heart for praise and worship but finding themselves stymied by an inability to lead God's people through the medium of music. Our churches desperately need musically proficient people whose hearts are ablaze with a godly anointing. This present work, therefore, is an attempt to blend the devotional and practical aspects of praise and worship into a cohesive whole. It will explore the many facets of praise, progress to a careful study of worship and what becoming a worshiper means, and then conclude with a practical section which will provide suggestions on how to lead people effectively into new releases in praise and worship.

The title, *Exploring Worship,* carries the flavor of my own personal pilgrimage in worship, with the obvious implication that this book is not the final statement on worship. These chapters are not sealed but should serve as catalysts for further insight and exploration. Make this the beginning of your own notebook. Since God is infinite, so too are the depth and meaning of worship. This book does not pretend to provide simple answers to the many complex problems that church leaders face in their worship services. In fact, some of the ideas put forth here will not be readily welcomed because they will demand more commitment and energy than some may be willing to give. But many practical issues will be discussed, and I trust that sincere questions will find possible answers within these pages.

I have been somewhat hesitant to publish a book on worship because I have come to understand that the more I learn about worship, the more there seems to remain undiscovered. It is so easy for us to think we are beginning to get a "handle" on worship, and we thereby confine the Holy Spirit to our own conceptions of worship. It is this very pitfall that has brought widespread stagnation in the worship styles of many in the body of Christ. So this volume is written in the humble hope that it will be an innovative and provocative source of blessing for many, as we continually face the challenges and joys of *Exploring Worship.*

Bob Sorge
Zion Fellowship
236 Gorham Street
Canandaigua, NY 14424

ACKNOWLEDGEMENTS

Warm thanks must be extended to those who through their assistance have helped make this book possible. I thank Graham and Pamela Truscott for their graciousness in encouraging me in my first attempts at writing.

I owe much to Cheryl Tipon and my brother, Sheldon, for their editorial help.

This book would not exist without the support of Bill Hein, whose willing contribution and professional counsel have blessed me exceedingly.

A big thanks to Louise Genetti for the cover photographs, as well as to Michael Jahn for the front cover layout. And I thank the worship team of New Covenant Tabernacle, Tonawanda, New York, for posing for the photos.

Finally, I thank my wife, Marci, for her patience and support throughout the long months of writing.

CHAPTER 1

WHAT IS PRAISE?

It is not uncommon to hear references to "praise and worship" as though they were identical entities, or at least combined to form one complete whole. Praise and worship are mutually cooperative activities and are frequently very similar in the way they are outwardly expressed, but they are not one and the same. Each has its own nature and purpose. Some churches are very vocal in their praise but quite withdrawn when it comes to worship. And for others, it seems relatively easy to enter into a sweetness in worship, but they have not yet learned the dynamics of praise. Balancing the two is easier once we recognize the distinctives and functions of both praise and worship.

THE ESSENCE OF PRAISE

Praise is not a difficult concept to understand, for it is part of our everyday lives. We "praise" our children when they please us; we "praise" employees for a job well done; we "praise" dogs when they perform tricks nicely. But above and beyond all that, praise is something we direct toward God or something we express to others about God. Some of the definitions given for "praise" in the dictionary highlight its simplicity: "to commend; to applaud; to express approval or admiration of; to extol in words or in song; to magnify; to glorify." Notice the bi-directional focus of praise inherent in these definitions: we praise God directly by extolling him or expressing our admiration to him; we praise God indirectly by commending him or magnifying him to others. Praise can be given directly to God, or it can

1

be expressed to others in reference to God.

Praise is preoccupied with who God is and what he has done. It focuses on both his incomparable character and his wondrous acts on behalf of his children. When God does something glorious for us, we love to lift high his praises. And yet praise is not simply our thankful response to his provision; praise is also very fitting even when we have no specific gift of God in mind. He is worthy to be praised solely for who he is.

One distinctive of praise concerns its extroverted nature. It is characterized by celebration and exhilaration and is expressed through singing, shouting, speaking forth, playing of musical instruments, dancing, and other external forms. In a most fundamental sense, praise could be defined as "raising much to-do about God." A study of the Old Testament, especially the Psalms, clearly reveals that the Hebrew people were very emotional and vocal in their expressions of praise and adoration before their God. May it not be testified of us that we were too modern or too sophisticated to rival their enthusiasm about God. We have a gloriously dynamic God, and he deserves our energetic acclamation!

He who has merely contemplated the wonders of God has not yet entered into praise. Meditation is not praise. Praise begins with a mind set upon God, but then those thoughts must be put into action in order to qualify as praise. We have some dear folks in our churches who cross their arms, lower their heads, purse their lips, and say, "This is just my way of praising the Lord." Wrong! First of all, there is no such thing as "my way" of praising the Lord; there is only "God's way," and his way has been shown to us clearly in the Scriptures. And second, the Bible shows us that praise is to be *declared* or *manifested*. Psalm 66:8 exhorts, "Let the sound of his praise be *heard.*" Praise is not praise until it is vocalized or shown forth. In other words, it is impossible to praise with the mouth shut, and the body slumped forward! In that posture we might be worshiping, or meditating, or praying, or sleeping, but we are not praising! The prophet cried, "Lift up thy voice with strength; lift it up, be not afraid!" (Isaiah 40:9, KJV). There are both vocal and non-vocal forms of praise, but whatever the form, praise is demonstrated — others are aware that praise is taking place!

Some saints are afraid to lift their voices in the congregation for fear that someone might hear them, or for fear that they might be recognized as poor singers. But God's praises are not restricted to those with fine voices! If one is not capable of singing, God's praises should be spoken. If someone cannot speak (that is, if someone is mute), God's praises can be shown forth in the countenance and bodily expression.

It is worth repeating that we do not praise God in our own way. Some churches take pride in providing a free context where people can praise the way they want to. That is fine and good, but Christians need to do more than simply praise according to their own feelings and desires. We will never grow and mature in our expressions of praise until we are willing to praise in a manner pleasing to the Lord — the way *he* wants us to praise. The Scriptures clearly enumerate for us the various ways God expects us to praise. The biblical forms of praise comprise for us the spectrum of possible ways to praise the Lord, but God does not want us to clone his praises by legalistically conforming to his demands. Rather, he wants us to praise him' authentically and genuinely, incorporating the scriptural forms of praise as a willing sacrifice. Therefore, if lifting the hands is not "my way of praising God," then we need to make it our way of praising! We need to do it until it becomes a natural and genuine part of our expression to God.

Many times praise is a function of the will. We must will and determine to praise the Lord, even when we do not feel like it. Praise is not contingent upon our feelings — it is based upon God's greatness, and that never changes! Notice how David spoke to his own soul: "Praise the LORD,

O my soul; all my inmost being, praise his holy name"
(Psalm 103:1). Sometimes we are "down in the dumps" or
dry spiritually, and it is at those times that we must serve
notice to our soul and say, "Soul! Bless the Lord!" Praise
must function according to our will and not our emotions.

"But how can I praise," you may ask, "when I feel completely deflated emotionally?" We can find an answer in the
Psalms, for they were written by men who, like us, experienced deep emotional valleys. One psalmist described his
feelings in this way: "My soul is downcast within me." So
he asked himself, "Why are you downcast, O my soul? Why
so disturbed within me?" Then he proceeded to get tough
on himself: "Put your hope in God." His next statement so
beautifully shows the discipline of praise: *"For I will yet
praise him"* (Psalm 42:5-6). The Lord wants all of us to
come to that same point where we determine to praise him
regardless of our feelings and circumstances. "I *will* bless
the Lord."

When we are truly impacted with the greatness of God,
praise comes easily. One delightful way to concentrate on
the character of God is by studying the names of God. Old
Testament praise occupied itself with the name of God. "I
will praise your name, O LORD, for it is good" (Psalm 54:6).
"Glorify the LORD with me; let us exalt his name together"
(Psalm 34:3). The Hebrews praised God's name because
for them a person's name was indicative of his character. I
once heard Dr. Judson Cornwall say that the Hebrews
would even wait a few years to name their children so they
could choose names in keeping with the children's personalities. God liked that custom and decided to reveal his
character to the Israelites by giving them a variety of
names for himself.

This is what happened in Exodus 15:26, when the Lord
said, in essence, "You can call me 'Jehovah-Raphah,' because I am the Lord who heals you!" In Genesis 22, God
revealed himself as "Jehovah-Jireh" when he wanted to
show that he would provide for his people. In the last verse

of the book of Ezekiel, God gave his name as "Jehovah-Shammah," which means "The Lord is there" (Ezekiel 48:35). God was revealing his omnipresence — he will never leave us or forsake us! It is appropriate, therefore, for praise to focus on all that is represented by the various names of God given in Scripture.

JUDAH AND PRAISE

In keeping with the Hebrew tradition of naming children according to their character, Leah gave the name "Judah" to the fourth son she bore Jacob. Her reason for calling him "Judah" (literally translated "praise") is given in Genesis 29:35: " 'This time I will praise the LORD.' " Leah, whose husband did not love her as he loved Rachel, praised the Lord on this occasion because he had given her a fourth son. So this son was known as "praise." And God took a liking to the name! In fact, he decided to show special favor to Judah, for it was from the tribe of Judah that the Messiah was born. The Scriptures allude to the tribe of Judah more than to any other of the twelve tribes, and one reason was because this tribe was known as the "praisers."

Since Judah means praise, there are many valuable lessons we can learn about praise by studying the occurrences of the word "Judah" in numerous passages. Let us look at just a few.

"Judah became God's sanctuary, Israel his dominion" (Psalm 114:2). God makes his sanctuary among the praisers! Notice the distinction made between Israel and Judah. All of Israel is God's domain, but he sets up his sanctuary in Judah — in the company of praisers!

"In Judah God is known; his name is great in Israel" (Psalm 76:1). This verse also distinguishes between Judah and Israel, Israel being typical of all the church, and Judah, of the praisers. God is great in his church today, but he is known in a special way by those living a life of praise.

". . . who says of Jerusalem, 'It shall be inhabited,' of

the towns of Judah, 'They shall be built' " (Isaiah 44:26).
". . . all the ravines of Judah will run with water" (Joel
3:18). "The LORD will inherit Judah as his portion in the
holy land and will again choose Jerusalem" (Zechariah
2:12). These and many other verses refer to the restoration
that God intends specifically for those who praise him. God
is restoring praise today as never before! God has purposed
to raise up a praising church in these last days, and nothing
will hinder him!

"Judah is my scepter" (Psalm 108:8). Reworded, this
could read, "Praise is God's scepter." That statement
becomes very meaningful when applied to the story of
Queen Esther. Because of Esther's beauty, Xerxes held out
his golden scepter to her to show her he loved and accepted
her and was inviting her into his chamber *(see* Esther 2:17;
5:2). To personalize the application, when God sees us in
the beauty of his praises he raises his scepter to us and bids
us come into his chamber.

The fifth chapter of 2 Samuel gives the story of how
David ruled over the tribe of Judah for seven years before
he was given the monarchy over all the tribes of Israel.
David had been called by God to be king over all Israel; he
had been anointed to that position by Samuel, and Judah
was the first of the tribes to officially recognize David as
their God-appointed king. It took the other tribes seven
years eventually to make David their king. The same thing
can be seen in today's praisers. The praisers are still the
ones who will most readily accept the new things that God
is doing and will embrace them with their lives. We should
be challenged to become the praisers God would have us be
so that we might be ready to flow with him in these days of
visitation.

WHY SHOULD WE PRAISE THE LORD?

First of all, we praise him because we are commanded in
his word to do so. "Praise *ye* the LORD" (Psalm 150:1,

KJV). Have you noticed that God has not *asked* us to praise him? That is because kings do not ask — they command! "Why does God demand our praise?" you may ask. "Is he some sort of egomaniac who feeds off our adulation?" No, it is not that God needs our praises, but he knows that we need to praise him! Ultimately, praise does not benefit God (he is God, whether we choose to praise him or not) — God has commanded praise for our own good. Not until we praise him are we able to come into proper relationship with him. Without a thankful and praising heart, we will never grow in the grace of Christ Jesus.

A second reason for praising is because God is enthroned in our praise *(see* Psalm 22:3, NASB). He loves our praise! He is so pleased with our praise that he literally surrounds himself with and bathes in our praise. We praise him because he loves it!

In this connection I want to focus on a verse that is foundational to much that will be said later in this book. Isaiah 60:18 contains a key that will unlock many passages for us as we study this subject of praise. This verse says, "But you will call your walls Salvation and your gates Praise." The key is this: in many passages that speak of *gates* we will find a principle relating to *praise.* Let us fit this key into a related verse: "The LORD loves the gates of Zion more than all the dwellings of Jacob" (Psalm 87:2). The Lord loves the praises (gates) of Zion more than he loves all the abodes of Jacob. There is no doubt that God responds to us when we praise him!

Third, there is power in praise. When we stop trying to fight our battles and simply begin to praise the God who has said he will fight for us, God is free to release his power and provision on our behalf. We will expand this thought in the section on praise as a weapon in spiritual warfare and will see how praise brings victory, power, deliverance and blessing.

We also praise God because it is a good thing to praise the Lord *(see* Psalm 92:1). It is a pleasant thing for the upright to praise him *(see* Psalm 135:3). It is fitting for his holy ones to bless him.

A fifth reason for praising God is simply because he is worthy of our praise. "Great is the LORD, and most worthy of praise" (Psalm 48:1). "Thou art worthy, O Lord, to receive glory and honour and power: for thou hast created all things, and for thy pleasure they are and were created" (Revelation 4:11, KJV). Consider these beautiful words of Martin Luther: "A person cannot praise God only, unless he understands that there is nothing in himself worthy of praise, but that all that is worthy of praise is of God and from God. But since God is eternally praiseworthy, because he is the infinite Good and can never be exhausted, therefore they will praise him for ever and ever."

Sixth, we were created to praise him. The Shorter Catechism expresses this as "Man's chief end is to glorify God, and to enjoy him forever." This is clearly brought out in the Scriptures. Jeremiah 13:11 shows us that God called the house of Israel unto himself specifically for his praise, renown, and honor. This is echoed in 1 Peter 2:9, which tells us, "But you are a chosen people, a royal priesthood, a holy nation, a people belonging to God, that you may declare the praises of him who called you out of darkness into his wonderful light." We have been chosen of God for the express purpose of declaring his praises! Isaiah capsulized this so beautifully: " 'The people I formed for myself that they may proclaim my praise' " (Isaiah 43:21).

Many people in the world today are longing for fulfillment and are searching desperately for it in all the wrong places. They will never find complete fulfillment in their innermost beings until they come into proper relationship with God through praise. A.W. Tozer has so aptly said, "The purpose of God in sending his Son to die and live and be at the right hand of God the Father was that he might restore to us the missing jewel, the jewel of worship; that we might come back and learn to do again that which we were created to do in the first place — worship the Lord in the beauty of holiness." Praise should not be a difficult and arduous task to master, but it should flow from our lives in a most natural way, for it is in fact a normal tendency inherent within our very fiber, placed there purposely by our Creator/Father. Praise is one of the most natural things we can do!

WHEN SHOULD WE PRAISE?

We praise, first of all, when we feel like it. "Is anyone happy? Let him sing songs of praise" (James 5:13).

We also praise when we do not feel like it *(see* Psalm 42:5). Sometimes people accuse us, "Your praise is simply emotionalism!" But emotionalism is following the dictates of one's emotions. Praise is a discipline that requires our initiative regardless of our emotions. Emotionalism surfaces when we enter into praise only when we feel like it and refrain when we do not feel like praising. To refrain from praising when we do not "feel up to it" is true emotionalism: allowing our emotions to dictate our level of praise. True praise is the antithesis of emotionalism; we praise God enthusiastically whether we feel like it, or whether we don't!

Please note, though, that while praise is not *emotionalism,* it is *emotional.* It is most fitting to praise the Lord in an emotional manner. God created our emotions, and praise is the noblest way to release our emotions. In her Magnificat, Mary said, " 'My soul glorifies the LORD and my spirit rejoices in God my Savior' " (Luke 1:46-47). Both "soulish" and "spiritual" praise are proper. In fact, we often exercise our soul and spirit simultaneously when we praise the Lord.

As a third consideration, a good time to praise the Lord is *now.* Sometimes we tend to rationalize our lack of praise in this way: "Lord, you know that I really praised you with all my heart last Sunday. I really let it all hang out last week! And I know you understand, Lord, that I am tired today. Truly my spirit is willing, but my flesh is weak. Since

I praised you so wholeheartedly last Sunday, I know you won't mind, Lord, if I relax a bit today and take it easy." Now who among us has never convinced himself that he has earned a day off from praise? We all have! And yet we find that the Bible makes no provision for us to perform a week's worth of praise in one day. The human body has no way to store up vitamin C — it either burns it up or discards it. Similarly, we cannot store up praise. *Now* is the time to praise the Lord.

The writer of Psalm 42 found himself in the "last Sunday" syndrome: "These things I remember . . . how I used to go with the multitude, leading the procession to the house of God, with shouts of joy and thanksgiving among the festive throng. Why are you downcast, O my soul?" (Psalm 42:4-5). In essence he was saying, "Last Sunday I was in the thick of the praise, singing and shouting the most loudly, playing the tambourine, and leading God's people in praises. It was a glorious worship service last week, Lord! But this week . . . what's wrong with this week? Why am I so grumpy and out of sorts?" Has it ever been your experience that when coming off one of those mountain experiences in God, you encounter a deep emotional valley? If so, that is not the time to rely on past experience and think, "I paid my dues last week." That is the time to say along with the psalmist, "I will yet praise him."

In this same psalm, the writer cried, "My soul thirsts for God, for the living God. When can I go and meet with God?" (Psalm 42:2). Have you ever called on God, trying to praise him, and yet feel like he is 500 miles away? I heard one brother refer to this as "the omnihiddence of God." Although God is omnipresent (everywhere, at all times), he is also "omnihidden." God can choose to hide himself from man, or he can choose to show himself to man. Psalm 19 says, "The heavens declare the glory of God," and yet how many people look at the heavens without ever seeing the glory of God! That is because God remains hidden from natural man and reveals himself to whom he wills. Sometimes God seems to be far removed from us, but even in those times when we feel completely estranged from his presence, it is still fitting to praise the Lord.

Fourth, the Scriptures speak of rising up early to bless the Lord. "Awake, my soul! Awake, harp and lyre! I will awaken the dawn" (Psalm 57:8). The Bible also speaks of praising the Lord late at night: "At midnight I rise to give you thanks for your righteous laws" (Psalm 119:62). The Levites in the time of David ministered before the Lord twenty-four hours a day. These musicians "were responsible for the work day and night" (1 Chronicles 9:33). Imagine being on the midnight shift with the duty of offering up continual praise before the Lord! Those men certainly knew what it meant to praise the Lord without any goosebumps! The Lord has called us, as a New Testament priesthood, to *"continually* offer to God a sacrifice of praise" (Hebrews 13:15), which is made feasible through the fullness of the Holy Spirit.

The point is this: we are to praise the Lord at all times. "I will bless the LORD at all times: his praise shall continually be in my mouth" (Psalm 34:1, KJV). No matter what time of day it is, and regardless of where we find ourselves, it is always fitting to bless the Lord.

But is it appropriate to praise the Lord in the hard times, when everything is going wrong? The answer resounds from the hills: *Yes!* The Old Testament prophet Habakkuk gave his remedy for times when everything is going wrong:

> Though the fig tree does not bud
> and there are no grapes on the vines,
> though the olive crop fails
> and the fields produce no food,
> though there are no sheep in the pen
> and no cattle in the stalls,
> yet I will rejoice in the LORD,
> I will be joyful in God my Savior
>   (Habakkuk 3:17-18).

A modern rendition of this passage might read like this:

Though the economy is unstable,
    and unemployment is rising,
though Communism may be growing,
    and terrorism is rampant,
though the car is broken down and my wife is
    stranded downtown,
though my kid just broke his arm and the medical
    insurance ran out,
yet I will rejoice in the Lord,
    I will be joyful in God my Savior!

It is not hypocritical to praise the Lord in hard times; that is precisely the time we need to lift our voices in praise to God! It is God's will that we offer up thanks in every situation in which we find ourselves.

WHERE SHOULD WE PRAISE?

If we are to praise the Lord at all times, it follows that we should praise the Lord everywhere. One verse even speaks of praising the Lord while we're at home in bed *(see* Psalm 149:5)!

Psalm 113:3 declares, "From the rising of the sun to the place where it sets the name of the LORD is to be praised." At first glance this would appear to mean that from dawn until dusk the Lord is to be praised. That is an appropriate application of that text, but there is still another way of interpreting that verse. Since the sun rises in the east and sets in the west, this verse declares that from the east to the west, across the entire horizon, the name of the Lord is to be praised. If we could ever travel far enough to pass beyond the east or the west, we would then be in a land where we need not praise the Lord.

The Scriptures make it clear that there are some specific places where praising the Lord is particularly appropriate. It seems that God places primary importance on praise in the congregation of the saints. He seems to derive particular pleasure from our congregated praises. Many verses in the Psalms readily bear this out:

> I will declare your name to my brothers; in the congregation I will praise you. From you comes my praise in the great assembly; before those who fear you will I fulfill my vows (Psalm 22:22,25).

> I love the house where you live, O LORD, the place where your glory dwells. My feet stand on level ground; in the great assembly I will praise the LORD (Psalm 26:8,12).

> One thing I ask of the LORD, this is what I seek: that I may dwell in the house of the LORD all the days of my life, to gaze upon the beauty of the LORD and to seek him in his temple (Psalm 27:4).

> I will give you thanks in the great assembly; among throngs of people I will praise you (Psalm 35:18).

> Your procession has come into view, O God, the procession of my God and King into the sanctuary. In front are the singers, after them the musicians; with them are the maidens playing tambourines. Praise God in the great congregation; praise the LORD in the assembly of Israel (Psalm 68:24-26).

> Zeal for your house consumes me (Psalm 69:9).

> Let them exalt him in the assembly of the people and praise him in the council of the elders (Psalm 107:32).

> I rejoiced with those who said to me, "Let us go to the house of the LORD" (Psalm 122:1).

Many benefits result when we praise God in the great congregation, and these will be discussed later. But surely the Lord is pleased with the unity and variety characteristic of congregational worship. A special sort of unity comes when God's people lift their voices with the same melody and words at the same time in praise to God. And yet there is room for much diversity of expression in our congregational praise and worship. Some would suggest that we should all stand together, sit together, raise our hands together, clap together, speak together, and sing together, all the time. Occasionally that may be appropriate, but the Spirit of God will inspire that unity — we do not have to demand it. Frequently it is very fitting for a wide variety of praise and worship expressions to be ascending simultaneously.

The incense used in the holy of holies of Moses' tabernacle was compounded from several different fragrances in order to produce what God desired. Symbolically, this shows us that the variety of praise in a congregation is very pleasing to him. Some may be standing; others may be kneeling; some may have their hands raised; others may be dancing. This is not disorder — this is orderly variety.

Some people fail to distinguish between *unity* in the body of Christ and *uniformity* to one set standard. We have been created as individuals with unique personalities, and the Lord is pleased when each of us expresses our heart to him in a way that is consistent with our personality. The Lord is not pleased with uniformity, because that can be achieved only through social control and manipulation. He is pleased with the unity that comes in the Spirit, when all are joined to one Lord in adoration and love. So let us lift up our voices together with the saints in the congregation — not neglecting the assembly of the saints — and with one accord magnify and exalt his name together!

A second place where it is especially fitting to sing God's praises is before all men and nations. "Declare his glory among the nations, his marvelous deeds among all peoples" (Psalm 96:3). "He put a new song in my mouth, a hymn of praise to our God. Many will see and fear and put their trust in the LORD" (Psalm 40:3). From these and other verses it becomes clear that God's praise has never been intended exclusively for the ears of saints. God has always purposed that his praise be declared before unbelievers, before the world, in order that they might hear of the mighty works of God and observe his glorious praises being sung. We have just read what will happen when sinners are confronted with God's praises: they will see and fear, and will put their trust in the Lord!

HOW SHOULD WE PRAISE THE LORD?

As we said earlier, we do not praise the Lord our way; we praise him his way. And his way has been expounded throughout the Scriptures for our benefit. Let us look at the Bible to determine just how God wants us to praise him.

The *lifting of our hands* is a common form of praise found in numerous Scriptures *(see* Nehemiah 8:6; Psalms 28:2; 63:4; 134:2; 141:2; 1 Timothy 2:8; et al.). Have you ever wondered just why the Bible tells us to lift our hands unto the Lord? Following are some of the foremost reasons why the Lord has impressed this form of praise upon us.

Let us first go back to the Old Testament tabernacle, where Moses met with God. Numbers 7:89 calls this the "Tent of Meeting," where Moses would speak with the Lord and the Lord would speak with him. This verse says that the Lord would speak to Moses "from above the mercy seat that was on the ark of the testimony, from between the two cherubim" (NASB). 1 Samuel 4:4 describes the Lord Almighty "enthroned between the cherubim." The wings of these cherubim were spread over the ark of the covenant with the mercy seat, and the tips of the wings touched at the top. When we raise our hands to the Lord, we could visualize our action as a modern representation of those cherubum, with our outstretched arms being the counterpart to their wings. And it is there — between the wings of the cherubim (our raised hands) — that the Lord said he would meet with us. 1 Chronicles 13:6 speaks of "the LORD, who dwells between the cherubim, where his name is proclaimed" (NKJV). As we lift our hands to him, we speak his name, he speaks with us, and we commune together.

I saw a second reason for the lifting of hands in the way my son greeted me when he was a toddler. When I would come home from the office at suppertime, he would greet me at the door with both hands outstretched and with a look that would say, "Pick me up, Daddy!" He wanted me to hold him! He wanted to be embraced up close. And similarly, when I reach out my hands to the Lord, I am saying, "Pick me up, Daddy God! Hold me close to your heart! I want to be near you!"

During my personal prayer time, I discovered a third value in the lifting of hands. I found that when my hands were raised to the Lord, I was better able to concentrate on the task of praying, and my mind was not so prone to wander onto other irrelevancies. Many struggle with having their minds wander when in a praise service, and the lifting of hands will help curb this tendency.

As a fourth consideration, ask yourself what you would do if someone were to walk up behind you, stick a revolver in your back, and say, "Reach for the sky, Buster!" What would you do? Right — you would lift your hands! A gunman demands that position because when our arms are lifted we are in an unprotected and vulnerable posture. A fighter will bring his arms down across his chest in order to protect himself from the blows of an opponent. When we cross our arms, we are assuming a self-protective stance. By lifting our hands, however, we are indicating to the Lord that we want to open up our hearts and lives to his Holy Spirit. But this is one of the most difficult things for us to do. We have been conditioned all our lives to "look out for Number One." We quickly learn to keep others at arm's length, and we are very selective in whom we really allow to get close to us. If we truly want to please the Lord in our praise and worship, we will take down our defenses and give him access to the inner recesses of our hearts. Many times we can discern how open people are being with the

Lord simply by observing their bodily stance and whether their arms are crossed or raised unto the Lord.

Finally, by lifting our hands we symbolically receive everything God is doing in our lives. A football receiver stretches out his arms in order to catch the ball; it is a position that enables him to make a reception. Similarly, when we lift our hands we indicate our willingness to accept and receive all that God has for us. Some people struggle with God, wondering why they are going through hard times, thinking God is out to get them. These people need to open their arms and receive the loving discipline of the Lord, resting in the assurance that he knows more about their situation than they do and that he is working in their lives for the good. By reaching out to the Lord, we show with what great yearning we long for all of him.

Another common form of praise in the body of Christ today is the *clapping of hands*. Only one verse in the entire Bible speaks directly of people clapping their hands in praise to God: "O clap your hands, all ye people; shout unto God with the voice of triumph" (Psalm 47:1, KJV). (There are some references to the trees clapping their hands *[see Psalm 98:8; Isaiah 55:12*.]) Is it possible that the lack of references to the clapping of hands may give us some insight into the relative importance and value of this form of praise? Clapping our hands in praise is certainly appropriate, but perhaps we overdo it sometimes or place too strong an emphasis on it. I have been in praise services where there was much clapping and tambourine playing, but when the clapping stopped and the noise subsided, there was nothing left. It was like a "sounding brass" or a "tinkling cymbal." There was no depth to the praise — it was just noise. It is important that we link the clapping of hands with a heart that ascends unto the Lord, because the clapping of hands without a heart involvement is really very empty. In studying Hebrew forms of praise, one does not get the impression that this "clapping of hands" was intended to be a "keeping of the beat." It was intended, rather, as just another form of making a "joyful noise" unto the Lord. Those Hebrew folks were noisy in their expressions of praise unto the Lord, and it is still appropriate for us today to raise clamorous acclamations of praise to God. When our heart is overflowing in praise to God, the normal human response is to try to give expression to that praise in a loud and jubilant form such as clapping. We do want to be careful, however, that our praise constitutes more than just noise but also reaches the depth of heart response to God.

The Old Testament is replete with references to the *playing of musical instruments* in praise to God. Entire pamphlets and articles have been written to try to show why we should *not* use musical instruments in our churches today; most of these statements were written by folks who were raised in a historic church setting where the playing of instruments is forbidden. One could almost pity those members in the body of Christ who have allowed isolated ideas in this regard to rob them of the joy of praising with and through musical instruments.

Those of us who use musical instruments in praise must be careful not to become too dependent upon those instruments so that when the music stops, the praise and worship immediately cease! Our praise should ascend to God even when no instruments are readily available. But God has ordained that musical instruments be used to help facilitate our praises. He has created us with musical sensitivities that immediately respond to good musicianship, and he has shown us that the proper response to music should take the form of praise. The Old Testament shows that musical instruments are more than merely things that are played to accompany worship; they are in and of themselves a praise to God: "Praise him with the sounding of the trumpet . . . with the harp and lyre . . . with tambourine and dancing . . . with the strings and flute . . . with the clash of cymbals . . . with resounding cymbals" (Psalm 150:3-5).

Another form of praise is that of *standing*. In the tabernacle of the Old Testament, God gave explicit instructions for many pieces of furniture to be made according to specifications and placed in the interior of the tabernacle. But there was one piece of furniture for which God made no provision: a chair! The priests continually stood before the Lord as they fulfilled their ministry. Standing is a very appropriate expression of praise for us today, we who are the New Testament priesthood. Once again, there are so many verses in the Bible showing us that standing is a proper posture for praise and worship. *(See* 2 Chronicles 5:12; 7:6; 29:26; Psalm 135:2; Revelation 4:9-11 for starters.)

Standing serves two particularly strong functions in praise. First, it speaks of respect. If we were together at a meeting of dignitaries and the president of the United States walked in, we would all stand out of respect for his office. How is it then, brethren, that when we gather together to celebrate the presence of the King of kings, we are found sitting? In the heavenly worship scene in the book of Revelation, the King is seated on the throne, and all others are standing around the throne. He sits — we stand!

Second, standing indicates alertness. I find that when I sit down, my ability to concentrate on the service tends to decrease. My mind switches into neutral and has the tendency to wander. An amazing variety of pertinent thoughts can come to mind when it is time to pray or to praise the Lord! Satan's battleground is in our mind, and he is delighted if he can distract us from worshiping by causing us to mull over concerns and problems. We are exhorted, "Do not give the devil a foothold" (Ephesians 4:27), and standing can help us ward off the devil's tactics by remaining mentally alert. When praise is vibrant and real, people can't be made to sit down; when the service is dragging, they begin to drop like flies. Standing and praising go hand in hand, because when we stand we are stimulated in our minds to remain a wide-awake and alert contributor to the service.

Kneeling, bowing, and prostration are highly apropos in praise or worship. "Come, let us bow down in worship, let

us kneel before the LORD our Maker" (Psalm 95:6). "The
twenty-four elders and the four living creatures fell down
and worshiped God, who was seated on the throne" (Revelation 19:4). The overwhelmingly obvious form of worship
that is seen in heaven throughout the book of Revelation is
falling in prostration. Many of our songs will make references to our bowing before the Lord in worship, and yet it is
the rare church that will practice that form of worship while
singing those songs. I am told of one church that would
sing, "Stand up, stand up for Jesus, ye soldiers of the
cross," while sitting down! It is appropriate to put into bodily action what we are saying unto the Lord! If we are singing about lifting our hands to the Lord, let us lift our hands
unto the Lord; if we are singing about bowing and falling on
our faces before him, then it is fitting for us to do so.

Some of our churches have no problem with rejoicing
before the Lord, but they rarely seem to enter into a dimension of reverential awe in the presence of God. But one
verse brings these two poles together in a unique way:
"Serve the LORD with fear and rejoice with trembling"
(Psalm 2:11). All of our joy and rejoicing must flow out of an
attitude of both love and fear before the Lord Most High.

Singing is probably the most common form of praise we
employ today. The Scriptures are so full of admonitions to
sing unto the Lord that I will not cite any references here,
but the Psalms in particular are a rich storehouse.

But some may ask, "Why can't we just speak our praise?
Why do we have to sing it?" The answer lies in the beauty
of music. Suppose, for example, that we were to congregate
and chant, "Alleluia . . . alleluia . . . alleluia." That would
not do much for any of us, would it? But picture what happens when we couple those simple words with the lovely
tune we all know so well. Our hearts are lifted to the Lord,
and our spirits are moved in the presence of God.

This is an "ultra-rational" experience in which one plus
one equals three, in which words plus music equal "more"
than just words and music. The words of the song may be

very meaningful, but when they are coupled with an en-hancing melody, the message of the song can be expressed with so much more meaning. God has given us this medium of music as a very special gift because he knows how much it helps us in lifting our hearts in praise to him.

How should we praise the Lord? *Audibly!* Praise is not praise until it is heard, made audible, vocalized: "proclaim-ing aloud your praise" (Psalm 26:7). When our son Joel was being potty-trained, we used praise as positive reinforce-ment to indicate our approval of his using the commode. If we had merely watched him and thought wonderful thoughts about his performance, he would have remained in diapers a lot longer. By speaking aloud those thoughts of admiration, we invoked the tool of praise and he responded favorably. The way we fussed over him, you would have thought the New York Yankees had just won the World Series! We did not actually engage in praise, however, until we vocalized our praise to him. Similarly, our thoughts of God must be made audible before they qualify as praise.

Praise must be manifest before it is praise. The only ex-ception to audible praise, then, is visible praise. If praise is not heard, then it must be seen. Praise can be spoken, or it can be shown and expressed through animated bodily movement. This is why the quietness of *dancing* is a proper form of praise. Yes, dancing *is* a bona fide expression of praise. Some people have problems with this being a valid form of praise, but a quick look in any concordance will show that dancing is found throughout the Scriptures — for example, Exodus 15:20-21; 2 Samuel 6:14-16; Psalms 30:11; 149:3; Acts 3:8.

One pastor vocalized his problem with dancing by saying that we have only one time recorded in the life of David when he danced before the Lord, and that was in the bring-ing up of the ark to Zion. It was his contention that dancing should thus be a rare expression of praise in our services.

I know that others have their problems with dancing be-cause they think it looks "silly" to outsiders. Well, I agree, but so do many of our expressions of praise. And after all, these expressions are not for outsiders; they're for God. Once we forsake scriptural concepts for the sake of propriety, we are headed for trouble.

We should not feel that dancing must be a part of every service. After the crossing of the Red Sea, Miriam led the Israelite women in dancing, but let me postulate that we would dance too if the Lord had just drowned our "Egyptian army"! We may not have many Red Sea experiences in our lifetime, but we need to be willing to respond in a fitting manner when those times come.

Another pastor told me he had no problem with dancing provided that the person also danced in his or her personal devotional life. He seemed to think that that would be necessary to make the expression of dance in the congregation consistent with the life-style of the individual. I rather doubt that this pastor was encouraging dancing in one's devotional life; he was most likely discountenancing the use of dancing in the congregation. His argument was insufficient for me. Should the drummer not be permitted to play in the worship service until he uses the drums in his quiet time with God? Should no one be permitted to clap his hands in praise without doing so in private prayer times? Although dancing and clapping and playing musical instruments may not be a regular part of one's private devotions, they are nonetheless very fitting expressions of praise in the congregation of the saints. The dynamics of our individual devotional lives differ from those of corporate worship.

For some folks, dancing is a very meaningful form of praise, so consequently it is only natural for them to emphasize it. I am not a "dancer," so I tend to put little emphasis on dancing. Occasionally I will dance when I find that nothing else seems to express fully my heart before the Lord, but I do not do it in such a way as to display it before others, since I am a rather clumsy dancer and not at all inspirational to watch. I do not dance in order to be observed by anyone else but only to express my heart unto God. However, trained, capable dancers can be very delightful to observe in their praise.

Some churches have a "dance troupe" ministry — a group of trained dancers who perform choreographed moves in accompaniment to a song. If the dance troupe ministers in every service, the congregation will soon grow accustomed to it, and it will lose its effectiveness. Such rehearsed dances should be performed only occasionally so that there is an impact when they are done. Some dance troupes minister very effectively, but others are comprised of young people who simply love to dance and have found this an acceptable outlet in their particular church. This is not an activity for those who "just love to dance"; it should be considered a ministry and should require that one have the special ability to inspire worship in others through graceful body movements. Because dance is so highly visible, it becomes difficult to make these rehearsed dances a bona fide ministry that exalts Jesus rather than displays the beauty and dexterity of those involved. It is a challenge that can be met, though, and the fruit can be rewarding.

One pastor confided that he found the choreographed dance moves distracting during the worship service. Rather than lifting his heart to God, the dancers diverted his attention from the Lord and onto them. Several have expressed to me their feeling that the ministry of dance troupes has at times blessed them but that the same troupe has at other times been a distraction from worship. Some churches have found a balance in this by using their dance troupe during musicals and special presentations and restricting dancing in the congregational worship services to individual expressions of spontaneity. Musicals and presentations are staged with the expectation that people will watch and be inspired, so the visibility of the dance troupe is very natural. Worship services are held in the expectation that people will lift their eyes unto the Lord, and some have found dance troupes to be counterproductive to that goal.

Churches with dance troupes should avoid an attitude of

superiority over those who prefer otherwise. Let us not fall
into the trap of thinking that having a dance team in our
church is the earmark of being on the "cutting edge" of
what God is saying today! Some churches give the un-
mistakable impression that one must become liberated in
the dance before being accepted as truly "free" or
"spiritual." The wise pastor will foster an atmosphere of
magnanimity in the congregation so that those not yet comfortable with dancing will not feel threatened or excluded
because of their non-involvement.

The value of dancing is the physical release it demands.
It requires us to set aside our inhibitions and "go for it"
with all our body. The apostle Paul made a statement that
casts interesting light on this truth. He said, "The spiritual
did not come first, but the natural, and after that the
spiritual" (1 Corinthians 15:46). The order is first the
natural, then the spiritual. We must initiate a physical
release if we would know a subsequent spiritual release.
The goal is the release in our spirits, but sometimes it will
not be achieved until we engage our bodies; hence the value
of lifting our hands, bowing, dancing, etc.

The Lord himself told us that we are to love the Lord our
God with all our heart, soul, mind, and strength (Mark
12:30). How many of us have ever wished that we could express our love to the Lord in a fuller measure — yes, even
with all our strength? Dancing is one way to do that! David
danced before the Lord with all his might because it was the
only way he could give full expression to his heart. Someone
who wants to praise the Lord with all his strength in the
congregation should not get down on the floor and do some
push-ups. That is not a biblical form of praising God with
our strength. But dancing is! We are very physical
creatures, and the Lord is delighted when we praise him
with everything that we are, spirit, soul, and body.

The caution has been given to dancers: "After you hop,
be straight in your walk." Dancing praisers naturally draw
more attention to themselves than others employing more

conservative forms of praise, and so any spiritual inconsistencies in the life of the dancer become more immediately glaring. "I know that sister is having problems with smoking, and now look at how she dances as though she were the most perfect saint on earth!" But nowhere do the Scriptures suggest that one must attain a preset level of spirituality before engaging in certain expressions of praise. We praise not because we are "spiritual" but because God is worthy!

Some pastors are afraid to allow dancing in their church because they fear it will get out of hand. But how far has conservatism gotten them in the past? It is easier to restrain a fanatic than to raise a corpse. Too many of God's saints have been hindered from entering into a deeper experience in the Lord simply because they were not willing to initiate a physical release. I have a stronger word of caution for those who do not dance or would like to throw a wet blanket on those who do: be careful what you say against it! If God is in it, no one will prosper by maligning it. Let us learn from Uzzah, who touched the ark of God and died. We must be careful not to touch anything that is of God, because something will die in us spiritually if we try to stop what God is doing.

Dancing has no inherent value in and of itself, but the spiritual release it can bring is valuable. Generally, if we are reserved physically before the Lord, it is a sign that we are probably reserved spiritually before him as well. And God is hindered by any reservations in our spirits. If we hold back in our hearts, we limit the extent to which God is able to move in our midst. But if we will remove our physical restraints and be simple enough to dance before the Lord with all that is within us, we will find that our spiritual restraints will crumble as well, and God will have a greater freedom to move among us.

Shouting is also a form of praise. The Scriptures exhort us to "shout unto God with the voice of triumph" (Psalm 47:1, KJV). Where the King James Version says, "Make a joyful noise unto the LORD" in a number of psalms, the New International Version more accurately translates that expression as "Shout for joy to the LORD" *(see* Psalms 66:1; 81:1; 95:1-2; 98:4-6; 100:1). The Hebrew word *hillel,* from which we get the universal word "hallelujah," means "to cry aloud or break out into a cry, and especially a cry of joy."

At a worship seminar I attended at a certain church, there was a sense of heaviness prevailing. We did not break through in the Spirit until we were led of the Lord to shout aloud in his presence with the voice of triumph. As the people lifted their voices in a glorious shout of praise, we experienced a beautiful release that continued for the rest of the seminar.

The Israelites were famed in Canaan for their battle cry. When they lifted their voices in the shout, the enemy began to tremble with fear. How well they knew what that shout represented and how, beginning at Jericho, this battle cry initiated Israel's victory. It was the shout of praise! Brothers and sisters, it is a sad day for the church when the shout of praise is no longer heard in the camp!

Speaking in tongues is a beautiful way to praise the Lord. How deeply we cherish the precious gift of the baptism of the Holy Spirit that Jesus has given his church, together with the sign of speaking in tongues. What a beautiful release we find when we are able to express our praises to the Lord directly from our spirits unto him! Truly this experience is to be coveted for all those who have not yet had the release of speaking in tongues. A certain dynamic and flow will be missing in praise until one knows the blessing of praising in other tongues as the Spirit gives utterance.

No matter when, where, or how we praise the Lord, we are to praise with our entire beings. "Bless the LORD, O my soul: and all that is within me, bless his holy name" (Psalm 103:1, KJV). In Mark 12:30 Jesus highlighted for us the foremost commandment of all: " 'Love the Lord your God with all your heart and with all your soul and with all your mind and with all your strength.' " This is the pinnacle of praise: to love and praise him with everything that is within us.

Often when we sing Psalm 103:1, I have watched people sing the words "And all that is within me, bless his holy name" in a most unconvincing way. It is time that we stop mouthing empty cliches in praise, dear saints, and start reinforcing our words with bodily expressions that reflect an overflowing heart. This is the bottom line on how to praise: doing it with everything that is within us!

CHAPTER 2

ENTERING THE PRESENCE OF GOD

If we have a heart which desires God, we naturally desire to come near to him. We want to be in his presence. So one of the foremost priorities of believers is to congregate with other saints for the purpose of meeting with God. But what is the proper way to enter into the presence of God as a congregation? Should we start with fast, handclapping praise songs, or should we come in reverence, singing slow, worshipful songs? Are there scriptural guidelines?

When we speak of entering "the presence of God," we should remember that there are varying *manifestations* of the presence of God. There are at least three levels to consider. First, God is omnipresent; his presence is everywhere, all the time. This is a very general aspect of his presence. Second, Jesus told us that where two or three are gathered in his name, he is there in the midst of them *(see* Matthew 18:20). This is a more particular manifestation of his presence. And third, 2 Chronicles 5:13-14 gives an account of the cloud of glory filling Solomon's temple when the singers and musicians lifted their hearts in praise to God. This cloud of glory (the presence of God) so filled the room that the priests could not even stand to perform their service! Truly that was a very special manifestation of the presence of God, and it is that same type or nature of manifestation that we seek today!

The problem with this last statement is that many of us will remain unhappy with our worship services until we see a literal cloud in our church. Such an attitude would not please the Lord, because in essence we would be saying,

"We're not happy with loving you, Lord, in the way we've been doing it. We'll feel fulfilled in our love for you when we see the cloud of your presence in the sanctuary." And the Lord simply wants us to love him — now — for who he is! The lesson we can learn from this passage is very meaningful, though. When that cloud filled the temple, the people and priests could not see anyone or anything around them, because all that was visible to them was the presence of the Lord. And for us today, the goal for our worship should be that we come to the point where we do not see anyone or anything around us, but we become totally taken up with God. That is the supreme goal of worship: to see only the Lord. There is no higher fulfillment for us, nor will there ever be.

OUR APPROACH TO GOD'S PRESENCE

The majority of Scriptures containing any clue to the general approach of the Israelites in Davidic times give the impression that they came before the Lord with songs of celebration and praise. The following passages speak of entering God's presence with praise: "Let us come before him with thanksgiving and extol him with music and song" (Psalm 95:2); "Serve the LORD with gladness; come before him with joyful songs. Enter his gates with thanksgiving and his courts with praise" (Psalm 100:2,4). *(See* also Psalms 42:4; 45:13-15; 68:24-26; Isaiah 30:29; 35:10.)

Other portions of Scripture, however, seem to indicate that worship is the fitting expression of those who enter the Lord's house. Consider the following passages: "Ascribe to the LORD the glory due his name. Bring an offering and come before him; worship the LORD in the splendor of his holiness" (1 Chronicles 16:29; Psalm 96:8). "But I, by your great mercy, will come into your house; in reverence will I bow down toward your holy temple" (Psalm 5:7). " 'Let us go to his dwelling place; let us worship at his footstool' " (Psalm 132:7). *(See* also Ecclesiastes 5:1-2.) So which is the fitting way — praise or worship? Is there a formula for our services?

No, there is no formula for what we call the "worship service." A worship service can be started with either fast songs of praise and thanksgiving or with slow songs of worship and adoration. Either approach is scriptural. From the weight of scriptural evidence, we might say that it is more common to come before the Lord with praise songs, but we need to shun the idea that there is a formula for conducting worship services, namely, starting with fast, upbeat praise songs, then moving into slower, more worshipful songs.

Some services will have that order inverted; other services will have only slow songs or only fast songs. The Scriptures do not give us a rigid approach to worship for the simple reason that God does not want us to come up with a formula for our services. If God had a proper ritual or pattern, then he would have given it to us. But Jesus made it clear that worship is not to be the performance of a ritual or a formula but is a matter of spirit *(see* John 4:23-24). The point is this: no matter what our form of approach may be, the Lord is looking for those who will come to him in spirit and in truth, with hearts that seek diligently after him.

There is no "right" way or "wrong" way to enter the presence of the Lord — there is only God's way. And his way is probably different every time! A worship leader must have a deep prayer life and must cultivate a sensitivity to the Spirit of God in order to discern the way of God for each service.

INDIVIDUAL VERSUS CORPORATE WORSHIP

The Scriptures seem to differentiate between the approach of a single worshiper to the Lord and the approach of the congregation before the Lord. Individual worship is quite different from corporate worship, and so must our approach be. In writing about worship, many authors have suggested that Isaiah chapter 6, gives us an outline for corporate worship. The problem with their idea is that that was

a very special encounter of Isaiah with God — a special encounter of *one individual* with his God. Perhaps Isaiah 6
gives us some insight into our private devotional life, but I
would question whether we can consider it to be a pattern
for corporate worship. These writers point to the total un-
worthiness that Isaiah felt in the presence of God and go on
to say that our worship should be preceded by repentance.
There are times when repentance is very appropriate to
worship, but that is the exception and not the norm. Psalm
100 would be a better chapter to read to gain insight into
our approach before the Lord. It is a clear reference to corporate worship.

Let us also keep in mind that praise is not so much God
coming into our presence as it is our going into his presence.
"Enter *his* gates with thanksgiving and *his* courts with
praise"; "praise God in *his* sanctuary" (Psalms 100:4;
150:1).

Furthermore, it is not that God descends to meet with us
when we praise, but rather that we ascend unto him.
" 'Come, let us go up to the mountain of the LORD, to the
house of the God of Jacob' " (Isaiah 2:3). "Who may ascend
the hill of the LORD? Who may stand in his holy place?"
(Psalm 24:3). If we are having a "bad" worship service, our
first thought is that we need the presence of God. The fact
is that God is already with us — what we need is to do something, for us to ascend unto the Lord in our hearts. The
problem is never with God, for he is always ready; the problem is with us, every time.

Perhaps we need to take a fresh look at Psalm 22:3:
"But thou art holy, O thou that inhabitest the praises of
Israel" (KJV); "Yet Thou art holy, O Thou who art enthroned upon the praises of Israel" (NASB). Based upon
this verse, some have thought that praise gives us access to
the presence of God. It has been expressed this way: "We
know how to produce the presence of God." Certain well-
intentioned Christians teach that we can have the presence
of God in our churches if we will only praise. When God's

presence is not sensed, if we will just praise him, he will come down and join our service. If we still do not sense his presence, we need to praise harder and more loudly and with more sincerity. (That almost sounds like the priests of Baal, who cut themselves in an effort to invoke the good will of their god!) They see this verse as saying that God will come and take up his abode with those who will praise him.

I would like us to entertain a different interpretation of this verse. It is true that God inhabits our praise, that he dwells and abides in our praise, in the sense that he loves our praises, bathes in our praises, and surrounds himself with our praises. He so delights in and relishes our praises. And note the NASB rendering, which is truer to the original Hebrew: he is "enthroned" on our praises. He is made King when we praise him, for we are declaring his Kingship and Lordship to a world that does not recognize him as Lord. By singing, "He is the King of kings, he is the Lord of lords," we are testifying to the heathen (and to the saints, too) of his Lordship and thus are "enthroning" him with our praise.

The former interpretation would see that verse as conditional: *"If* we praise, we can be assured of the presence of God." But we cannot coerce or induce the presence of God. It is a heathen concept to think that we can. Praise does not flatter God in order to incur his favor. God is never conditioned by our praise. I once heard someone complimenting a certain worship leader by saying, "He really knows how to bring the presence of God into a meeting!" I am sure the brother to whom this person was referring is a tremendous worship leader, but nonetheless he does not have the ability to bring God's presence. Sorcerers will attempt to do that sort of thing, but God will not be aroused through sorcery. That worship leader cannot produce God's presence, but he probably does have a special ability to lead God's people up to Mount Zion, the eternal tabernacle of God.

Psalm 132:13-14 gives a more accurate understanding of

how God inhabits our praises. "For the LORD has chosen Zion, he has desired it for his dwelling: 'This is my resting place for ever and ever; here I will sit enthroned, for I have desired it.' " Here the Lord himself says that he has determined to manifest his presence in Zion, and he is dwelling there both now and forevermore. He does not abide in Zion only when we praise — he has taken up permanent residence in Zion! When we gather together, he is already there, and he will always be enthroned in Zion as we praise him. It is not a condition — it is a fact.

We must not attempt to command the presence of God by whipping God's people into a lather of praise. 1 Chronicles 13:7 tells us that Uzzah and Ahio "drove" the cart on which the ark was being transported — and Uzzah was killed when he touched the ark. We cannot "drive" God's presence.

THE RESPONSIBILITY OF THE INDIVIDUAL WORSHIPER

Most Christians attend church not with an attitude of contributing but with the purpose of getting as much out of the service as they possibly can. In keeping with that mindset, pastors and worship leaders are expected to see that all the components of the service flow together cohesively and meaningfully. "That's the pastor's job — that's why we hired him!" If something goes wrong, the pastor or worship leader gets the blame, and both are likely to hear about it! The weight of the responsibility for the service is thus seen to fall on the shoulders of those on the platform, and the individual in the congregation is relatively free from feeling any responsibility for the service. But if we truly believe that all Christians are active members of the New Testament priesthood — that all of us are ministers before and unto the Lord — then we must begin to accept the proper responsibility for our role as ministers in the congregation.

The first and foremost responsibility of every worshiper

is to *minister unto the Lord.* The Bible says, "Praise *ye* the
LORD" (Psalm 150:1, KJV). The responsibility to praise and
worship does not rest on the pastor or the worship leader; it
is my responsibility, your responsibility, the responsibility
of each person to offer up an individual "sacrifice of praise"
to the Lord.

Each of us also has the responsibility to *prepare ourselves
for worship.* One beautiful way to do that is to get up early
on Sunday and spend some time in prayer and praise. We
could play a cassette of praise songs and sing along in the
car on the way to church. Prayer and meditation can be a
beautiful prelude to a worship service. When we come into
the sanctuary, we may find it appropriate occasionally to
spend some time in prayer rather than to visit with others.
Staying up late Saturday night to watch a "horror flick" is
not a good way to prepare for Sunday worship. We want to
come with hearts already attuned to the Spirit of God.

One excellent way to prepare for worship is to deal with
any known sin in our lives before we get to the service. If at
the outset of the service we are trying to come into right
relationship with God, we can lose precious moments that
could have been spent in vibrant praise or worship. Or if we
try to sweep that sin under the carpet, we will not find a full
release in worship. We will experience what happened to
David following his sin of adultery with Bathsheba. When
David made that right with God, he confessed, "For I know
my transgressions, and my sin is always before me" (Psalm
51:3). He tried to worship the Lord with all his heart, but
that sin would flash across his mind again and again, and he
would find his heart cold toward the Lord. If we attempt to
live in unconfessed sin, then we too will find that sin coming
to mind just when we want to worship the Lord. We can circumvent the ploy of the enemy to distract us from worshiping by repenting beforehand, receiving God's gracious forgiveness, and then refusing any condemnation.

We have a responsibility to *invest ourselves in prayer* for
the service ahead of time. Dr. Judson Cornwall has said that

prayer is to the believer as communication is to a marriage — absolutely vital. He defines prayer as communication with God and suggests that the prayerless saint will never be a worshiper.

Jesus gave us a principle that applies here: where your treasure is, there your heart will be *(see* Matthew 6:21). If we invest ourselves diligently in prayer for the worship service, we will be amazed at our level of concern for and participation in the service. If we spend quality time praying for the service, we will be eager to see a return on that investment and will be ready to become involved to help make it a glorious session.

We also need to *frequent the place of worship.* The Scriptures exhort us not to neglect the assembling of the saints *(see* Hebrews 10:25). We all need the strength and encouragement we receive by fellowshiping with others in the body of Christ. We are only small members in the body; by ourselves, cut off from that body, we will die spiritually.

When coming into the presence of God, we ought not to come for a handout but should rather *bring an offering.* Someone has aptly said that many of God's people are "professional beggars in the courts of the Lord." But Psalm 96:8 says, ". . . Bring an offering and come into his courts." Rather than coming to see how much we can receive from God, let us endeavor to give unto God, to minister to him, and to bless his name. Others will come with some money for the offering plate and then think they are "off the hook" because they have "paid their dues." We have a responsibility to come with an offering, but that involves much more than merely a financial contribution. We must come into God's presence by offering up a sacrifice of praise, and we should be prepared to reach out in ministry to other brothers and sisters as the Holy Spirit would divinely direct us. God is not trying to grow lazy leeches who know how to sponge off the pastor and the congregation. God loves givers — people who come to the congregation intent upon contributing.

Psalm 66:2 gives us all a mandate: "Make his praise glorious" (KJV). That requires us to *invest energy*. Have you ever been in a praise service that was a "dud"? The instrumentalists could not seem to get together on the same tempo; the pastor appeared to be reciting his sermon in his mind; the ushers had retreated to some haven in the narthex; half the congregation was trying to muster some quickly depleting energy, while the rest of the people had outright given up on the praise time. How we wish such stories were confined to "Ripley's Believe It or Not," but in fact most churches struggle with an occasionally poor praise service. Does this happen because God likes to withdraw his Spirit and watch us dangle? No, the problem is not with God but with us. The emphasis of Psalm 66:2 is that we *make* his praise glorious. Our praises are not automatically glorious. Praise is not a magical wand that when waved will guarantee a glorious service. If we do not invest any effort, we will miss a tremendous secret of praise. Glorious praises become the domain of those who make them so. We serve a wonderful God, and he deserves the most glorious, lavish amount of fanfare and adulation that we can muster. Praise is not the response of those who have waited for some heavenly shower; it is initiated by those who approach God with a spiritual sacrifice.

We also have a responsibility to *be self-motivated in our praise and worship.* Ben Patterson has said that God is, at the very least, unimpressed with merely spontaneous worshipers. How true! "Spontaneous worshipers" are folks who know how to praise and worship when they feel like it, when the goosebumps begin to trickle up and down their spines, or when the worship leader really hits their "worship button." How we all love those times of spontaneous worship when it is so easy to lift our hearts unto the Lord! But if we operate at that level only, we have not learned the discipline of being a worshiper. Have you ever "itched" a dog? If you scratch it in the right place, the mutt is likely to involuntarily flail its paw at the same time. Some people sit around like lazy dogs, waiting for the worship leader to scratch them in precisely the right spot so that they can involuntarily worship. One "fruit of the Spirit" is self-control. If more individuals would exercise self-control in worship and be self-motivated to enter into God's praises, we would probably have fewer worship leaders attempting to use crowd control to elicit a response. A worshiper worships at every given opportunity and does not demand some horizontal stimulus from the pastor or worship leader before entering into praise.

With this, we should *enter readily and wholeheartedly into the praise of God.* Far too many of us are "slow starters" on Sunday morning. We are like a cold engine on a wintry morning, and the worship leader is like the driver of an old classic who is trying to get the thing started by cranking up the engine. Crank it up — a few sputters — then nothing. Crank it again — sputter, cough, sputter, cough — it dies. Crank it one more time — and finally something seems to "take."

New sports cars are sometimes rated according to how quickly they accelerate: "zero to fifty in 8.6 seconds." I wonder how our services might be rated on a similar scale: "zero to fifty in twenty-five minutes. . . ." My, how we waste precious time in our services, waiting for the slow starters to "get with it"!

Following his resurrection, when Jesus met two disciples on the road to Emmaus, he said to them, " 'How foolish you are, and how slow of heart to believe all that the prophets have spoken!' " (Luke 24:25). When Jesus called them "slow of heart," he did not intend it as a compliment! And it is not commendable before heaven to be known as a "slow starter" in praise and worship. We are slow starters because we are slow of heart. We are just like those disciples — and the Lord would give us a similar rebuke. We must stir up our own souls when it is time to praise the Lord. "Bless thou the Lord, O *my* soul!" We must motivate ourselves to praise and enter enthusiastically into the worship service.

We are also to do more than just sing songs. The Psalms exhort us to "sing praises unto God." Just because we are singing songs, we are not necessarily singing praises. It is possible for us to sing without having our hearts in it at all. Our responsibility is to *make our songs a praise from our hearts* unto God.

It is our obligation to "brighten up" and *be cheerful* when coming into his presence. Have you noticed what a young lady does when she is preparing for a date? She spends hours fixing her hair, putting on her makeup, and selecting the right outfit. And when her date rings the doorbell, she welcomes him at the door with a pretty smile and a bouncy voice. She may have had the worst day in her life — everything may have gone wrong that day — but when he arrives, she looks like the queen of England! Similarly for us, when we first come before the Lord, that is not the time to spew out all our problems and cares upon him. What a terrible way for God to have to start the service! When we first come in, we are to put aside those concerns, block out all the emotional upheavals of the week, put on a garment of praise, put a smile on our faces, and lift up our hearts in thanksgiving and praise to God!

Worshiping despite distractions is also incumbent upon us. How easy it is to blame others for our lack of praise! "The worship leader just isn't flowing with the Spirit of God today!" "What's the pastor doing — he doesn't look like he's enjoying the worship service at all." "My, that was a sour note on the piano." "When are the drummer and pianist *ever* going to get it together?" "This worship leader obviously doesn't know what he's doing."

There are "a thousand and one" reasons why we do not praise God. But the responsibility to praise must inevitably return upon us. God never told us to praise "if you like the style of the worship leader" or "when a song you really like comes along." What does Scripture say? "I will bless the LORD at all times" (Psalm 34:1) — even when the worship leader is off key, the pianist does not know the song, and the drummer is too harsh. This comes as an injunction to all of us as worshipers: we must not allow ourselves the luxury of becoming distracted by the sincere but faltering efforts of the musicians or leaders. We may be very accurate in our analysis of their deficiencies, but we will rob ourselves of the privilege of blessing the Lord.

We must *be worshipers all week long.* A worshiper does not enjoy worshiping only on Sunday in the congregation; his life is a continual praise and worship unto God twenty-four hours a day. Once we have learned that life of worship throughout the week, it is easy to come together in the congregation and praise him! When worshipers assemble, the praise ascends immediately. If the level of praise in our congregation is poor, we can be sure the problem is that the people have not learned to live a life of praise throughout the week. We have been called to more than "just visiting" in the house of the Lord. The Scriptures say, "He that *dwelleth* in the secret place of the most High shall abide under the shadow of the Almighty" (Psalm 91:1, KJV). Let us abide in his presence continually.

It is easy to confuse *worshiping* with *being a worshiper.* Just because someone worships, it does not necessarily follow that he or she is a worshiper. Virtually anyone can worship as the occasion might demand, but relatively few seem to manifest the life-style of a worshiper. When God asks us to be worshipers every day, he is not asking us to do nothing but sing songs all week. He knows we must do other things besides vocalize our worship. But God does ask us to live a life consistent with that of a worshiper seven days a week. Once we adopt that life-style, we will inevitably find a song of praise frequently welling up from within. We will begin to realize that everything we do truly constitutes an act of worship unto the Lord, for our daily activities are but an expression of our dedication to God.

Having worshiped in the congregation, we are responsible to go out and live a life consistent with our confession at church. Someone has said, "Don't 'lip' it unless you live it." That statement is not intended to discourage any from worshiping, because we know we all fall short of God's ideal from time to time. We do not wait to praise God until we are living a perfect Christian life, or else none of us would ever praise! But as we confess the Lord with our mouth, our life slowly comes into line with that confession. That is the process called "sanctification." Horatius Bonar penned these fitting words:

> Not for the lip of praise alone
> Nor e'en the praising heart
> I ask, but for a life made up
> Of praise in every part.

> Praise in the common things of life
> Its goings out and in
> Praise in each duty and each deed
> However small and mean.

Someone else put it succinctly: "Your walk talks, and your talk walks, but your walk talks further than your talk walks." May the intimacy of our worship before God on Sunday so affect our lives that the change is evident throughout the week!

THE SACRIFICE OF PRAISE

Many times when we come before the Lord, it is very easy to lift up our hearts in praise, but there are other times when praise is anything but easy. Sometimes it is the last thing we want to do. At such times it becomes necessary to offer up "a sacrifice of praise."

This term "sacrifice of praise" is taken from Hebrews 13:15: "Through Jesus, therefore, let us continually offer to God a sacrifice of praise — the fruit of lips that confess his name." Peter said that we are a spiritual priesthood, offering up spiritual sacrifices to the Lord *(see* 1 Peter 2:5). The Psalms also refer to "sacrifices of thanksgiving" and "sacrifices of joy" *(see* Psalms 27:6; 54:6; 107:22; 116:17).

The New Testament uses the word "sacrifice" as a counterpart to the original temple sacrifices. Even back in Old Testament days, the Lord made it clear, in the Psalms and Prophets, that he was looking not simply for animal sacrifices but for sacrifices from the heart. The Mosaic law demanded animal sacrifices, and it was while still under the old order that an inspired David wrote, "You do not delight in sacrifice, or I would bring it; you do not take pleasure in burnt offerings. The sacrifices of God are a broken spirit; a broken and contrite heart, O God, you will not despise" (Psalm 51:16-17). Today we offer up the fulfillment of the Old Testament type: sacrifices of praise.

A sacrifice speaks of something costly, the giving of something that is dear to us. This is illustrated so beautifully in 1 Chronicles 21. Satan had incited David to number the children of Israel, and since David did it in a way that displeased the Lord, God punished the nation. The Lord sent a plague on Israel and 70,000 people died. When the destroying angel came to the threshing floor of Araunah, God told the angel, " 'Enough! Withdraw your hand' " (verse 15). David was then commanded by the angel to build an altar to the Lord on Araunah's threshing floor, at the precise place where the destroying angel stopped the killing of any more Israelites. David approached Araunah to purchase the site in order to make his sacrifice unto the Lord, but Araunah said he wanted to give the altar site to David, along with oxen and wood for the burnt offering. Notice David's response: " 'No, I insist on paying the full price. I will not take for the LORD what is yours, or sacrifice a burnt offering that costs me nothing' " (verse 24).

A sacrifice is not a sacrifice until it costs us something! How glibly we sing, "We bring the sacrifice of praise," without really offering God anything sacrificial at all. Many times we think we are offering up a sacrifice of praise when, in fact, we are praising because we feel like it. In the Old Testament, a sacrifice called for death. And the New Testament sacrifice of praise calls for a death, too — a death to our comfort, our "pity party," our ego, our desires.

THE COST OF PRAISE

Praise is not a free commodity. It involves cost to those who involve themselves in it. First, there is the cost of energy. Sometimes we are tired after a full week of hard work, and we come to church on Sunday morning in order to relax. We do not feel like lifting our hands or standing too long — we do not have the energy for it. At such a time, it is fitting to offer up a true sacrifice of our energy and bless the Lord with our heart, soul, mind, and strength.

Second, there is the cost of preparation. Sometimes we sense the need to receive cleansing and renewal in order to be freer in the presence of God. "Who may ascend the hill of the LORD? Who may stand in his holy place? He who has clean hands and a pure heart" (Psalm 24:3-4). This passage shows us that the Lord requires purity of those who will minister unto him. If we truly want to minister unto the Lord in an intimate way, we may first be required to purify our heart through confession and repentance.

Third, there is the cost of time. Is our time of high importance? Is there never enough time in a day to get everything done? Time is my most precious commodity, I think. Ask me for twenty dollars, and I will give it with a small inner wince. But ask me for two hours of my time? That is precious! But living a life of praise will inevitably require a sacrifice of time. We cannot always dash in and out of the presence of the Lord; there are times when we need to stay and commune for a while. After the wedding day, husbands learn very quickly that it takes more than five minutes to have a time of fulfilling intimacy with one's spouse. How much more that is so with our heavenly Lover.

"A sacrifice of praise" is not something fun to experience. It might be fun to sing about, but when it actually comes time to offer up that sacrifice, it will cost something.

And yet this is an integral part of living a life of praise and being one who abides in God's presence. We are solemnly warned, "Woe to you who are complacent in Zion" (Amos 6:1). May we not be a complacent company, but may we be among those who are willing to stir themselves and offer up a sacrifice of praise in the midst of adverse circumstances.

Our attitude toward and involvement in praise and worship are keys to entering God's presence. We bring our praise with no ulterior motives, no attempt to "twist God's arm" to come to us. In his presence we find fullness of joy. We also find that our praise becomes a powerful weapon against the enemy.

CHAPTER 3

PRAISE: A WEAPON FOR SPIRITUAL WARFARE

The New Testament unquestionably tells us that the Christian is involved in a battle, a struggle, a veritable war. We are told that we fight, not human forces, but spiritual principalities and powers that inhabit the atmosphere around us. Furthermore, we are enjoined to clothe ourselves with the armor of God, in order that we might be able to effectively withstand the attacks of the evil one (see Ephesians 6:10-18).

Spiritual victories are won through a variety of methods, such as intercessory prayer or the confession of God's word. But there is another form of spiritual warfare available to us that is beginning to receive more serious consideration, and it is the medium of praise.

When we talk about praise, we could talk about a large spectrum of subjects. And when we speak of warfare, there are many different areas that could be discussed in that regard as well. But in this chapter we are confining ourselves to that area that is shared by both these subjects, namely, the use of praise as a weapon in spiritual warfare.

THE SCRIPTURAL BASIS FOR WARFARE THROUGH PRAISE

This theme can be traced throughout the Scriptures, beginning back in the book of Exodus. Imagine the scene after the Israelites' crossing of the Red Sea. Egypt's army had just drowned in the rushing waters, and the people were safe on the other side. Miriam grabbed a tambourine and led the women in singing, "I will sing unto the LORD, for he hath triumphed gloriously: the horse and his rider hath he thrown into the sea" (Exodus 15:1, KJV). On that occasion Moses and all Israel sang a tremendous song of triumph unto the Lord, and within that song is contained an exciting revelation: "The LORD is a man of war: the LORD is his name" (Exodus 15:3, KJV). The New International Version says, "The LORD is a warrior." After seeing how God dealt with Pharaoh and his armies, the Israelites knew they had witnessed a great battle strategist in action!

Joshua was given a similar revelation of God's character. As he was about to lead Israel into Canaan to conquer Jericho, a man appeared to him with a drawn sword. "Joshua went up to him and asked, 'Are you for us or for our enemies?' 'Neither,' he replied, 'but as commander of the army of the LORD I have now come' " (Joshua 5:13-14). The Lord was then, and still is, a warrior, Commander-in-Chief of heaven's armies!

Some might counter that that was an "early" revelation of God, and he has progressively revealed himself throughout history so that now we know him as a kind, gracious, loving heavenly Father. True; but he is the same yesterday, today, and forever. We know him as a loving and tender heavenly Father, but he still remains a man of war! So long as his enemy is loose in the earth, God will be known as a warrior.

We find several examples in Scripture where the Lord wrought a tremendous victory for his people in response to praise. One of the foremost instances was in the days of King Jehoshaphat, when the Edomites were attacking Judah *(see* 2 Chronicles 20). Jehoshaphat became totally alarmed and called all of Judah together to the temple to seek the Lord. In his prayer he confessed, " 'For we have no power to face this vast army that is attacking us. We do not know what to do, but our eyes are upon you' " (verse 12). We are then told that the Spirit of the Lord came upon Jahaziel, who was a Levite, a descendant of Asaph (the chief musician at the time of King David). Jahaziel proclaimed, " ' "Do not be afraid or discouraged because of this vast army. For the battle is not yours, but God's" ' " (verse 15).

Through Jahaziel, the Lord then gave the battle plans. After worshiping the Lord for the promised victory, Jehoshaphat said to all the people, " 'Listen to me, Judah and people of Jerusalem! Have faith in the LORD your God and you will be upheld; have faith in his prophets and you will be successful' " (verse 20). Jehoshaphat then proceeded to appoint a group of men to sing praises and to say, " 'Give thanks to the LORD, for his love endures forever' " (verse 21).

Let us get the story in perspective. Over on the right Jehoshaphat lined up his army in ranks. Then he said, "Now where are the singers?" So the singers came out and lined up on his left. Jehoshaphat then did something very ludicrous: he told the singers to go in front and sing praises unto God at the head of the army! He placed the choir as the vanguard in front of the army! He knew who his true warriors would be that day — the praisers would win the battle!

Off they went to war, with the choir in front singing God's praises, and the army following. "As they began to sing and praise, the LORD set ambushes against the men of Ammon and Moab and Mount Seir who were invading Judah, and they were defeated. The men of Ammon and Moab rose up against the men from Mount Seir to destroy and annihilate them. After they finished slaughtering the men from Seir, they helped to destroy one another. When the men of Judah came to the place that overlooks the desert and looked toward the vast army, they saw only dead bodies lying on the ground; no one had escaped. So Jehoshaphat and his men went to carry off their plunder, and they found among them a great amount of equipment and clothing and also articles of value — more than they could take away. There was so much plunder that it took three days to collect it" (2 Chronicles 20:22-25).

Jehoshaphat's soldiers looked at one another, glanced down a little sheepishly at their swords and spears, shrugged, put down their weapons, and sauntered in to clean up the plunder. The real warriors on that occasion were not the soldiers in the army but the singers in the choir! As they sang praises to God, he fought for them, and the soldiers did not even so much as lift a finger. What an awesome victory!

Look again at the song these praisers were singing: " 'Give thanks to the LORD, for his love endures forever' " (verse 21). It is interesting to note that they were not calling down fire from heaven, or invoking God's wrath upon the heathen. Too much of our "spiritual warfare" gets distracted with rebuking the enemy, or with calling on God to act for us in some specific way. But these singers were not recommending a battle strategy to God, nor did they bother to curse the enemy. In its essence, their song of praise said, "Lord, we recognize that you are the omnipotent God and that you have promised to fight for us today. So we thank and praise you for the victory, rejoicing in what we know you have already determined to do on our behalf." Words like that release God to act in the way he knows is best. Warfare through praise does not dictate to God what he should do — it praises him for his wisdom and might, recognizing that he is capable of settling the problem in the best possible manner. We do not focus on the battle or the enemy; we look only to the solution — God! "But the people that do know their God shall be strong, and do exploits" (Daniel 11:32, KJV).

Paul and Silas experienced the effectiveness of praise while in the Philippian jail. They had been flogged and put in an inner cell, with their feet fastened securely in stocks. Around midnight, Silas said, "Paul, did we miss God today? My back hurts, and my feet hurt, and I just don't feel like putting up with all this. Should I invoke a curse on the jailer for treating us like this, or perhaps we should just call down fire on this whole place!" Paul groaned a little as he turned his aching body toward Silas and said, "Silas, I think we should praise the Lord! Let's thank him that we're still alive! Let's thank him that he's going to bring something good out of this situation!" So at midnight Paul and Silas began to pray and sing hymns unto God! Midnight is the very time for prisoners to lift their hearts in praise to God.

Paul and Silas were not crying out to God for deliverance. They were not rebuking the stocks nor casting demons out of the jailer. They were simply praising God for his greatness and goodness. And what happened? "Suddenly there was such a violent earthquake that the foundations of the prison were shaken. At once all the prison doors flew open, and everybody's chains came loose" (Acts 16:26). The story ends with the jailer and his entire household confessing their faith in Jesus Christ. God responded to their praise and not only freed them from jail but also delivered an entire family from the clutches of Satan!

THE SHOUT IN WARFARE

The Bible contains other instances of God responding to praise. "Shouting" is a specific form of praise, and there were two special occasions when the Lord responded to the shout. The first is recorded in Joshua 6, when Joshua led the Israelites to conquer Jericho. For six days they tramped around the city; on the seventh day they arose early to march around the city seven times. After the seventh time, "When the trumpets sounded, the people shouted, and at the sound of the trumpet, when the people gave a loud shout, the wall collapsed; so every man charged straight in, and they took the city" (Joshua 6:20).

Scientists have since offered an explanation for what happened there. They say that as the Israelites lifted their voices in the shout, they hit the resonant frequency of the walls of Jericho, and so the walls collapsed. I don't think so! God responded to their shout of praise on that occasion, and it was not a natural phenomenon but a supernatural miracle. God worked a strong victory on their behalf that day!

Remember Gideon? He was the commander of an ever-decreasing army. God chopped his numbers down until he had only 300 soldiers left " 'in order that Israel may not boast against me that her own strength has saved her' " (Judges 7:2). Gideon led his 300 men to the edge of the Midianite camp. At the appointed time, per Gideon's specific instructions, the 300 men blew their trumpets, broke the jars they were holding, lifted their torches, and shouted, " 'A sword for the LORD and for Gideon!' " (Judges 7:20). In response to their shout, the Lord again fought for Israel, and the Midianite army turned on itself, killing one another. Israel went forward to a mighty victory, all because they had the shout of victory in the camp!

In some circles we have thought of silence as being more reverent than sounds of praise, and others have thought a "shout" to be uncultured. But it is a sad day for the church when the shout is gone from the camp, when spiritual Israel no longer shouts for joy in the power of her Deliverer.

God intends this weapon of praise to be used today in releasing his power on our behalf. There are times for prayer, and there are times for intercession, but there are also times for warfare through praise. In praise, we no longer attack the problem or the enemy forces — we simply confess and rejoice in Christ's Lordship. We rejoice in the fact that he is Lord and victor in our current dilemma. When we rejoice in his strength, he goes to battle. We praise; he fights! As we confess him as Lord in that situation, our faith begins to rise to the level of our confession, and God says, "Why, my children really do believe that I am God and Lord in this situation! In that case, I will display my strength and glory!" God responds by granting us a great victory!

We need not become militant or adopt a warring spirit. God has ordained us to be emissaries of peace. If there is any fighting to be done, let God do it. The apostle Paul made it very clear in Ephesians that the armor designed by God for the Christian soldier is not for the purpose of attacking, but rather for standing firm against the devil's schemes. "Therefore put on the full armor of God, so that when the day of evil comes, you may be able to stand your ground, and after you have done everything, to stand. Stand firm then . . ." (Ephesians 6:13-14). We do not pretend to have power over the enemy in ourselves, but we do rejoice in the God who does. "But even the archangel Michael, when he was disputing with the devil about the body of Moses, did not dare to bring a slanderous accusation against him, but said, 'The Lord rebuke you!' " (Jude 9).

There are many Scriptures that reveal God's intention for praise as a weapon to release his power. Note these verses:

"When you go into battle in your own land against an enemy who is oppressing you, sound a blast on the trumpets. Then you will be remembered by the LORD your God and rescued from your enemies" (Numbers 10:9). (God says that in response to the trumpet blast [praise], he will bring the victory.)

"Judah, your brothers will praise you; your hand will be on the neck of your enemies" (Genesis 49:8). (Judah means "praise," so under a prophetic anointing Jacob declared that the hand of the "praisers" will be on the neck of their enemies.)

After the death of Joshua, the Israelites asked the LORD, "Who will be the first to go up and fight for us against the Canaanites?" The LORD answered, "Judah is to go; I have given the land into their hands" (Judges 1:1-2). (The "praisers" were to go first, leading Israel into Canaan, into victory, into blessing. Let us send the praisers first today, too!)

From the lips of children and infants you have ordained praise because of your enemies, to silence the foe and the avenger (Psalm 8:2). (God in his wisdom has determined to have praise come from those with no battle experience: children! They are utterly naive when it comes to fighting battles the world's way, but they are childlike enough to lift their voices in praise and watch the Lord fight for them!)

Open to me the gates of victory; I will enter by them and praise the Lord. This is the gate of the Lord; the victors shall make their entry through it (Psalm 118:19-20, NEB). (The way to victory is through the gates of praise [see Isaiah 60:18]! Those living in victory have learned how to enter effectively through that gate.)

Let the high praises of God be in their mouth, and a two-edged sword in their hand; to execute vengeance upon the heathen, and punishments upon the people; to bind their kings with chains, and their nobles with fetters of iron; to execute upon them the judgment written: this honour have all his saints. Praise ye the LORD (Psalm 149:6-9, KJV). (God has given us a twofold combination with which to defeat our enemies: the praise of God in our mouths, and the word of God in our hands!)

HIGH PRAISE

Psalm 149:6 is the only verse in the Bible that contains a reference to "high" praise. I believe this has at least three meanings.

In many of our churches, the level of praise at 11 a.m. on Sundays is not very high at all; it is skidding somewhere around floor level. But most of us have experienced times when praise began to ascend, and our hearts were lifted in thanksgiving and praise to God; and before long the praise had ascended to a high level of intensity. There are levels of praise, and "high" praise is first of all a reference to an intense level of praise.

Second, we need to be reminded that we are not the only

ones who are offering up praise and worship unto the Lord. Even now, around the throne in the heavenlies, cherubim and seraphim and angels and creatures and the saints of all ages are lifting their voices to sing the holiness of our God. Thus "high praise" is a reference to the praise that is occurring high above us right now, the praise that is ascending to the Father from before the throne. I believe it is possible for us, here below, to participate now in that "high praise." By listening with our spirits, we can discern the type of song being sung around the throne. As "Holy, holy, holy" resounds in the heavenlies, the earthly choir can join in and sing, "Holy, holy, holy." When the angels are singing, "Praise befits his majesty," the saints here can also sing, "Praise befits his majesty!" We can have a two-part antiphonal choir: the heavenly choir sings praises unto the Lamb, and the earthly choir responds with songs of praise. May we have that "high praise" today, "in earth as it is in heaven"!

Finally — and this is our focus — there is a type or level of praise that ascends into the heavenlies and wars on our behalf. We all recognize that spiritual forces of wickedness inhabit the heavenlies. Daniel learned this in a very specific way on one occasion while praying. A "man" appeared to him in a vision; according to the description of this "man," he was possibly the Lord himself, although the text does not say so specifically. When Daniel had first prayed, this man was sent to Daniel with the answer to his prayer but was detained for twenty-one days by the evil prince of the Persian kingdom. Michael, "one of the chief princes" in heaven, was then sent to help this man in his battle against the prince of Persia, and because of their united fight, this man was able to break through the spiritual barrier and visit Daniel with the answer *(see* Daniel 10).

The Scriptures make it clear that evil powers hover over nations, cities, households, and even individuals. Various forms of spiritual warfare can be waged against these evil forces. In the example of Daniel, he prayed through to vic-

tory. But the Lord has given us another precious tool for
engaging in warfare: high praise!

Psalm 149 links this "high praise" with the "two-edged
sword," or the word of God. There is a beautiful relationship between the singing of God's praise and the preaching
of the word. Coupling the praises of God with a dynamic
and fresh word from God produces an unbeatable combination! Churches that are moving in these two dimensions of
ministry are flourishing and growing, and they will not be
stopped.

This psalm also speaks of executing "vengeance upon
the heathen, and punishments upon the people." A New
Testament understanding of this passage is in order, because God does not usually respond to our praise by pouring
out his wrath and judgment on the heathen. In a New Testament sense, God is saying, "There is an inheritance for the
church in the nations, but it is not yet claimed. Go forth and
bind the satanic powers that blind the hearts of men, and
reclaim for the kingdom that portion of the body of Christ that
has yet to be brought in." You see, the main thrust of warfare
through praise is *evangelistic.* God's heart beats for the lost,
and he wants us to become part of the action.

Praise operated as a tool for evangelism in the New Testament. On the day of Pentecost, the God-fearing Jews from
many nations who were in Jerusalem heard the Christians
speaking in unknown tongues — "declaring the wonders of
God" — in essence, giving praise to God in other tongues.
As a result of hearing this "high praise," followed by
Peter's sermon ("two-edged sword"), about three thousand
people came to Christ that day! As is typical of praise, there
were two types of responses on that occasion: "Amazed and
perplexed, they asked one another, 'What does this mean?'
Some, however, made fun of them and said, 'They have had
too much wine' " (Acts 2:12-13). God has not called us to
worry about man's responses. We are called to sing his high
praises and declare his word; the harvest belongs to him.

God has given us the tools and the opportunity to become involved, for God releases his conviction and repentance as we praise. The church has an unclaimed inheritance in the nations! We must lift high the banner of praise and by faith witness the release of God's word and power in all the earth, until the body of Christ is full and complete!

"Every stroke the LORD lays on them with his punishing rod will be to the music of tambourines and harps, as he fights them in battle with the blows of his arm" (Isaiah 30:32). This is an activity in which instrumentalists are to participate! Get out the tambourine! Get out the guitar! Let the pianist sit down, and let the drummer take his place. It is time to go to war! It is time to lead God's people in high praise, to declare that he is victorious in all the earth — and this Scripture shows us that as we do, God tightens his fist and gives the enemy a left hook, and then a big right cross to the jaw!

God wants to punish the kingdom of darkness by rescuing from Satan's hand many souls who are now doomed to destruction. Every time a soul is snatched from darkness and brought into God's kingdom, a death blow is administered to sin, the purposes of Satan are frustrated, another carnal nature is put to death, and a newly born saint emerges! If interceding for that unsaved husband for many years has brought weariness of the battle, stop fighting and start praising! Praising and rejoicing and confessing God's sovereignty release God to fight, and what was not accomplished in years may happen in just a matter of months or weeks!

Isaiah declared, "On this mountain he will destroy the shroud that enfolds all peoples, the sheet that covers all nations" (Isaiah 25:7). Which mountain was this? It was Mount Zion! Mount Zion was famous as a place of praise. Moses' tabernacle was known as a place of sacrifices, but David's tabernacle (Mount Zion) was known as a place of singing, music, and praise. On that mountain of praise, the Lord will destroy the blanket of darkness that covers cities and families. How many of us have tried to witness to someone, only to be met with a completely blank face? That person could not understand a thing being said, because Satan has blinded people's minds so that they cannot receive the truth of God's word, even if they might want to. Praise breaks through that barrier!

Some young people who have participated in Youth With A Mission (a worldwide evangelistic outreach) told me that they have experienced times when their personal evangelism seemed to be hitting a cement wall. At such times they would get out the guitars and start singing the praise of God wherever they were. The spiritual walls would begin to crumble, and they would have a breakthrough at that locality! We have a wonderful weapon in praise because God has ordained that through his praising church (Mount Zion) he is going to tear through the spiritual barriers that cover the nations!

" 'So the LORD Almighty will come down to do battle on Mount Zion and on its heights' " (Isaiah 31:4). The "heights of Zion" are the high praises of God's people! When our hearts are lifted up in high praise to the Lord, our spirits ascend the heights of Zion. As we raise our voices in that level of high praise, God will respond in might and power. "In Zion his battle-quarters are set up" (Psalm 76:2, NEB).

"Hear that uproar from the city, hear that noise from the temple! It is the sound of the LORD repaying his enemies all they deserve" (Isaiah 66:6). What uproar is coming from the city of God? What noise is in God's temple? It is praise — high praise and worship. That sound of praise is the sound of the Lord bringing retribution upon his enemies!

THE SOUND OF WAR

Ezekiel had a magnificent experience in which he was caught up into the heavenlies and heard the heavenly worship. Notice how he tried to express what he heard: " . . . like the roar of rushing water, like the voice of the Almighty, like the tumult of an army" (Ezekiel 1:24). This was Ezekiel's best attempt to describe the sound of the heavenly praise. The apostle John, in a similar experience, described the heavenly worship this way: "Then I heard what sounded like a great multitude, like the roar of rushing waters and like loud peals of thunder, shouting, 'Hallelujah! . . .' " (Revelation 19:6). To find out what heavenly worship sounds like, gather the saints together in praise and worship! That is the sound! It is like the voice of the Almighty. It is truly the tumult of an army, the army of the Lord. It is like loud peals of thunder — that is the sound of the Lord repaying his enemies all they deserve! The sound of praise is the sound of war.

God will continue to respond to prayer and intercession, but the time will come when he will whisper in our hearts and say, "Stop asking, stop striving, stop interceding, and start praising me for the victory!" Praise does not dictate to God *how* the answer should come. Many times our prayer requests limit God because we ask him for things when he would want to answer in a different and fuller dimension. But praise takes the lid off the possibilities, because it simply confesses and rejoices in the absolute ability of God to be exactly who he is in the situation at hand. Praise God that he is in control and that he is glorified in this situation. When we confess God's supremacy through praise, our faith rises to the level of our confession, and he responds!

The problem is not God's ability to deal with the situation, nor is it a matter of trying to convince God to display his glory. The problem is with us. We limit God with our puny conceptions of who he is! When we sing, "Let God be magnified," we are not attempting to make God any bigger than he already is. But we are desirous of having our conception of him enlarged!

THE ROLE OF FAITH

Faith plays a strategic role in warfare through praise, so this is a key concept. When we go to war in praise, there is the added dimension of faith. By faith we lift our hearts unto the Lord and say, "Lord, I'm singing this song of praise specifically to release you to be God in this situation. By faith I make my praise ascend into the heavenlies, to do warfare in spiritual places." We actually can send forth — commission — our praise to an intended goal. Psalm 118:26 reads, "From the house of the LORD we bless you." "You" in this verse is plural in the Hebrew and therefore is a reference not to God but to people. From the house of God we can, by faith, virtually send forth or commission a blessing to come upon someone who is not present in the congregation. In the same way, by faith we can send our praises like shafts of light, commissioning them to do combat in heavenly realms.

To an outsider, warfare through praise would not really appear to be very different or unique. When going to praise in warfare, we might sing the same song that we sang in last week's praise service. Last week that song was simply a praise unto God; this week it becomes a tool of war. What is the difference? — faith! The song is offered up to God from a completely different posture of the heart.

A WORD FROM GOD

We go to war through praise only at a word from God. Usually this word will come through the spiritual leadership of the group that is meeting. For instance, in the middle of a service, one of the elders might feel it is time for the church to go to war, through praise, on behalf of a family that has been suffering an attack of sickness from the evil one. The musicians will take their places, the worship leader will rise, and God's people will lift their hearts in praise. God will respond in delight over the praises of his people and will rebuke the devourer for the glory of his name.

In the story of Jehoshaphat that we read earlier (2 Chronicles 20), the people received a very specific word from God. All they had to do was obey. So it must be with us.

When we attempt to engage in spiritual warfare without a word from God, several negative things can happen. First of all, it is possible to be found buffeting the air. If we are not engaging the enemy, we are fighting a phantom battle! I am convinced that much of today's "spiritual warfare" is little more than a buffeting of the air. If our "spiritual warfare" bears no concrete results, we must question how effectively we are engaging the enemy. Second, we might end up attacking brethren. We must understand that the enemy is not the Baptist church down the road. Third, we can miss the timing of God and, by entering prematurely into a situation, can miss the full potential of what God intended. And finally, it is possible to attack things that God never intended for us to conquer. For example, we might want to engage in spiritual warfare against a certain pornographic shop down the street, when the Lord might in fact be saying, "None of your business!" But when we receive a word from God to do battle through praise against such a place, we will be thrilled with what he will do. We must make ourselves available to hear a word from God. Once we are available, God will speak to us in his timing, and we will have the certainty of moving in his will.

PREPARING FOR WAR

We must prepare for this type of warfare. If we are not prepared and battle-ready, then God will not commission us. Jeremiah 12:5 reads, "And if in the land of peace, in which you trusted, they wearied you, then how will you do in the flooding of the Jordan?" (NKJV). "If you were wearied in the easy times," Jeremiah was asking, "how will you be able to make it when the hard times hit?" And in the area of praise, the question is this: "If you are having a hard time praising the Lord when everything is going well for you, how will you muster the strength to enter into warfare through praise when the hard times come?" You see, many churches in America today are struggling to enter just into praise — let alone warfare through praise. But this new dimension of warfare through praise gives us a motivation to "get it together" when it comes to praising the Lord. Indeed, we *must* get it together if we want to be used at all in this greater dimension. Therefore, now is the time to prepare for warfare through praise. We prepare by learning to truly make his praise glorious now in the time of peace; then when it is time to sound the trumpet and go to war, we are capable of offering up a glorious and triumphant praise to God.

Proverbs 24:10 puts it another way: "If you falter in times of trouble, how small is your strength!" When the hard times hit — and they will hit — our strength is truly tested. Have we learned the lesson of praise? Will we offer up sacrifices of praise regardless of our circumstances? Unfortunately for us, God knows there is only one way we tend to discover the answer for ourselves, and that is through sending us some difficult circumstances. Trials and tribulations can be a test for us, even as they were for Job, to see if we will remain fervent in our praise in the midst of unpleasant situations.

The psalmist wrote, "Praise be to the LORD, my Rock, who trains my hands for war, my fingers for battle" (Psalm 144:1). The Lord wants to prepare and train musicians for the time of war. He will train their hands to play the drums; he will teach their fingers to play the piano. Is anyone out there being prepared for battle? Is someone in the middle of those tedious music lessons? Hang in there! It's God's training for wartime! If we are prepared musically, then we will be ready to lead God's people in glorious praises that can ascend to do spiritual battle in the heavenlies. God is looking for leaders who are ready to lead his people in spiritual warfare, for, as Costa Deir has said, "Only battle-ready leaders will ready soldiers for the battle."

We must guard against being unprepared in the day of battle. David once wrote, "For in the day of trouble he will keep me safe in his dwelling; he will hide me in the shelter

of his tabernacle" (Psalm 27:5). The safest place in the time
of war is in the shelter of his tabernacle — in proper relationship to the body of Christ, and specifically, to a local
church. There is safety in the body! Outside his tabernacle,
we become very vulnerable to the attacks of the enemy. We
must prepare now for that attack and unite ourselves in
spirit to a local body of believers.

I once asked a young man, "What church are you
from?" He responded, "None. I guess I'm kind of like a lone
ranger." One lesson we quickly learn as we mature in Christ
is that God does not have any "lone rangers"! It is imperative that we know the security and safety of the local
church, or else we become candidates for outside attacks.

Notice something else that Psalm 27 says: "Then my
head will be exalted above the enemies who surround me"
(verse 6). God never promised that our enemies would all
disappear or be annihilated, but he has promised that we
can be victorious in the midst of our enemies!

ENGAGING IN BATTLE

Some worship leaders think that their enemy on Sunday
morning is the congregation. They feel that the people
almost fight their attempts to let the praise resound. In fact,
sometimes that is exactly what happens. The people may be
so fearful of opening their hearts in praise that they harden
themselves against the attempts of the worship leader to
lead them. Worship leaders often ask, "What can we do
when there is a sense of heaviness in the congregation, as
though spiritual forces are holding the people back from
entering into that which their hearts truly desire?"

The answer is this: The worship team — leader, pianist,
organist, orchestra and choir, and pastor (if possible) —
should gather on a Saturday evening and proceed to do
spiritual battle in behalf of God's people. If Satan has bound
God's people in their freedom of praise and worship, then
that hindrance must be broken! It is not a time to rehearse

music — it is a time to enter into high praise and unitedly attack the spiritual shackles on God's people. If this is done, who knows what might happen on Sunday morning!

When directed of God, this weapon can also be used to invade enemy territory. Before an evangelistic team goes into the neighborhood, a session of high praise can prepare a pathway for the feet of those who are bringing the good news of our Lord.

Praise can also be used in spiritual warfare when we find it necessary to stand firm in our position against an attack. We are not the only ones waging warfare; Satan also will attack us, the church, or someone in the church. Go to praise! Go to war! Do not give an inch! Stand firm, and praise the one who always causes us to triumph!

Once we are ready for warfare through praise, the Lord will continually provide us with challenges to keep us battle-ready. He did the same thing to Israel: "These are the nations the LORD left to test all those Israelites who had not experienced any of the wars in Canaan (he did this only to teach warfare to the descendants of the Israelites who had not had previous battle experience)" (Judges 3:1-2). The Lord left some of the Canaanites in the land so that Israel would be kept on their toes, always ready for battle. Once we have seen a victory in warfare through praise, it is not time to settle back and relax — another battle may be just around the corner. This is God's way of keeping us "instant in season," always ready to follow his command.

It has been said that "we need less emphasis on rapture, and more emphasis on capture!" For too long the church has had a "hang-on" mentality, waiting for that day when we will be snatched out of this terrible mess. But God is speaking to us today because he wants to raise up a victorious, conquering, overcoming church!

When the Philistines captured the ark of the covenant, they placed it in the temple of their god Dagon. The next morning they arose to find Dagon fallen facedown before the ark. They put Dagon back in his place, but the next morning he was not only fallen before the ark but also had his head and hands broken off. The ark of the covenant is symbolic for us of the presence and glory of God, for over that ark God's presence resided in the Old Testament tabernacle. When we magnify God's name in praise and worship, the principalities and powers of the air will bow down to the Lordship of Jesus Christ.

We war in praise, and we praise when the victory is won! "It is finished!" is the triumphal cry. With that knowledge, and rejoicing in battles won, we come to our God not only in praise but in worship.

CHAPTER 4

WHAT IS WORSHIP?

There are so many concepts of what worship is (or is not), and so many interpretations of how worship is expressed or manifested, that answering the question "What is worship?" is a difficult task indeed. Many have struggled with finding an adequate definition of worship. Praise is not hard to define, but worship is another matter. No one definition seems to adequately express the fullness of worship — perhaps because worship is a divine encounter and so is as infinite in its depth as God himself.

Over a period of time, I have collected a number of "definitions" of worship. Though these are but attempts to put into words what essentially is a feeling, they should nonetheless help us begin to understand something of the basic nature of worship.

1. Worship is conversation between God and man, a dialogue that should go on constantly in the life of a Christian.

2. Worship is giving to God and involves a lifetime of giving to him the sacrifice he asks for: our total selves.

3. Worship is our affirmative response to the self-revelation of the triune God. For the Christian, each act of life is an act of worship when it is done with love that responds to the Father's love. Living should be constant worshiping, since worship may be said to provide the metabolism for spiritual life.

4. Worship was the outcome of the fellowship of love between the Creator and man and is the highest point man can reach in response to the love of God. It is the first and principal purpose of man's eternal calling.

5. Worship is one's heart expression of love, adoration, and praise to God with an attitude and acknowledgment of

his supremacy and Lordship.

6. Worship is an act by a redeemed man, the creature, toward God, his Creator, whereby his will, intellect and emotions gratefully respond in reverence, honor, and devotion to the revelation of God's person expressed in the redemptive work of Jesus Christ, as the Holy Spirit illuminates God's written word to his heart.

7. Worship means "to feel in the heart." Worship also means to express in some appropriate manner what we feel.

8. True worship and praise are "awesome wonder and overpowering love" in the presence of our God.

9. Worship is the ability to magnify God with our whole being — body, soul, and spirit.

10. The heart of true worship is the unashamed pouring out of our inner self upon the Lord Jesus Christ in affectionate devotion.

11. Worship is fundamentally God's Spirit within us contacting the Spirit in the Godhead.

12. Worship is the response of God's Spirit in us to that Spirit in him whereby we answer, "Abba, Father," deep calling unto deep.

13. Worship is the ideally normal attitude of a rational creature properly related to the Creator.

14. Worship is extravagant love and extreme obedience.

These definitions are all very good and give us much insight into worship; yet they all seem to fall short somehow. I once heard my father-in-law, Morris Smith, say, "Real worship defies definition; it can only be experienced." How true this is, for worship was never intended by God to be the discussion of textbooks but rather the communion with God experienced by his loved ones.

DIFFERENCES BETWEEN PRAISE AND WORSHIP

As an introduction to studying the meaning of worship, it would be helpful for us to gain a clearer perspective on some of the distinctives between praise and worship. They frequently operate in different realms. Sometimes, however, it is virtually impossible to differentiate between praise and worship; both may be expressed in a service by different individuals at the same time. When we are lifting our hands or dancing before the Lord, are we praising or worshiping? We could be doing either, because the outward forms that praise and worship employ are often identical.

It is almost as difficult to separate praise and worship as it is to divide soul and spirit. That the soul and spirit are two different aspects of man seems sure, but it becomes very difficult to identify the differences. When I feel a certain impulse, who am I to label that as coming from my spirit or from my soul? There is only one thing sharp enough to discern between soul and spirit, and that is the word of God *(see* Hebrews 4:12). I cannot even analyze the difference in my own self! Similarly, praise and worship are two different entities, but they are often impossible to separate.

The four expressions known as prayer, thanksgiving, praise, and worship are very closely related. Areas within each of these expressions overlap with one another. By seeing the overlap in the diagram below, perhaps we can begin to understand why it is difficult to completely separate these from each other.

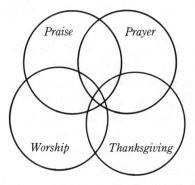

The differences between praise and worship in this chapter, therefore, are almost hypothetical. But we will gain a better grasp of the essence of worship by examining these "hypothetical" differences.

First, God does not need our praises; we need to praise him. God has commanded us to praise, not because of what it does for him but because of the changes it brings in us. It places us in proper relationship to God and is a necessary step for us in the process of self-abasement. God receives ample praise from his other multitudinous creations — he will manage quite well if you or I refuse to praise him. But the Father *seeks* worshipers *(see* John 4:23)! He seeks them because he needs them. Notice that God seeks "worshipers," not "worship." He does not need our worship, but he is fervently seeking those who have adopted the life-style and mind-set of a worshiper.

Second, praise can sometimes be distant, but worship is usually intimate. The heart of man need not be near to God for praise to occur. I have heard stories about men who have started to praise God while in drunken revelry. I have even heard of drunkards witnessing to one another, as though therein were some easing of their conscience. On one occasion Jesus said the rocks would cry out if his disciples did not praise him *(see* Luke 19:37-40). Rocks obviously do not have a relationship with God Almighty, and no interaction of personalities will ever exist between God and a rock, but praise is still possible. Anyone or anything can praise; the trees, mountains, rivers, sun, moon, and stars all praise the Lord *(see* Psalm 148:3-12), and yet God has no relationship with any of these.

Worship is different. It brings us close to the heart of God. Relationship is a requirement for worship because worship is a two-way street, involving both giving and receiving. It is possible for praise to ascend one way only, but worship involves communion and fellowship.

Next, praise is always seen or heard; worship is not always evident to an observer. There are times when worship is every bit as visible and evident as praise, but not always. Sometimes worship is quiet and visually unassuming. We are told that the elders fall prostrate before the throne in worship. I would imagine that they appear almost lifeless as they pour out everything of themselves in a self-effacing way before the Lord. It is not always possible to look at people and determine whether or not they are worshiping. One might venture to judge whether another is praising God, because praise is always obvious to others. But there is only One who knows whether or not we are truly worshiping.

Fourth, praise is largely horizontal in its purpose, while worship is primarily a vertical interaction. Much happens on a horizontal level when we praise; we speak to one another, and we declare his praise before each other. But worship is more private and is much more preoccupied with the Godhead. Praise does have some vertical functions, and worship has some horizontal elements, but these are not their primary directions.

Praise is often preparatory to worship. God will frequently attempt to teach us to praise before we enter into the fullness of worship, for once we have learned what it means to praise the Lord with all that is within us, it is then a fairly easy progression to become an extravagant worshiper. If we are inhibited in our praise, however, we will likely be bound in our worship also.

Praise can be conceived as a gateway to worship. Many times it is easier to praise than to worship. Therefore, if we're having trouble entering into worship, starting with praise will help worship flow more easily. We sing in order to enter into praise, and sometimes we praise in order to enter into worship. But singing does not guarantee praise, just as praise does not guarantee that we will cross the threshold into worship.

There are exceptions to this next point, but as a general rule, experience affirms that worship is usually accompanied by slower songs, and praise, by faster songs. It is not that a slow tempo always denotes worship, while a fast tempo equals praise; rather, the mood of slower songs is more conducive to worship, and faster songs lend themselves more readily to the activity that characterizes praise. Of course there is an occasional exception, but generalizations such as this can help us gain a better comprehension of the distinctives of praise and worship. Actually, one of the best ways to determine whether a song is a "praise chorus" or a "worship chorus" is to look not merely at the speed of the tempo but at the subject matter of the lyrics.

We must remember, however, that music is a catalyst for worship — it in no way guarantees or even denotes worship. Some might complain, "I don't relate to all this emphasis on worship because I don't like to sing." Enjoyment of singing is entirely irrelevant to worship. Many people cannot "carry a tune in a bucket," but they are adoring worshipers. In Luke chapter 7, the woman who anointed Jesus' feet is exemplary as a worshiper; she had no musical instruments being played before her, nor was she singing, but she was worshiping in a most notable and commendable way. Worship is not a musical activity but a function of the heart.

A final variance between praise and worship can be seen in that sometimes we need to plunge into praise with an aggressiveness. It is often necessary to stir up our flesh and our soul to praise the Lord. But worship seems to operate at a different level. Worship does not seem to involve human effort to the same degree. It is more often characterized by a quiet and unassumed basking in God's presence.

Our spirit is willing to worship, but our flesh is weak and reluctant. Since praise is expressed through the flesh, it requires a stirring up of the flesh. But since worship is more a function of the spirit, what is needed is not a stirring up of the flesh but an unlocking of the spirit.

These comments are not intended to imply that worship is superior to or nobler than praise. Both expressions are equally important, and both play a vital role in the life of every believer and congregation. If we think worship is more desirable than praise, the push will be on in every praise service to progress into worship. But it is frequently appropriate to remain at praise for a period of time or to bring a service to an apex by concluding with high praise.

Some people get preoccupied with the direction of their songs: "Is the song directed to myself, to my neighbor, or to God?" Songs that speak to God are not necessarily any better or more desirable than songs that speak about him. What matters to God is that we enter into sweet communion with him, regardless of whether the song is written in the first, second, or third person. Let us not get so introspective that we start worrying, "Am I praising right now, or worshiping?" Let's get our focus off the mechanics and concentrate on pleasing the Lord by simply expressing our love to him.

Some have made the mistake of equating praise with "the outer court" and worship with "the inner court." To place this strong a barrier between the two is artificial. Many of the bodily activities employed in praise, for example, are employed in worship also. When I lift my hands, am I praising or worshiping? Obviously I could be doing either, or even both. We typically think of dance as a form of praise, but I clearly recall one service in which I danced before the Lord with all my strength as an expression of worship. Shouting, clapping, singing — yes, all the outward forms of praise — can be used in worship. But worship can also transpire without any outward activity, whereas praise is always characterized by some form of physical manifestation. Which is the highest of these two expressions? — whichever is inspired by the Holy Spirit for the occasion.

A MISCONCEPTION

Some have espoused an alleged difference between praise and worship that needs some adjustment. The idea has been expressed in words similar to these: "Praise creates the presence of God, while worship is our response to his presence."

There are some problems with this statement. Praise does not "create" the presence of God; it does not induce or coerce or command the presence of God. God's presence is with us, based not upon our praise but upon his promise. He will never leave us or forsake us! And he has promised that where two or three are gathered, he will be with them *(see* Matthew 18:20).

When we praise, the Holy Spirit begins to stir our hearts, and we become more conscious of God's presence. His presence never comes and goes — we are the ones who change. Our awareness of his presence changes.

Not all services start with praise and end in worship once God's presence is manifested. Some services will begin with worship and end with a glorious sound of praise. Since God is already among us, it becomes totally feasible to start with worship.

Another problem with this statement is that worship does not result only in response to his presence. There are times when we feel very far from God, and yet we need to worship him. When Abraham was on the way to the mountain where he purposed to kill his only son, what did he say to the servants? " 'Stay here with the donkey while I and the boy go over there. We will worship' " (Genesis 22:5). In the mental anxiety of planning to kill his own son, when God no doubt seemed miles away, Abraham worshiped. He could not understand why God had commanded him to sacrifice his only son, the only true heir whom God had miraculously provided. But despite his inability to comprehend God's intentions, Abraham worshiped. His worship would not have been complete without his total obedience. Paul referred to this level of obedience in worship when he wrote, "Therefore, I urge you, brothers, in view of God's mercy, to offer your bodies as living sacrifices, holy and pleasing to God — which is your spiritual worship" (Romans 12:1).

Most of us are familiar with Job's tale of woe, when in one day his oxen and donkeys were stolen, his sheep were destroyed, his camels were carried off, his servants were slain, and his sons and daughters were killed when a house collapsed on them. Notice Job's first response: "At this, Job got up and tore his robe and shaved his head. Then he fell to the ground in worship" (Job 1:20). There were no "goosebumps" for Job on this occasion, when he worshiped. He was not responding according to a great sensation of the glory of God; quite to the contrary, he was in the lowest emotional pit of his entire lifetime. But regardless of his feelings, he fell prostrate in worship, affirming God's ultimate sovereignty in his life.

David had a similar experience. The son born out of his illicit relationship with Bathsheba was cursed of God and lay dying. David fasted and prayed for seven days, spending the nights lying on the ground, but on the seventh day the child died. When David learned of the child's death, his response was most remarkable. "Then David got up from the ground. After he had washed, put on lotions and changed his clothes, he went into the house of the LORD and worshiped" (2 Samuel 12:20). This was a devastating moment in David's life. At a time when God had said, "No," and his child had died, David worshiped. He was not shouting the victory, or dancing, or singing. But in this emotional valley he confessed the Lordship of his God. He worshiped the Lord Most High, whose understanding and justice were infinitely greater than his own and whose ruling of death was somehow right and good.

THE ESSENCE OF WORSHIP

Worship is not simply something that happens in the congregation when we feel the anointed presence of God. Worship can happen when we are in our darkest hour and we affirm his sovereignty regardless of our circumstances. Not until we go through an experience like David's or Job's can we prove to ourselves the essential quality of our worship. Only under stressful conditions are our true colors revealed, and we discover whether we are worshipers indeed.

The true worshiper will worship even under emotionally devastating circumstances. Until we know what it means to worship in the hardest of times, we have not grasped the most fundamental element in becoming a worshiper.

The dynamics and dimensions of worship are so many and so varied that no one definition of worship could possibly include all its ramifications and meanings. But what is the root idea of worship? What is the absolute essence, the common denominator, in all of worship? I believe it is seen in the lives of men like Abraham and Job, who worshiped in the midst of the most life-shattering circumstances. This is the fundamental essence of worship: regardless of negative circumstances or complete emotional turmoil, I bow my heart and life before God Almighty, acknowledging his supreme Lordship. The bottom line on worship is confessing his Lordship when everything that surrounds one's life screams, "God is unjust! He doesn't love you! He has forsaken you!" At such a time, the true worshiper says, "The Lord is God. Blessed be the name of the Lord."

Worship is learned. "Blessed are those who have learned to acclaim you" (Psalm 89:15). It is not a talent with which one is born, nor is it a special gifting for a select few. Worship is the art of expressing oneself to God, and we must learn that expression and open our hearts as channels of the Holy Spirit.

Just as preaching is an art that is learned, our ability to worship is developed through application and experience. Worship is not learned by reading books, or by taking classes, or by going to seminars. Like the art of prayer, worship is learned by doing it.

We should not be impatient with ourselves if we are not now able to worship as we would desire. Learning the fullness of worship is a lengthy process and does not come easily. The lessons God brings into our lives to teach us worship can sometimes be as dramatic as those of Abraham, Job, and David. Responding positively in worship rather than bemoaning the trying circumstances will cause us to grow as worshipers. In many churches we have been taught to work, and we have been taught to witness, but we have not been taught to worship.

Perhaps this is what the psalmist meant when he said, "Deep calls to deep in the roar of your waterfalls" (Psalm 42:7). In the context of that verse, the writer was speaking of deep emotional turbulence in difficult times. When everything seems to be crashing down upon us like a roaring waterfall, we must resort to the deep-down faith that we have in God. When we feel overwhelmed and do not know why God has allowed this situation to come into our lives, we must reaffirm our basic faith in God. "Though God slays me, I will trust him!" This is the deep within us — that expression from the depths of our soul that affirms our trust in God regardless of the vicissitudes of life. Worship is the deep within us calling out to the deep in God.

Sometimes this level of worship is best expressed in quietness. " 'Be still, and know that I am God' " (Psalm 46:10). This verse has nothing to do with praise, but it certainly applies to worship. There are times when our worship will not constitute the forming of words and phrases but will involve the humble prostration of our souls before God, revering his greatness in silence and stillness. Since worship is an expression of love, it frequently functions very similarly to marital love. Love does not need to be verbalized in order to be expressed or appreciated. Sometimes more is said simply through eye contact than could ever be expressed verbally. Worship involves "eye contact" with God — worship is staring at God.

When facing turbulent circumstances, we have a tendency to complain now and postpone the worship for later. But Jesus said, " 'The hour . . . *now is,* when the true worshipers will worship the Father' " (John 4:23, NKJV). Worship operates in the present tense. Worshipers are not satisfied with waiting for the euphoric praises of the redeemed around the throne in heaven. The fact that we may have worshiped in the past, or that glorious worship awaits us in the future, is unsatisfactory. Now is the time to enter into true worship.

Although worshipers are not satisfied with waiting for heaven, they will take a cue from heaven. We have a blessed peek into the nature of heavenly worship through the Apocalypse of the apostle John. Set before us in the book of Revelation is a glorious example worthy of our emulation. I am keenly anticipating that day when our worship around the throne will be free from all hindrances and shackles of self-consciousness! Heaven is noisy and passionate in its demonstration of praise and worship to God. God himself is fiercely and passionately emotional, and he responds to us accordingly! We will never go wrong in using the heavenly prototype of worship as a pattern today. As we gain insight into the heavenly worship, we can then pray that we experience worship "in earth as it is in heaven."

Heaven is certainly spontaneous in its worship, and spontaneity can also play a key role in our worship. Husbands will experience times of loving their wives in a determined, almost perfunctory manner, but spice is added to a marriage when love "just happens." A husband might decide to buy flowers on a whim or take his wife out for ice cream. Similarly, spontaneous expressions of worship are particularly pleasing to the Lord. It is proper to respond to a small impulse, even though it may be a new way of expressing love to God.

Any desire to worship, whether spontaneous or mechanical, is placed in us by God. We must understand that worship is born in the heart of God. The Holy Spirit initiates worship in the heart of man, and he is vitally involved in our worship.

THE HOLY SPIRIT AND WORSHIP

Since intimacy in worship is impossible without the inspiration of the Holy Spirit, unregenerate men never can and never will worship in love. The Scriptures do contain examples of heathen men "worshiping," and they make it clear that men from all nations will come and worship before him, for his judgments will be made manifest (Revelation 15:4). Every knee shall bow and every tongue confess that Jesus Christ is Lord (Philippians 2:10-11). Heathen men are capable of recognizing the awesomeness of God and of worshiping him accordingly. But they will never know the intimacy of worshiping him in spirit and in truth. Spiritual worship is the exclusive privilege of those who have been quickened by the indwelling Holy Spirit. David acknowledged, " 'Everything comes from you, and we have given you only what comes from your hand' " (1 Chronicles 29:14). Paul asked the question, "What do you have that you did not receive?" (1 Corinthians 4:7). Paul also said, "For from him and through him and to him are all things" (Romans 11:36). John the Baptist said, " 'A man can receive only what is given him from heaven' " (John 3:27).

The Holy Spirit is an integral part of our worship, and congregational worship is successful only as we submit to him as our divine Worship Leader. The flow of the Spirit in worship is uniquely pictured in Ezekiel's account of an awesome heavenly vision: "When the living creatures moved, the wheels beside them moved; and when the living creatures rose from the ground, the wheels also rose. Wherever the spirit would go, they would go, and the wheels would rise along with them, because the spirit of the living creatures was in the wheels" (Ezekiel 1:19-20). Ezekiel was seeing how the heavenly worship was being guided and directed by the heavenly Worship Leader, the Holy Spirit.

Many worship leaders are frustrated because they have not learned to follow the Holy Spirit's guidance in the context of a worship service. God wants to do specific things in each worship service, and unless we move with him, we can miss his purpose. It becomes vital, then, that we be sensitive to the gentle promptings of the Spirit as the service is in progress. (On occasion that may mean forsaking our preplanned list of songs and moving with God.)

Numbers 9:15-23 gives the account of the Israelites following the cloud of God's glory. When the cloud moved, they moved; when the cloud stayed, they pitched their tents and stayed. When the Spirit of God is not ready to move on, no one should violate his sovereignty by saying, "You may be seated, and will the ushers please come forward?" Conversely, when God moves on in our worship services, all should be prepared to pack their bags and move with him! Many services have suffered because of our insensitivity to realize the "burden" of the Spirit for the worship time has lifted. Any singing beyond that point is an anticlimax at best.

The Song of Solomon describes the Lover (our Lord) knocking at the door of his Beloved (us — the church), in order to share love. But the Beloved is reticent to open the door because she has taken off her robe and washed her feet, and she is on the verge of falling asleep. She is not sure she wants to respond to the beckoning of the Lover. Finally, she goes to the door to greet her Lover, but lo! he is gone! She hesitated too long. This shows us how easily the Holy Spirit can be grieved when we reject his overtures. When he beckons us and calls us unto God, we must be quick to answer and to follow his way.

God has promised, "I will instruct you and teach you in the way you should go; I will counsel you and watch over you. Do not be like the horse or the mule, which have no understanding but must be controlled by bit and bridle or they will not come to you" (Psalm 32:8-9). We can apply this passage to our present study — the Lord will guide us in the way we should go in worship. But he pleads with us that we not be slow to understand and respond to his promptings. God does not yank us around, the way we would handle a horse or a mule. He refuses to hit us on the head and yell orders in our ears. Rather, he speaks softly and gently to us. So if we are to hear the counsel of the Spirit in our worship, we must be continually sensitive to his voice.

WORSHIP IN SPIRIT AND IN TRUTH

In John 4, Jesus gave us the greatest revelation of worship, and to understand the heart of worship we must carefully consider his words. "Jesus declared, 'Believe me, woman, a time is coming when you will worship the Father neither on this mountain nor in Jerusalem. You Samaritans worship what you do not know; we worship what we do know, for salvation is from the Jews. Yet a time is coming and has now come when the true worshipers will worship the Father in spirit and truth, for they are the kind of worshipers the Father seeks. God is spirit, and his worshipers must worship in spirit and in truth' " (verses 21-24).

Jesus was showing that worship would no longer be bound to a certain time or place (neither in Jerusalem, where the Jews worshiped, nor Mount Gerizim, where the Samaritans worshiped); rather, it was going to be a function of the spirit of man reaching out to the Spirit of God. Jesus knew the time was shortly to come when Mosaic sacrifices at Jerusalem would be outdated, and worship would occur within the New Testament temple — man himself *(see* 1 Corinthians 3:16). Worship can now happen any time, wherever a Spirit-inhabited person may be.

Jesus also indicated that as a function of the spirit, true worship is more than just an outward ritual. Worship is our spirit corresponding with God's Spirit. Under the old covenant, worship was a series of outward ceremonies that did not necessarily involve the heart response of the participants. Through Isaiah, God lamented, " 'These people come near to me with their mouth and honor me with their lips, but their hearts are far from me. Their worship of me is made up only of rules taught by men' " (Isaiah 29:13). Jesus has inaugurated a new and better covenant so that our worship might become more than merely the mouthing of empty cliches but can be the upright expression of a pure heart. God no longer wants ceremonial worship at a fixed locality; he now desires worshipers who will worship in purity of spirit.

Jesus was further showing that our worship would one day be greatly enhanced through the fullness of the Holy Spirit. One beautiful reason why Jesus gave us the Holy Spirit, together with the gift of speaking in tongues, is that we might be released in a greater measure in our worship. There is a certain element in worship that will always be absent for those who do not accept the fullness of the Holy Spirit, with speaking in tongues, as a reality in their lives.

The sought-after worshipers will worship not only in spirit but in truth, Jesus said. In this John 4 passage, he definitely distinguished between *ignorant* worship (" 'you Samaritans worship what you do not know' "), and *intelligent* worship (" 'we worship what we do know' "). When Jesus spoke of worshiping in truth, he meant that worship must involve the mind. Worship that involves only the spirit is insufficient; the mind must also be exerted. Some people wait for a floaty, ethereal feeling to come over them before they are sure they have really worshiped. They fail to realize that worship involves all of one's mental faculties and is experienced at the height of mental awareness. The more we exert our minds in worship, the more meaningful our worship is likely to be. Some have lamented the use of hymns, complaining they require so much mental concentration that worship is encumbered. Nonsense. Such an attitude only points up our need to sing more hymns, for they might help us engage our minds as well as our spirits in worship. Too much of our worship is stymied because of our inability to enter mentally into the content of worship.

The second obvious application of worship in truth is that worship must be through Jesus Christ, who is the truth (John 14:6). Those who do not recognize the mediation of our great High Priest cannot approach God and therefore cannot find that intimacy of relationship which fosters worship.

Third, we are to worship out of a heart that is true to God, with a life that displays truth and purity. Simply put, this means we are to worship with integrity.

True worship, furthermore, is to be distinguished from hypocritical worship. We have an example of hypocritical worship in the life of king Saul, after the Amalekite battle: "Then Saul said to Samuel, 'I have sinned. I violated the LORD'S command and your instructions. I was afraid of the people and so I gave in to them. Now I beg you, forgive my sin and come back with me, so that I may worship the LORD.' But Samuel said to him, 'I will not go back with you. You have rejected the word of the LORD, and the LORD has rejected you as king over Israel!' As Samuel turned to leave, Saul caught hold of the edge of his robe, and it tore. Samuel said to him, 'The LORD has torn the kingdom of Israel from you today and has given it to one of your neighbors — to one better than you. He who is the Glory of Israel does not lie or change his mind; for he is not a man, that he should change his mind.' Saul replied, 'I have sinned. But please honor me before the elders of my people and before Israel; come back with me, so that I may worship the LORD your God.' So Samuel went back with Saul, and Saul worshiped the LORD" (1 Samuel 15:24-31).

The motivation of Saul in wanting to worship the Lord was hypocritical. Saul was interested only in saving face before the people, who knew that it was traditional for Samuel to accompany the king and for them to worship together. If Samuel had not returned with Saul, the people would have known that Saul was out of the good graces of both Samuel and the Lord. So Saul wanted to cover up the true state of affairs and make things appear to be all right. He was not interested in truly worshiping the Lord; he was just trying to maintain his reputation and standing in the eyes of the people.

Saul should not be castigated too severely, for we too fall into the same trap of hypocritical worship. Things may not be at all well between us and God, but we come into the congregation and pretend that nothing is wrong. We put on a good "front," and nobody can discern that we are really churning inside. God is not pleased with forms of worship that are actually hypocritical in nature. He wants us to come before him with hearts that are pure and true. When things are not right between us and God, we must be honest before God and get everything out in the open. It is not hypocritical to praise the Lord despite negative feelings or known sin so long as we are willing to acknowledge and deal with those problems. In contrast, hypocritical worship attempts to cover over the inner maladies by putting on a spiritual front, all the while denying the Holy Spirit access to the recesses of our hearts. True worship gazes honestly into heaven and invites the cleansing presence of the Holy Spirit.

Finally, in saying we should worship in truth, Jesus intends that we worship in accordance with the truth of God's word, for " 'your word is truth' " (John 17:17). It is not enough to worship in sincerity; we must also worship in truth. There are millions on the earth today who worship in sincerity, but since they do not worship according to the revealed truth of God in his word, he does not hear them. When Muslims worship Allah, they believe they are worshiping the one true God. But the true God's name is not Allah! These highly sincere people refuse to worship him according to the biblical guidelines. Therefore, their worship is ineffectual and in vain. No matter how sincere it may be, it is not acceptable.

We can know we are a worshiper of the true God by getting to know him through the Scriptures. Worship flows out of relationship, and our relationship with God is strengthened by learning of him through his word. Jesus described the Samaritans as worshiping " 'what you do not know' " (John 4:22). It has been said that our worship is no higher than our knowledge of God. Obviously, then, we must grow in our knowledge of God, and this comes through diligent study of the Bible.

Jesus had a remarkable ability to pack numerous thoughts into but a few choice words: " 'The true worshipers will worship the Father in spirit and truth' " (John 4:23).

What a simple and yet profound summation of the essence of worship! As we enter into these depths of worship intended for us by God, our times of worship will become transformational. Mortals cannot help changing when in the presence of Almighty God. Worship inevitably works a changing and purifying within. In order to maintain deep communion with God, one must first be cleansed from the filthiness contracted from the world *(see* 2 Corinthians 7:1). Intimate fellowship with God will of a certainty bring a refining in our lives; the inner recesses of our hearts will be illuminated by the Holy Spirit, and the dross will be purged, for "our God is a consuming fire" (Hebrews 12:29).

THE SIMPLICITY OF WORSHIP

With so many books written about worship and so many teachings available on this subject today, it is possible to be overcome with the sheer magnitude and seeming limitlessness of it all. Worship can become a high and lofty goal toward which we strain, and we find ourselves consumed with attempting to execute it properly. We labor to engineer a level of worship exceeding the intensity of last week's level. And my, how we labor! How we strain! But worship is simple! And not only is it simple, but it is for the simple. It is for those who are childlike enough to just open up their hearts and respond to God in sincerity and honesty. Worship is not work — it is fun! Worship is enjoyable and relaxing. Worship should be renewing, invigorating, therapeutic. We must relax if we are to enjoy the simplicity of worship.

When Jesus gave the tremendous revelation that we are to worship in spirit and truth, he first gave that mighty revelation to a Samaritan woman. The woman who anointed the feet of Jesus was a known sinner in her hometown. If worship were so lofty, intricate and complicated, God would not have used these two ordinary women to illustrate its beauty. Worship is nothing more than opening one's heart to God and enjoying a relationship of loving communion with him.

Some worship leaders exert emotional pressure on their people to try to "get into" an emotionally high state of praise or worship. Other leaders have found great success in becoming very relaxed during their praise and worship, without trying to "work up" their people to reach some high point. Everyone enjoys "peak" times of praise and worship, but no one likes the feeling of being pressured to enter into high worship. Every congregation should experience "high" times in God, but not every worship service is titillating and ecstatic; in fact, most are not. And there is very little that we can do to control the level of ecstasy we experience during a given worship service. God alone regulates that, by his Spirit. So if God is regulating the degree to which he will manifest his glory, then why should we strain to enter into a euphoric level of worship? We may as well relax, delight in being with God, and enjoy the degree of glory we presently know. We must find an internal motivation to give energetic praise to God, but then we must relax and worship him in simplicity and thankfulness.

Worship leaders, does it take a great spiritual experience on the heights of Zion to make us happy with a given worship service? If we derive our fulfillment from the intensity of each worship service, we are sure to be frustrated. If we must attain some spiritual "high" in order to be at peace with ourselves, then everything we do is tainted with energy, concern, effort, and worry. If the service does not "take off" according to our expectations, we increase our level of exertion or "hype." We must find our joy and peace in something other than the intensity of praise and worship attained in a service. Our peace must be drawn from Christ and from a personal relationship with him that is not affected by the vicissitudes of worship services. We must find contentment in a "simple" expression of praise and worship and rest on the unmoving Rock, Christ Jesus.

In his book *Celebration of Discipline,* Richard Foster

aptly points out that our spirits can become weary from straining after God, even as our physical bodies get tired from manual labor. Straining, yearning, and striving are characteristics of activities wherein we actively seek God, such as prayer and intercession. But worship falls into a different category. Even praise could be characterized by strenuous intensity as we seek to declare his glories with enthusiasm and energy; but not so with worship. Worship can be intense, but it is an intensity initiated by God rather than by man. Intense times of worship just "happen," without any human manipulation or effort, simply because God's Spirit moves sovereignly upon his people. Worship, therefore, should not be a function of straining and striving in the sense of trying to enter into something climactic, but it should be characterized by relaxation, enjoyment, celebration, ease, enthusiasm, and rejoicing. Ivan Q. Spencer, the founder of Elim Bible Institute, once said, "When you work, God rests. But when you rest, God works." Let us relax and simply enjoy his presence!

EXCLUSIVE WORSHIP

Although this book is directed for the most part to congregational praise and worship, the church is not the only place where worship transpires. A complete understanding of worship acknowledges that worship takes place (ideally) every day of our lives, in and through all we do. There is a distinction, however, between loving and doing, between worship and service. In their hustle and bustle of serving the Lord, some folks have neglected times of simply loving the Lord. Jesus reflected on this when he said, " 'For it is written: "Worship the Lord your God, and serve him only" ' " (Matthew 4:10). The order our Lord gave was first worship, then service. Remember Mary and Martha? Martha was displeased with Mary, who was sitting at Jesus' feet listening to him, because Martha was having to prepare the meal by herself. Jesus eventually chided Martha because in her busyness of serving, she had not taken time to worship. We do the same thing today, excusing our lack of worship by pointing to the many things we do for God. In our hurry to serve God, we neglect to worship him.

We must be reminded repeatedly of the priority of being a worshiper. Some folks are concerned about having too much emphasis on worship because they fear it will cause the church to become an inverted "bless-me club." They are afraid that churches which emphasize worship are likely to neglect evangelistic outreach. Nothing should be further from the truth. True worship should cause us to lift our eyes unto the fields of harvest. A worshiper is one whose perspective is being expanded, whose focus is decreasingly on self, and whose interests are flamed by the passion of God himself. So worshipers should be the best servants! But the greatest service will never be a substitute for worship.

We are to worship God alone. This is so important a truth that God made it the first of the Ten Commandments. The Lord also said, " 'I will not give my glory to another' " (Isaiah 42:8). God demands exclusive worship. There is another — called Satan — who also seeks exclusive worship. This was the nature of the ambitious pride that entered his heart in heaven, for he desired the worship of Almighty God. Satan is delighted when he can distract us from giving our worship exclusively to the Lord. His cause is aided when we allow other things to gain a priority in our hearts and desires — when we give an inordinate amount of time and affection to our careers, our hobbies, or our own personal pleasures and desires.

I wonder if some deliverance ministries might not, in an indirect way, allow worship of Satan. I have seen some deliverance ministries operate in such a way that Satan has people foaming at the mouth, rolling under the pews, screaming and flailing about like uncontrollable maniacs. This type of scenario brings much attention to the power of Satan and his demons and hence almost causes us to revere and worship

Satan's power. I have seen many saints gripped with the fear of demonic influence following these "deliverance" sessions, and Satan gloats in the attention! Rather, we should place the focus of our attention and desires upon the Lord. Even as a bride saves herself for the exclusive enjoyment of her groom, so also we must save ourselves from any other affections in order that we might give exclusive worship unto the Lord our God.

Few Christians are tempted with worshiping Satan. The temptation to worship things other than God usually comes in a much more insidious fashion. Morris Smith once said, "To lower your eyes from God to any work of God, worship included, and to try to reproduce it or program it, in Holy Scripture is called idolatry." Too many have fallen into idolatry by worshiping worship. It is very easy to become so consumed with wanting better worship that we put our eyes on the form or style and lose sight of the object of our worship — the Lord God. We have nothing to gain by scrutinizing worship; we have much to gain by gazing upon the Lord. Isaiah said, "In the year that King Uzziah died, I saw the Lord . . ." (Isaiah 6:1). David wrote, "My heart says of you, 'Seek his face!' Your face, LORD, I will seek" (Psalm 27:8); "and I — in righteousness I will see your face; when I awake, I will be satisfied with seeing your likeness" (Psalm 17:15). Truly that is worship! It was said of Jesus that he knew how to please the Father *(see* John 8:29). As we learn to submit any inordinate desires to the Lordship of Christ, we will learn that nothing pleases the Father more than unconditional and exclusive worship.

In worship, we partake of the very river that flows from the throne of God. The psalmist wrote of that river, "There is a river whose streams make glad the city of God" (Psalm 46:4). This is an allusion to the waters of Siloam (Shiloah), whose several different courses ran underneath and through Jerusalem and supplied the city with water. Similarly, the Holy Spirit provides us with renewing waters as we worship from our innermost beings. Through worship, the river of God washes over our souls with cleansing and refreshment. When Ezekiel was caught up in this divine river, the waters rose from his ankles to his knees and then to his waist, until he could no longer walk in the current. During this experience, Ezekiel was told, " 'And it shall be that every living thing that moves, wherever the rivers go, will live. There will be a very great multitude of fish, because these waters go there; for they will be healed, and everything will live wherever the river goes' " (Ezekiel 47:9, NKJV). As the river of God begins to flow during our times of worship, it brings life, abundance, and healing, washing over broken hearts and restoring parched souls.

How wonderful worship is! How glorious it is! But in all the wonder and glory of learning about worship, we must realize that it is possible for us to come to a good understanding of the dynamics of worship without ever making an application to our lives. It is one thing to know what worship is — it is quite another to become a worshiper.

CHAPTER 5

BECOMING A WORSHIPER

We know from Jesus' own declaration that the Father seeks worshipers (see John 4:23). God delights in the lifestyle of worshipers; nothing pleases him more than the quality of life displayed by a worshiper. It is incumbent upon us, then, to endeavor to please him by learning to become increasingly Christlike in every way. We want to be worshipers, but sometimes we do not fully understand all that that entails. The New Testament does not have a large number of references specifically to worship, but it does contain some excellent examples of what it means to be a worshiper. One of the most outstanding instances of worship in the New Testament is seen in the story of the sinful woman who anointed the feet of Jesus. Let us explore this account in Luke 7:36-50 to see more clearly the qualities that characterize a worshiper.

> Now one of the Pharisees invited Jesus to have dinner with him, so he went to the Pharisee's house and reclined at the table. When a woman who had lived a sinful life in that town learned that Jesus was eating at the Pharisee's house, she brought an alabaster jar of perfume, and as she stood behind him at his feet weeping, she began to wet his feet with her tears. Then she wiped them with her hair, kissed them and poured perfume on them.

> When the Pharisee who had invited him saw this, he said to himself, "If this man were a prophet, he would know who is touching him and what kind of woman she is — that she is a sinner."

Jesus answered him, "Simon, I have something to tell you."

"Tell me, teacher," he said.

"Two men owed money to a certain moneylender. One owed him five hundred denarii, and the other fifty. Neither of them had the money to pay him back, so he canceled the debts of both. Now which of them will love him more?"

Simon replied, "I suppose the one who had the bigger debt canceled."

"You have judged correctly," Jesus said.

Then he turned toward the woman and said to Simon, "Do you see this woman? I came into your house. You did not give me any water for my feet, but she wet my feet with her tears and wiped them with her hair. You did not give me a kiss, but this woman, from the time I entered, has not stopped kissing my feet. You did not put oil on my head, but she has poured perfume on my feet. Therefore, I tell you, her many sins have been forgiven — for she loved much. But he who has been forgiven little loves little."

Then Jesus said to her, "Your sins are forgiven."

The other guests began to say among themselves, "Who is this who even forgives sins?"

Jesus said to the woman, "Your faith has saved you; go in peace."

The first lesson to be learned from this drama is that worshipers are givers. This woman gave Jesus some very costly ointment thought to be valued at roughly a year's wages. Today the value might be from fifteen thousand to twenty-five thousand dollars. In those days, there were no banks where currency could be saved, so people would invest in valuable articles like this jar of perfume as a means of building up financial security. The jar represented this woman's entire savings; perhaps she had planned to retire on the money it would bring her.

This flask of ointment was not like our jars of perfume today. Our perfume bottles have spray pumps that dispense only a little liquid at a time; or we can unscrew the bottle lid and dab a little perfume here and there. But this jar was made of stone, so the only way to get to the contents was to break the jar. Furthermore, once the jar was broken, all the contents had to be used, as there was no way of saving them. So in bringing the jar of perfume to Jesus, this woman knew that there was no way to give only part of it; it was all or nothing. But she manifested no hesitancy or reticence. What a beautiful act of lavish love this was.

It is very scriptural to bring a gift when coming to worship the Lord. Psalm 96:8-9 exhorts, "Bring an offering and come into his courts. Worship the LORD in the splendor of his holiness." In the Old Testament sacrificial system, the worshipers were instructed to bring a lamb (or a goat, or ram, or turtledove). They were not to appear before God without a gift to present to him. " 'No one is to appear before me empty-handed' " (Exodus 23:15). Some folks think they can worship although they do not pay a full tithe. Some try to be "freeloaders" in God's kingdom, but a freeloader will never learn the joys of becoming a worshiper.

Many church leaders have struggled with the problem of finding meaningful ways to collect offerings. Although giving is very much a part of our worship, it always seems to become divorced from the worship service so that it is viewed as an activity apart from worship. We need to work at ways to make our offerings truly a part of our worship. Some pastors place offering plates at the front of the church, and before starting the worship, they tell the people that each family is to come forward together and give their offering unto the Lord during the worship. Whenever the members of the congregation desire, as others are singing and worshiping, they can come forward as a family, kneel at the altar, and give their offering in worship unto the Lord.

It is also good to encourage people to give cash sometimes, rather than a check, to the Lord. It is a proven fact
that stores can increase sales by as much as 20 percent if
their customers will use credit cards rather than cash, for it
is much easier to slap a card on the counter and say,
"Charge it!" than it is to relinquish those "greenbacks"
from one's billfold. It's psychological — those tens or twen-
ties are *real* money, unlike a credit card or a check, either of
which has much less personal connotation. Similarly, when
we give, our giving might be more meaningful if we would
give cash — something "real" and in essence part of us —
unto the Lord, laying the bills on the altar as an expression
of worship. If we can make our offering times more meaningful, we will find a new and added dimension in our worship.

When this woman came into Jesus' presence, she was
weeping. This was the outward manifestation of a heart
that was deeply stirred before her Lord. She was repentant,
overcome, unreserved. This was not a show. Our Hollywood actresses today learn to cry at the drop of a hat, but no
emotion is involved. This woman's tears were sincere. I will
confess that as a man I find it very difficult to cry. Few are
the times when I come to tears before God. And that concerns me, because I ask, "Lord, is my heart too hard before
you? I want to be soft and tender in your presence!" The
times of worship that have been most meaningful to me are
the times when I cried before God. Brokenness and tears
are truly key elements in worship.

We see also that this woman kissed Jesus' feet. This is a
beautiful aspect of worship, for the Greek word for worship
— *proskuneo* — means "to kiss the hand toward; to do reverence or homage by kissing the hand; to bow one's self in
adoration." The derivation of *proskuneo* is thought to
come from the Greek word for dog. Thus the original meaning was "to kiss, like a dog licking his master's hand."
When I first discovered this, I was somewhat repulsed by

the idea. I asked God, "Lord, am I like a dog before you? Is that all I mean to you?" But then the Lord began to show me some beautiful lessons through the etymology of this word.

Although I have always been a dog lover, I had a dog for only a few years while I was growing up. Among my fondest memories of "Buster" are the times when we would come home from church and be greeted by him at the door. From outside we could hear his tail thumping against the wall and his paws scratching at the door. And when we stepped inside, he was all over us! Jumping, licking, wagging, thumping, twirling — you would have thought he hadn't seen us for weeks! As I remembered those royal welcomes, the Lord whispered to my heart, "How excited are you about being with me again, when you enter the house of the Lord?"

Anyone who has ever had a dog knows what it is to be sitting, perhaps reading, and look over to see the dog just lying there staring. "What are you looking at, mutt?" He seems to talk back with his eyes, "Silly, you know what I want." Finally, tired of being scrutinized, the dog's master asks, "Do you want to go outside?" Thump, thump, thump. That is what he was waiting for! Similarly for us, there is an element of waiting in worship — simply staring at the Lord. Perhaps God gets tired of our continual chattering before him. At times he would call us to be quiet in his presence, and this too is worship. My wife and I do not need to be talking all the time in order for communication to occur between us. Sometimes a look can say much more than a thousand words. We should cultivate the habit of staring at God, so that when he stirs, we are aware of it.

Then there is the time when the dog comes over to sit by the chair. But he isn't satisfied with sitting next to his master; he has to plop his body right on top of his master's feet. Dogs desire the closeness of physical contact with their masters. And for us, let us not be satisfied just with being near the Lord; let us come close to his heart in worship and lean upon his breast!

Since Luke described this woman as "sinful," many biblical scholars believe that she was a prostitute. When she had washed Jesus' feet, she let down her hair — a common way at that time for prostitutes to seduce their clients. No doubt the disciples were aghast. Could it be that she would attempt to seduce the Master? When this woman first entered the room, everyone pretended not to notice. But when she let down her hair, they were all nervously watching out of the corners of their eyes.

Worshipers cannot go unnoticed. They will attract attention to themselves. For this very reason, many have refrained from entering into the fullness of worship. They are afraid of what others might think of them. Peer pressure affects worship. It has held back countless saints from the blessing of opening their hearts to the Lord. Some folks might say, "Oh, that's just Sister Brown doing her thing again." Others might shake their heads and think, "Straaaange." But this is part of the cost of being a true worshiper.

Obviously this woman was not following the conventional forms of worship. There is no mention in the Psalms of pouring perfume on our Lord's feet. Weeping and kissing and hair — David gave no guidelines concerning these things. So we must consider how tolerant we are of unique or "overboard" expressions of genuine worship. There are no formulas for worship because worship is a function of the heart, and the heart will find expression in a variety of external forms.

She had tried to fill her longing for love in men. Now she had found the Lover of her soul. Many of us find it very difficult to express love unashamedly to others. If we have difficulty expressing love to one another, how can we claim to be open with God, whom we have not seen? We need to open up in our relationships with our brothers and sisters so that we can enjoy a greater depth of relationship with the Lord.

Another insight into worship can be seen in Simon's derogatory thought: " 'If this man were a prophet, he would know who is touching him and what kind of woman she is — that she is a sinner' " (Luke 7:39). A worshiper will no doubt receive the defamation of some and the acclamation of others. When David escorted the ark of the covenant to Zion, and while dressed in a linen ephod and dancing before the Lord with all his might, he was assailed by Michal, " 'How the king of Israel has distinguished himself today, disrobing in the sight of the slave girls of his servants as any vulgar fellow would!' " (2 Samuel 6:20). Because of her criticism, Michal was barren for the rest of her life. Likewise, if we become critical of genuine acts of worship, we are in danger of spiritual barrenness.

In the church today, nothing is quite so controversial as worship. Entire churches have been split over matters of worship and the proper way to conduct it. That is because true worship will invoke the criticism of the spiritually barren. But real worshipers are willing to pay the price!

A choice is set before us: we can choose to please man, or we can decide to please God. It rarely seems possible to do both. This sinful woman was willing to endure the censure of others for the sake of hearing the Master's "Well done."

At last Jesus turned to the woman. All along the disciples were surely thinking, "Why doesn't Jesus do something? This woman is obviously out of order! Why doesn't he rebuke her? Why is he letting this thing drag on?" And when Jesus finally did give her his attention, the disciples heaved a sigh of relief. "It's about time he took control of this situation!" But rather than rebuking her, Jesus commended her. What a beautiful assurance this is that when we worship, he will respond! He will turn to us! He will speak to us, for he is eager to do so.

This story illustrates some of the differences between a worshiping and a non-worshiping church. The Pharisee could represent a non-worshiping church — perhaps a church that takes greater pleasure in its historical roots than in its expression of worship. The Pharisee was the teacher. He

was the man who had the word studies down pat. He was
the one with the coherent, dogmatic theology of worship; in
fact, he may have written the latest book on worship. But
what matters is not a proper theology of worship; what is
important is a loving heart that cries out to God!

Having sat at the feet of Jesus, the disciples had much
head knowledge about worship; but it took a sinful woman
— someone who was uneducated in the many ramifications
of worship — to emulate being a worshiper before those disciples. Spiritual maturity does not exempt one from being a
worshiper. We will never grow to the point where we are
"above" worshiping the Lord. Psalm 107:32 says, "Let
them . . . praise him in the council of the elders." In the
book of Revelation we read of the elders repeatedly falling
down in worship before the throne of God *(see* Revelation
4:9-11). In truth, there should be a greater responsibility incumbent upon elders and the spiritually mature to worship
the Lord and to be examples of worship to others. The disciples should have been the examples of worshipers in this
story, but, sadly enough, they needed an example themselves. No one should assume that just because he or she
has attained great spiritual stature, he or she has become a
worshiper. The unfortunate fact is that in many of our
churches, the elders are the most inhibited in their worship!
Rather than stimulating worship by example, many in leadership positions actually stifle the worship of others by their
negative attitudes. They are in places of spiritual influence
and are honored as model Christians by many young and
tender hearts. Pastors, elders, deacons — all church leaders
— must respond to their divine duty of leading the saints to
responsiveness in worship by setting an example.

A few days after this experience, Peter was walking the
streets of the city, looking for Jesus, when suddenly he de-
tected a familiar odor. It was the fragrance of the perfume
the sinful woman had poured upon Jesus. Peter hurried
around the corner, expecting to see the Master, but he was
not there. Instead, there was the woman! For days after

that anointing, she carried with her the fragrance of Christ! The glory of true worshipers is carrying the aura of Christ with us after we have poured ourselves out in worship.

WORSHIPING WITHOUT GUILT

The last words of Jesus to this woman — " 'Your sins are forgiven' " — contain a beautiful lesson. The woman worshiped, and then she received forgiveness and cleansing. The point here is that it is possible to approach God in worship, even if there is sin in our lives, and become purified. But too often we allow feelings of guilt to rob us of this blessing. All Christians struggle with guilt and condemnation at some point in their walk with the Lord. For some of us, condemnation has played a key role in keeping us from God's best for our lives. We are experts in self-condemnation. If we cannot think of a reason to feel guilty, we will invent one! The commandment of Jesus seems impossible to attain: " 'Be perfect therefore, as your heavenly Father is perfect' " (Matthew 5:28).

Nothing will debilitate our witness more quickly and efficiently than condemnation. This is a principal reason why many of God's chosen remain frozen in their ability to live a victorious Christian life. It really is possible to be freed from the shackles of guilt and condemnation and be released to worship the Lord in purity and freedom!

Romans 8:1 rings loudly and clearly: "Therefore, there is now no condemnation for those who are in Christ Jesus." Period. The King James Version adds a phrase to that verse: "who walk not after the flesh, but after the Spirit." This is a most unfortunate addition to the original text. That phrase is intended to occur in verse 4 of that chapter, but it was somehow duplicated at the end of verse 1. Other versions do not include this phrase as a second part to verse 1. In the past, Romans 8:1 has been just one more reason for condemnation! We read the comforting words, "There is therefore now no condemnation to them which are in

Christ Jesus" (KJV), and we lift our hearts in thanks to God, because we know we are in Christ Jesus. Then we read on, ". . . who walk not after the flesh, but after the Spirit." Condemnation galore! After all, who is so spiritual that he or she no longer walks after the flesh? This becomes one giant stipulation for freedom from condemnation, and it is a condition we feel incapable of meeting. The sword is given yet one more twist, and we are left to writhe in a morass of hopelessness.

There is but one condition for freedom from condemnation: being in Christ Jesus. The Scriptures make it clear that when we truly are "in him," God's righteousness is credited unto us. "But now a righteousness from God, apart from law, has been made known, to which the Law and the Prophets testify. This righteousness from God comes through faith in Jesus Christ to all who believe" (Romans 3:21-22). Jeremiah spoke prophetically of the Lord Jesus, saying, " 'This is the name by which he will be called: the LORD Our Righteousness' " (Jeremiah 23:6). Paul declared that Jesus Christ "has become for us . . . our righteousness" (1 Corinthians 1:30) and that "God made him who had no sin to be sin for us, so that in him we might become the righteousness of God" (2 Corinthians 5:21).

This righteousness is not earned through good living but is the reward of faith. Through faith in Christ Jesus, therefore, we are the righteousness of God. God literally sees us clothed in the righteousness of Jesus Christ! It is no longer something we need strive to reach; it is a historical fact, once we place our faith in the Lord Jesus. The commandment of Jesus to "be perfect" is no longer an impossibility for us! Through Christ, we *are* perfect with the perfection of God himself! This truth must sink into our hearts if we are going to enter into the liberty of worshiping God without guilt.

There was a time in my life when I was struggling with a specific, recurring sin that I had difficulty conquering. And oh, the guilt, when it was time to worship! I could not find a release in my spirit because I felt like a failure before God. I withdrew from God, supposing that he was not interested in fellowshiping with a sin-ridden son. For years I allowed guilt and condemnation to rob me of the blessedness of continual communion with my Father!

I had to learn that I must never allow sin to deter me from intimate fellowship with God. God is never shocked by sin in our lives. He never condemns us for sinning. And he never holds us at arm's length when we do sin. God does convict, but he never condemns. Conviction and condemnation are poles apart. Conviction leads to repentance; condemnation leads to despair. Conviction culminates in victory over sin; condemnation culminates in abject defeat. Conviction motivates us toward God; condemnation leaves us deflated and powerless. God convicts; we condemn. Jesus said, " 'For God did not send his Son into the world to condemn the world, but to save the world through him' " (John 3:17). Jesus' statement to the woman caught in adultery, after her accusers slipped away one by one, was " 'Neither do I condemn you. Go now and leave your life of sin' " (John 8:11).

Guilt and condemnation are among the greatest hindrances in our worship services. And for too long we have heard the wrong solution! We have been told, "Repent before the Lord first, receive his cleansing, and then come into worship. Don't come before God unless you've first been purified." But God has never said that to us! That is a human solution. The Lord made his solution very real to my heart one day as I was meditating on this passage in Luke 7. I was impressed with the fact that not until *after* this sinful woman had worshiped our Lord in such a beautiful and extravagant manner did Jesus declare her sins to be forgiven. The progression was this: first she worshiped, and then she was forgiven!

Jesus never says to us, "Wait a minute. There's sin in your life! Don't try to get close to me and love me in that condition!" On the contrary, he says, "Come close to me;

lean upon my breast, and let us commune together." Then his promise comes: "And you will be purified as you worship me!" We do not get purified in order to worship — we worship and are consequently purified. The only time it is inappropriate to worship God with sin in our life is when we have no intention of changing. To worship while purposefully maintaining a sinful life, without any intentions of repentance and change, is hypocrisy. But to worship despite any known sin, when we acknowledge it and desire to receive God's strength to gain victory over it, is the first step toward the solution.

I am not espousing a new brand of "cheap grace." God hates our sin! No sin can survive in God's presence. But this is precisely why, when we need cleansing, we must flee into his presence. There we receive healing, cleansing, holiness, and purity. This was the message of Charles Wesley when he wrote:

> Jesus, Lover of my soul,
> Let me to Thy bosom fly
> While the nearer waters roll,
> While the tempest still is high!

> Plenteous grace with Thee is found,
> Grace to cover all my sin;
> Let the healing streams abound,
> Make and keep me pure within.

Too often when in the throes of guilt and condemnation, we have turned and hidden ourselves from our source of healing and forgiveness. Condemnation has driven us away from the very Balm that would heal our souls!

Condemnation will rob us of the blessed purification that will come through worship. Condemnation is a whirlpool that will siphon our spiritual vitality until we are consumed. The more we abstain from worship, the greater will be our defilement; with greater defilement comes greater condemnation, and hence a greater separation between us and God. It is our blessed privilege as God's redeemed to draw near to him in times of sin and uncleanness and receive of the cleansing power that flows from his presence.

HINDERING ATTITUDES IN WORSHIP

Though we may have dealt with condemnation and guilt, the pitfalls and hindrances to worship remain many. The foremost deterrent to worship is in wrongly formulated attitudes of the mind and heart.

No doubt a major problem that debilitates our worship is pride. Pride is probably the greatest hindrance to worship. Pride has ruined far more worship services than all the forces of hell combined. It is pride that gravitates toward conservative, low-key worship, because the ego is never fed by all-out worship. It is pride that restrains us from lifting our voices without fear in the congregation. Pride will rob us of the joy and release that come when we dance or lift our hands or bow in the presence of the Lord. Pride will incarcerate us in a self-conscious prison of spiritual bondage. Pride comes up with excuses such as "Well, that's just not my style of praise." And pride never takes the blame or acknowledges the fault. It is one of the most insidious hindrances to worship because it is so difficult to discern. The flesh will never proffer the solution by saying, "The problem is pride, old buddy!"

The very essence of worship is self-abasement and humility. Worship is the humbling of self and the exalting of God. We have developed the remarkable ability, however, to worship the Lord without sacrificing our own sophistication. How is it that we are able to say, "I exalt the Lord!" without once humbling ourselves? There was a time in this century when it took a lot of humility to raise one's hands or clap or dance. But these expressions of praise are now accepted as common fare in most pentecostal and charismatic circles. It is possible for contemporary believers to lift their hands and sing in tongues without sacrificing personal pride, simply because that has become socially acceptable behavior in many circles. But are we prepared to express our worship in a different manner if we sense the impulse of the Spirit, regardless of what others might think?

Pride is highly susceptible to peer pressure in worship. We tend to be more concerned about the opinions of others than we are about the Lord's opinion, at precisely the time when the Lord should fill all our thoughts. Pride is sin. Let us be willing to cast aside our charismatic sophistication and worship the Lord with all our hearts, giving no heed to self and the maintenance of a "spiritual" image. Some of the best advice I've heard is this: "Never do anything because others are looking at you, and never refrain from anything because others are looking at you."

Our worship often suffers from a sort of "reverse hedonism." Hedonism is the modern philosophy of life that says, "If it feels good, do it." "It's your thing, do what you want to do." We live in a hedonistic society, for everywhere around us people are seeking to satisfy the cravings of their sensual desires. Conversely, if it doesn't feel good, don't do it. Carried over into worship, this reversed attitude says, "If you don't feel like worshiping, don't worry about it. God understands your weakness — he won't zap you!" "The spirit is willing but the flesh is weak." But we *must* participate in worship, especially during those times when we do not feel like it. If we allow our worship to be controlled by our feelings, we will never gain victory in our Christian walk. We do not worship because we feel like it — we worship because Christ is worthy!

A third faulty attitude in worship is that of presumption. We saunter into the worship service and say, "Hi there, God — good to see you again this week." And God says, "The voice is familiar, but I don't recognize the face." We assume our right to approach him even after living selfishly all week long. How often we presume upon God's grace and expect his Spirit of blessing to be showered upon us without any sacrifice, investment of prayer, or humble repentance on our part.

A fourth malady in worship is "spectatorism." How easy it is for us to get caught up in watching the proceedings of a worship service and afterward find that we have done everything but worship! Paul made no mention of the ministry of surveillance in his epistles. We are called not to peruse but to participate.

Corporate worship too often resembles a spectator sport. Dr. Graham Truscott has compared worship with football. He describes American football as fifty million people needing exercise, watching twenty-two people needing rest. Some churches cater to a spectator-sport mentality in their worship services: so much transpires on the platform that the worshiper is required to contribute relatively little in order for the service to succeed. Perhaps this is why many have rethought their approach to what has been termed "special music." "Special music" in many circles has come to mean the performance of a musical piece that (under the guise of "ministry") does little more than titillate the ears of the "audience."

Worship is not performed by one party in behalf of another. No one can worship for another. We have all been called, as a spiritual priesthood, to offer up sacrifices of thanksgiving and praise to the Lord *(see* Romans 12:1; 1 Corinthians 3:16; 1 Peter 2:5-6; Revelation 1:6). A performer/audience orientation is completely foreign to the New Testament. None of us is a spectator, but we are all participants in raising high his glorious praise. True worship must eventually transcend the horizontal and become centered on the vertical dynamics of communion with God.

Sentimentalism can also stymie worship. We often become sentimental in worship when we become more taken up with the music than with the message of our songs. Overly familiar songs are in danger of becoming sentimental for us. These are songs that are so well known and common that they lose their effectiveness in stimulating our minds to worship. Worship leaders must understand the strong emotional pull of music and the easy way we can become sentimental over a favorite tune. We must not be satisfied with an emotional response alone; we need a complete response of body, soul, and spirit.

When Israel rejected the word of the Lord through his servant Ezekiel, the Lord said the following about Israel: " 'Indeed, to them you are nothing more than one who sings love songs with a beautiful voice and plays an instrument well, for they hear your words but do not put them into practice' " (Ezekiel 33:32). God knows full well how easily we get caught up in the beauty of a nice melody without the message changing us in the least. We should occasionally ask ourselves while praising if we are guilty of "jiving" to the music without giving any heed to the message of the song.

We have been created as humans to enjoy music. God has placed that sensitivity in us, and it is good. But God has intended that music help us to open our hearts and become more receptive to him. We are never to worship music or place inordinate emphasis upon it. Music is a vehicle, not an end in itself. St. Augustine observed, "When I am moved by the voice of him that sings more than by the words sung, I confess to have sinned."

A sixth wrong attitude in worship is the paying of mere lip service. How easy it can be to mouth the words of a song, all the while knowing our heart is not a part of the message. Nothing is more repugnant to the Lord than half-heartedness and hypocrisy. At one point in Israel's history, the Hebrews were sacrificing to the heathen gods and then were turning around and fulfilling the Mosaic sacrifices to God. Notice what God said to them through the prophet Amos: " 'I hate, I despise your religious feasts; I cannot stand your assemblies. Even though you bring me burnt offerings and grain offerings, I will not accept them. Though you bring choice fellowship offerings, I will have no regard for them. Away with the noise of your songs! I will not listen to the music of your harps' " (Amos 5:21-23). God would prefer that we keep our mouths shut rather than worship him ostensibly.

Another dangerous attitude is the fear of manipulation. We might think, "I'm not going to let this worship leader 'hype' me! He can try cheerleading if he wants to, but just see if he can get me to respond!" Whether or not the approach of the worship leader is proper is irrelevant; the problem is my refusal to enter into worship simply because I allow myself the luxury of being irritated with a worship leader's style. God is worthy of my praise regardless of any human foibles manifested by the leadership.

A final attitude we must change is wrapped up in the seven last words of a dying church: "We've never done it this way before." That is all the more reason to do it! Our worship is likely to improve if we will stir ourselves to be innovative, be willing to try new things, and be ready to experiment and explore all that God has for us in worship.

Becoming a worshiper is a privilege and a challenge. It is the one thing that delights the Father's heart above all else. Once people are prepared to enter into worship without reservation, however, the church leadership must come to a proper understanding of the role of worship in the congregation. Our services will be effective when our worship is conducted with a definite purpose.

CHAPTER 6

THE FULL PURPOSE OF CONGREGATIONAL WORSHIP

Inherent in the question "Why worship?" is another question: "What do we hope to accomplish in and through our congregational worship?" This is especially significant when we consider how much time and energy we give to this activity. Church leaders will admit that time is one of the most valuable commodities on Sunday morning. There usually doesn't seem to be enough time to accommodate everything that needs to be fitted in. And yet some churches will spend 30 to 50 percent of their congregated time in worship. We must formulate a philosophy of congregational worship that adequately defines why we devote precious blocks of time to this corporate activity and what the result of this outlay of time and effort should be.

Every pastor and local fellowship must determine this philosophy for themselves. It is no longer adequate to defend our worship services by saying, "Well, we've always done it this way." It is equally insufficient to conceive of our worship time as "the preliminaries," something to "condition" the people in preparation for the truly important part of the service: the sermon.

Since these reasons are inadequate, what reasons should we have for congregational worship? The answer can be divided into three general spheres in which our worship services minister. There is the *vertical* aspect of worship, the level in which the worshiper communicates with the Lord; there is the *horizontal* aspect of worship, the level in which the worshiper communicates with others in the congregation; and there is the *inward* aspect of worship, where the worshiper is personally affected by the worship service.

Each of these areas helps us to understand better the role of worship in the congregation.

THE VERTICAL ASPECT

The foremost reason for worship is *to minister unto the Lord.* The basic posture of the worshiper is not "Bless me, Lord," but rather "I will bless the Lord!" Most of us will affirm that this is not an unfamiliar concept, and yet we must admit that there are times when we go home from a worship service and complain because the worship did not do as much for us as it did the previous week. If someone asks us how the worship service was, we might answer, "Well, on a scale of one to ten, I'd put it right around five." But if the main purpose for worship is to bless and glorify the Lord, then why am I upset when it does not seem to bless me? The question is not whether the worship service blessed me but whether it blessed God. It is not what I thought of the worship service that counts — it is what God thought of it that truly matters! How did it rate on *his* scale from one to ten? Did he approve? Was he pleased with our "sacrifice of praise"?

Granted, when we bless the Lord, we get blessed in the process. There is an old Korean saying that goes like this: "If you want to smear the face of others with mire, you will have to smear your hands first." And the converse of this is true: if you bless another, then you too will be blessed. Proverbs 11:25 says, "He that watereth shall be watered also himself" (KJV). When we truly bless the Lord, we are automatically blessed. But the important thing is our motivation. We must minister to the Lord not with the ulterior motive of receiving a blessing but rather with the motive of blessing him whether he blesses us or not. If we will bless him with the proper motivation, he will also bless us!

We must guard against being sidetracked from this primary purpose of worship. There are many things that can pull our attention away from the Lord if we are not careful.

We can become so caught up, for example, in "What is God saying?" that we can miss the opportunity to minister to the Lord. If God wants to speak, he will; but our first priority is to minister to him. Or we can be diverted by the question "Is there sin in my life?" Some introspection can be good, but we can become so engrossed in introspection that we neglect the priority of blessing the Lord. The worship service is not the time for me to get into myself; it's the time for me to get into God! The problem with too many people is that their lives are completely self-centered, with everything revolving around personal interests, desires, and concerns. The worship service provides a welcome reprieve when we can forget about self and get taken up with God.

We can also be distracted by outside factors in a service. In some churches, the people must concentrate so much on following the worship leader that they are never able to lift their hearts unto God. Admiring a dynamic leader is never a substitute for a personal encounter with Christ. I can recall a certain lady approaching me after a Sunday service to say, "Bob, I just love the way you play the piano! I could just sit there for hours and listen to you play!" I thanked her politely, thinking that was a nice thing for her to say. But in retrospect, I saw that it was not a compliment at all. In actuality, that lady was so taken with my piano playing that she had not worshiped. My flourishing musical style had become a distraction to her, causing her to get her eyes off the Lord! I can no longer consider it a compliment when I realize my piano playing has distracted others from their primary ministry unto the Lord. Conversely, parishioners must avoid the tendency to get distracted with their admiration of talented human elements in a worship service. Those talents are being expressed exclusively as a stimulus to direct the worshiper Godward.

Sometimes we catch ourselves thinking, "The worship leader just isn't in the Spirit tonight." How easy it is to become a picky analyzer of worship — some of us are veritable connoisseurs of worship services — and bypass our heavenly ministry. We may be the sharpest spiritual detectives of all time, consistently hitting the nail on the head, detailing every flaw in the leadership, and imagining the perfect solution, but our negligence in worship would displease God. Let us not even allow our so-called ministry of "discernment" to deter us from blessing the Lord.

What can I give unto God, that he should repay me? What can I offer him that he does not already have? As awesome and marvelous as it seems, the Scriptures make it clear that I have something I can bring him. I can bring him my praise and blessing. I can bless the Lord! How amazing, that such a creature as I can bless the Lord God Almighty! I do not understand how that can possibly be, but I choose to believe it! Therefore, I will take frequent advantage of that blessed privilege, to minister unto the King of kings and Lord of lords!

We also worship in order *to better realize the manifest presence of God.* The Scriptures reveal that God is everywhere at all times (omnipresent), but yet there are different degrees to which God manifests his presence. He manifests himself on one level "where two or three are gathered." But when a group of God's people congregate to sing his glorious praise, he "inhabits" those praises and reveals his presence in a very particular way among his praising people *(see* Psalm 22:3).

Exodus 33 records an interesting conversation that Moses had with God. In this divine encounter, Moses was given a unique glimpse of the Lord such as no other man has ever had. God covered Moses in the cleft of a rock and then removed his hand to reveal his back to Moses. Before this took place, the Lord promised Moses, " 'My Presence will go with you, and I will give you rest.' Then Moses said to him, 'If your Presence does not go with us, do not send us up from here. How will anyone know that you are pleased with me and with your people unless you go with us? What else will distinguish me and your people from all the other people on the face of the earth?' " (verses 14-16).

This same question can be asked today. What distinguishes the church from the world? What makes our church services any different from the meetings of a Rotary Club or any other social organization? Is it because we are happy? They are happy, too. Is it because we have good fellowship? They have good fellowship, too. The difference is God's presence! *The presence of God is the earmark of the church!* If we do not have God's presence in our services, we may as well dismiss and have a picnic instead. But when sinners experience the presence of God in our midst, they will know we have something different.

Luke 5:17 speaks of an occasion on which "the power of the Lord was present for him to heal the sick." In the presence of God the power of God is revealed. As God's presence is realized among his worshipers, we should expect to experience a tremendous unleashing of his power. There is deliverance, cleansing, the fullness of the Holy Spirit, and much more when God is present in power. I once read that when a certain church experienced problems with its electrical system, the following notice appeared in the church bulletin: "Due to the lack of power, there will be no worship service tonight." But in many churches we might amend that slightly to read, "Due to the lack of worship, there will be no power in our services today."

A third reason for congregational worship, in this vertical sphere, is *to provide an atmosphere or seedbed for the expression of the gifts of the Spirit* and various spiritual ministries. The gifts of the Spirit are apportioned according to the sovereign will of God, and our praises do not cajole God into releasing his gifts. But a worship service will provide an atmosphere that is most conducive to the operations of the gifts of the Spirit. Without an atmosphere of worship, the gifts seem rarely to be manifested, but in a worshipful context the Spirit is able to operate more freely.

For instance, prophecies rarely come forth at the beginning of worship services. This is not accidental. First we worship, and then spiritual ministries begin to operate. God is not unwilling to speak prophetically to his people at the outset of the service, but often we are not ready to receive what he has to say! God has much to say to his people, but he waits until we are ready to receive his word. As our spirits become sensitive to the Spirit of God in worship, we become ready to flow in the gifts of the Spirit.

Finally, we worship *to open up the channels of communication between us and God.* Christians can look deceptively spiritual in their Sunday attire, but inside they can be feeling alienated from God. Some have not prayed or worshiped or communicated with God since the last service they attended. Perhaps we would be shocked to know how many Christians forget to read their Bibles or spend quality time in prayer in a given week. Others may come to a meeting harassed by guilt and depression. The worship service is their opportunity to find new strength in the presence of God.

We can be a fairly incommunicative lot before the Lord! He longs for our time and attention, but we are often too busy with life. There is a beautiful verse in the Song of Solomon that gives us insight into the heart of God: "My dove in the clefts of the rock, in the hiding places on the mountainside, show me your face, let me hear your voice; for your voice is sweet, and your face is lovely" (Song of Solomon 2:14). The Lord calls us his "dove" because the dove is somewhat nervous and is easily frightened. In this verse the Lord pictures us, his dove, as hiding in the clefts of the rock. And how much we really do try to hide from God! We are afraid of making ourselves vulnerable to his gentle hand. There is a pleading note in his voice as he says, "Show me your face! Let me hear your voice!" To many of us the Lord would say, "Show me your face!" We hang our heads low in the worship service, burdened with cares and concerns. He would be the lifter of our heads *(see* Psalm 3:3)! And he would add, "Let me hear your voice!" Some are afraid to lift their voice above a whisper for fear someone might hear them. But God delights in hearing our voices! He longs for us to open up and give expression to our feelings in his presence.

THE HORIZONTAL ASPECT

A great deal of interaction takes place vertically between us and God in praise and worship, but insufficient consideration has been given to the horizontal aspects of praise. These horizontal dynamics of praise comprise an integral part of the congregational experience — an element that is critical to the life of the believer, and yet absent in one's personal devotional life. Within the following points, the terms "praise" and "worship" are not used interchangeably. Some of these horizontal elements are operational in worship, but most are expressed through praise. Let us look at six ways in which worshipers interrelate in the context of congregated praise and worship.

As a first consideration of the horizontal dynamics of our services, we praise and worship in order *to enhance the sense of unity within a body.* From passages like Psalm 133, we begin to understand how important unity is to the Lord and how it pleases him. Since praise and worship contribute to unity, they must hold a special place in God's heart.

Singing can in itself unify a group in mind, activity, and stance, because when a group sings a song together, they are all saying the same words, doing the same thing, involving themselves in the same activity. Worship takes that natural medium of singing and becomes even more effective as a tool for unity.

Consider, for example, what happens when believers from various denominations, backgrounds, or churches come together for an ecumenical convocation. They cannot talk doctrine together, nor can they discuss church structure or government, and there may be little else on which they can agree. But one thing they can do together is to unitedly sing praises to the Lord! All believers have this one thing in common: they love the Lord Jesus Christ and can express their mutual faith together in song. How better can we catch a glimpse of the unity we truly have in Christ than to gather the saints together to praise God?

The bonds of unity we feel as brothers and sisters together in the body of Christ are strong and meaningful, but there is an even greater sense of unity that can come between co-worshipers. "Let me be one in heart with those who revere thy name" (Psalm 86:11, NEB). Sometimes in prayer services, as we see others expressing the depths of their hearts in worship, we sense a great rapport with them. As we see a sister crying openly in the presence of God, or a brother worshiping with great feeling, our hearts leap within us. These are worshipers indeed! After worshiping, we could have gone around and given everybody a warm embrace! That is the bond that can grow between people who are not afraid to open their hearts to God before others.

When we let down our guard and open our hearts to the Lord, we begin to realize properly just how much a part of one another we truly are. We do not feel a strong rapport with others when walls of insecurity and self-protection are erected, but we do identify strongly with the true inner person of other saints. Our fear of becoming vulnerable holds us back from being that open and transparent before God and others. We know that as we make ourselves vulnerable to God, we become vulnerable to others as well — our brothers and sisters will see us for who we truly are, without the spiritual facade. Since God knows all things anyway, we may not be threatened by the idea of becoming vulnerable before him. But before others? Why, we have a reputation to maintain! We would not want others to know the truth about our spiritual needs. But until we are willing to become vulnerable before men, we will not know a full openness before God. There is a level of unity that will never be realized until we learn to become completely open and vulnerable before both God and his people.

The Bible makes it clear that there is a distinct relationship between our love for God and our love for our fellow believers: "If anyone says, 'I love God,' yet hates his brother, he is a liar. For anyone who does not love his brother, whom he has seen, cannot love God, whom he has not seen" (1 John 4:20). The principle is this: our love for God can never transcend our love for one another. Put another way, we can never enjoy a measure of worship that exceeds the quality of relationship we have with our brethren. It is not possible to have a dynamic, personal relationship with God and be at odds with other Christians. If we are growing in loving worship of God, we will inevitably grow in our love for others, for worship causes us to grow in love and unity within the body of Christ.

Not only does worship cause us to grow in brotherly love, but it also gives us opportunity *to minister to one another.* There is no better time to minister to others than in the context of the worship service! To his admonition about brotherly love, the apostle John added, "And he has given us this command: Whoever loves God must also love his brother" (1 John 4:21). Worship in the congregation is intangible and somewhat ethereal. So God says to us, "You say you love me? Okay, prove it! Minister in love to your neighbor." That is the proof of our love for God. We should not tell God we love him if we are unable to show that love to others. When we congregate, we find ample opportunity to express our love for God in a tangible way to others.

We praise, further, in order *to teach and reinforce spiritual truth.* Notice how Paul worded this concept: "Speak to one another with psalms, hymns and spiritual songs. Sing and make music in your heart to the Lord" (Ephesians 5:19). In another place Paul said, "Let the word of Christ dwell in you richly in all wisdom; teaching and admonishing one another in psalms and hymns and spiritual songs, singing with grace in your hearts to the Lord" (Colossians 3:16, KJV). Paul made this horizontal function of praise very plain! He said clearly that we speak to one another in the songs we sing, and he specified how this happens, for we teach and admonish one another through praise.

Many of the songs we sing are actually intended to be sung to one another. We sing songs such as "Come and let us go up to the mountain of the Lord, unto the house of our God" or "Come, bless the Lord, all ye servants of the Lord, who stand by night in the house of the Lord." These are songs we sing to each other, exhorting each other to lift high God's praises. How often in our singing we admonish one another to "praise ye the Lord!" And it is right and proper for us to do so.

Much instruction is inherent within the lyrics of the songs we sing. How wonderful it would be if our children could gain an understanding of the inspirational content of the songs in our hymnals. As we sing Scripture songs and hymns, we are educating our young people to the truths of our faith. With many of the choruses we sing, we are actually memorizing Scripture, and what better way to memorize God's word? (Some folks, in attempting to better memorize the Scriptures, will actually compose melodies for large portions of the Bible — not for the purpose of public singing but for private memorization.) We could safely say that the songs we sing are in essence teaching our children the practical theology of the church.

As a fourth consideration, our praise *provides believers with an opportunity to profess their faith before others.* Congregational praise helps us become more vocal in expressing our faith, because praise is simply giving vocal affirmation to our love of and faith in the Lord Jesus. When we sing, "Jesus is my Lord, my Master, my Savior," the next step is to make that same confession outside the walls of the church building. If we will confess the name of Jesus in the worship service, we will find increased boldness to declare his name before unbelievers. If some are too shy to confess Jesus' name aloud among believers, they will never summon the courage to share their faith with unbelievers. As we lift our voices in the congregation, the Lord will increase our ability to vocalize our faith to others.

The fifth point is related to the fourth, for we praise in

the congregation *to declare the glories of God before unbelievers.* The unsaved actually do visit our worship services, and they give us the "once-over" when we praise. Often we need to be reminded that we are under scrutiny in our worship services! What impression do sinners get when they listen to our praises and watch our countenances? Do they respond by thinking, "I've got enough problems of my own already, without joining up with this morbid bunch"? Or do they witness a level of vitality and enthusiasm that convinces them we are participating in something genuine?

When unbelievers come into our worship services, they need to experience the reality of the glory of the Lord. Sinners do not need to understand everything they see and hear so long as they sense God's presence. We cannot worry about unsaved visitors misunderstanding our praise. Explanations of why we praise the way we do will not improve their first impressions, particularly if they are determined to be critical from the start. Sinners do not need to understand our praises; they simply need to experience the reality of Him whom we praise!

Psalm 108:3 declares, "I will praise you, O LORD, among the nations; I will sing of you among the peoples." God never intended that his praises be confined to the ears of believers. For too long God's people have been bashful about their praise. Some may think, for instance, "I'm not going to bring my neighbor to the Sunday evening service, because our church really gets carried away on Sunday nights, and I don't want my neighbor to get turned off." But a worship service can be the best place to bring an unsaved friend, because when God manifests his presence in the midst of his people, unbelievers will be apprehended by the convicting power of the Holy Spirit and drawn to the Lord.

Some churches almost give the impression that they are checking ID cards to make sure that all who enter are Christians. Then, when all the Christians are huddled together in a small circle, the door is locked, the shades are pulled down, and the praise service is started. No! Open up the doors of the church, lift the shades, prop open the windows, crank up the sound, and sing his praise before the world!

Hosea 6:11 says, " 'Also for you, Judah, a harvest is appointed.' " Since Judah means praise, the Lord was saying that praisers will reap a harvest. A large, thriving, evangelistic church is not too likely to have mediocre worship services, because when a church becomes a praising church, it will begin to reap a harvest of souls. Praise is evangelistic! Praise is intended to draw souls unto God. Modern sales managers have learned a principle that God knew all along: advertising works! When we praise, we are advertising our faith before the world. We are telling others about God's goodness, faithfulness, holiness, righteousness, mercy, gentleness, love, and so on. There is no better way to tell our unsaved friends about the great God we serve! As we lift high his praises, we are assured that the appointed harvest will come in.

As a final consideration, we find that praise and worship *foster a receptivity for the word.* I have asked a number of pastors across the nation, "Do you find it easier to preach after your people have opened up in worship?" The answer has invariably been an overwhelming yes! In the first place, after a pastor has worshiped with his people, he will gain a greater sense of the anointed presence of the Spirit. But more importantly, by worshiping, the people will become more open to receive the word of God.

There is a phrase in Hosea 10:11 which reads, "Judah shall plow" (KJV). We could read this as "Praise plows." Praise plows the soul of our hearts so that we are prepared to receive the implanted seed, the word of God. When a seed is planted, it requires immediate watering. David sang unto the Lord, "You visit the earth and water it, You greatly enrich it; the river of God is full of water; You provide their grain, for so You have prepared it. You water its ridges abundantly, You settle its furrows; You make it soft with showers, You bless its growth" (Psalm 65:9-10, NKJV). We experience the river of God in worship when his Spirit flows over our hearts and washes us anew. God's river and his heavenly showers soften the soil of our heart and prepare it to receive the word. That word will find a hearty reception in true worshipers, for they have a voracious appetite for it.

Music and worship also fulfill a role in preparing the pastoral leadership for the delivery of the word. The third chapter of 2 Kings tells an interesting story of a harpist being brought to Elisha to calm his troubled emotions. As the harpist played, Elisha's emotions were soothed, and he proceeded to prophesy. Preachers find the worship service very necessary in preparing their own hearts prior to pulpit ministry. Many other concerns flood their hearts and minds, but getting caught up in the Spirit enables preachers to get their emotions in tune with the Spirit, and they are readied to proclaim, "Thus says the Lord!"

THE INWARD RAMIFICATIONS OF WORSHIP

Having looked at what takes place vertically between the worshiper and God, and horizontally between co-worshipers, let us now consider what worship accomplishes inwardly in the individual.

The first thing worship does in this inward sense is to *release God's people in an uninhibited expression of their inner selves.* The key word here is "uninhibited." The Lord desires that we worship him without any holding back or any inner hindrances.

Some folks feel that if we do not dance, we have not experienced a full release in worship. Others react against that attitude and refuse to dance at all. I am not suggesting that everyone ought to dance all the time, nor am I saying we should refrain. The point I would like to make is this: no matter what outward form the worship takes, we should do it with all that is within us, without inhibitions. Some folks who never thought they were dancers may be the most extroverted in their expressions when they get to heaven, to make up for all their conservatism down here!

We will be completely uninhibited in our worship when we get to heaven — nothing will hold us back! So why should we not be that way down here, now? Uninhibited worship does not take any specific outward form, but it will allow us to be as completely transparent before the Lord as we will be in heaven.

We are so proficient, it seems, at barricading ourselves from the Lord and from one another. Psalm 24:7 says, "Lift up your heads, O you gates; be lifted up, you ancient doors, that the King of glory may come in." To what gates does the psalmist refer? They are the gates to the heart — barriers that each of us has put up inside. Our culture trains us to be self-protective, so we are preconditioned by society to erect walls of insecurity toward anyone who might try to get close to us. When God attempts to explore the recesses of our hearts, the barriers instinctively arise. If we would be willing to lift off those ancient gates that barricade our hearts, the King of glory would come in!

Worship also *provides a verbal expression of the feelings of our heart.* Some of us struggle with not always knowing how to express our feelings to the Lord. It can be difficult to vocalize just how much God means to us. At such times we need a little help to express ourselves, and congregational worship provides that. We have many hymns and choruses written by poets and writers of many ages who had a particular knack for expressing themselves with a pen. When words fail us, we can echo the words of Martin Luther: "A mighty fortress is our God, a bulwark never failing!" Thank God for men like Charles Wesley, who have left us a tremendous heritage in their great songs that have been preserved throughout the years. By singing these great songs of the church, we find that our feelings are provided a vocabulary, where choice words are coupled with an enhancing melody, and the song becomes a meaningful expression from our hearts to the Lord.

As a third element in the inward ramifications of worship, we find that worship *increases our faith.* When Jesus appeared to his disciples after his resurrection, "When they saw him, they worshiped him; but some doubted" (Matthew 28:17). The sad fact is that much of our worship is also mixed with doubt. But praising and worshiping God is one way to increase our faith.

We know that faith comes by hearing the word of God. Often when we praise God, we are speaking the word of God that we have learned. As we begin to confess God's word in praise and confess God for who he says he is, we will find that our faith will begin to rise to the level of our confession. We will truly begin to believe that God is as great and marvelous as our praise indicates! This world would be different if all Christians everywhere truly believed that God is as awesome and wonderful as they claim in their singing. His praises should be allowed to stretch our faith!

As we worship, we also *grow in holiness.* The best adjective to describe God is "holy," and his holiness should become a part of our lives through worship. Psalm 115 talks about the false gods of the heathen who cannot see or smell or walk or talk. It then adds that "those who make them will be like them" (verse 8). We learn a valuable principle here: we become like that which we worship. This is also true for the Christian, for as we worship the Lord we are changed into his very likeness!

Someone has said, "You are the company you keep." Those who spend enough time with the Lord will become like him! Some couples have been married so long that they begin to walk alike, talk alike, and even look alike! Oh, that we might know that quality of relationship with the Father!

Second Corinthians 3:18 is a beautiful verse about worship: "And we, who with unveiled faces all reflect the Lord's glory, are being transformed into his likeness with ever-increasing glory. . . ." When we worship with an uplifted countenance, we truly reflect the Lord's glory, and it is then that we are changed little by little, becoming more like the holy God whom we worship.

"Well, worship doesn't change me," some might say. "I go out of church the same as when I went in." If worship does not change a person's life, the reason is simple: that person has not unveiled his or her face before God! Those who will lower their inner barriers and pour out their hearts to God with tears of repentance and contrition will know life-changing worship.

The Bible gives us the assurance that "when he appears, we shall be like him, for we shall see him as he is" (1 John 3:2). Worship is seeing the Lord. And when we see him on that day, we will be like him! But I do not believe this verse is speaking exclusively of the hereafter. This verse also comes to us as a promise and guarantee that if today we will see him in worship, we shall be like him. It is healthy to keep the goal clearly in mind. Perhaps we would be tempted to despair in our Christian walk if we did not have the encouragement of knowing we are becoming more and more Christlike. The end of the book of Revelation is so encouraging, because it gives us insight into the beauty of the final product, the perfected Bride. John describes that glorious Bride of Christ as being "clear as crystal" (Revelation 21:11) — clear, without any shadow of sin, totally spotless in the holiness of God himself! That is the divine destiny of the worshiper!

Further, worship *inspires a greater commitment to a life of worship.* It is one thing to worship in the congregation, when the saints are gathered in joyful assembly, musicians are playing their instruments, and everyone is united in glorious praise; it is quite another to live a life of worship throughout the week, when the music is gone and the charged atmosphere is forgotten! Our congregational worship is intended to help inspire us to a consistent life of worship all week long. When the worship on Sunday is vibrant and real, we gain new impetus to go forth and live that during the week. The church service is practice time; out in the world we discover if we truly learned the lesson.

Finally, worship *prepares us* for the new thing God wants

to do. There is no doubt that God is continually doing new things *(see* Isaiah 43:19), and he wants to prepare us to flow with him in that. What is holding God back from sending his final outpouring that will see the culmination of the ages? Is God preparing the president of the United States, or perhaps Communist Russia, or maybe the world economy? No, but God is preparing people. Luke 1:17 reads, " '. . . to make ready *a people* prepared for the Lord.' " God is preparing his people, his church! The church is the only thing that is holding God back from bringing the fullness of his kingdom to earth.

Praise and worship have preparatory effects. " 'He who sacrifices thank offerings honors me, and he prepares the way so that I may show him the salvation of God' " (Psalm 50:23). Worship softens our hearts and sensitizes our spirits, so that when God moves, we will know it. When God does something new, it often comes in an unconventional or unexpected form. If we are not closely attuned to the Holy Spirit, we can easily reject the new thing God wants to do. But if we will behold him steadfastly in worship, we will see when he moves and which way he goes.

I am not suggesting that "worship" in and of itself is the complete end-time message that God yet needs to speak to the church in order to inaugurate his second return. But I do see worship as playing a vital role in preparing us so that no matter what God does, we will be ready to move with him. God wants us to be prepared, but that involves some initiative on our part. Revelation 19:7, speaking of this prepared church, says, " 'Let us rejoice and be glad and give him glory! For the wedding of the Lamb has come, and his bride has made herself ready.' " It would be a mistake for us to wait for God to do in our lives what we alone can do. The reins of our lives are in our own hands, and we can choose to become the worshipers God wants us to be. As we surrender our wills to him, he will make us into worshipers who are prepared to move with him.

It is possible for us to know what God is doing in the earth today. The writer of Psalm 73 complained about how the wicked seem to prosper and the righteous seem to suffer. He said, "When I tried to understand all this, it was oppressive to me till I entered the sanctuary of God; *then I understood* their final destiny" (Psalm 73:16-17). In coming into God's sanctuary the psalmist gained understanding. And this is how we today gain understanding in the ways of God: by worshiping in his sanctuary, in the congregation. When we congregate to worship, one comes with a word, another with an exhortation, another with a prophecy — and a picture begins to emerge and take form. By putting together the contributions of all the saints in the body, we can gain insight into what God is saying and doing in the earth today!

Psalm 77:13 reads, "Thy way, O God, is in the sanctuary" (KJV). An alternate marginal reading is "The understanding of your ways in the place of worship." Truly we begin to understand God's ways in the congregation, as praise and worship ascend to him! And one of the beautiful expressions we find in this congregational praise and worship, to teach us God's ways, is a flow of the prophetic ministry.

CHAPTER 7

MOVING PROPHETICALLY IN PRAISE AND WORSHIP

Praise and worship are natural complements to the functioning of the gifts of the Spirit *(see* 1 Corinthians 12:4-11), particularly prophecy. Both relate to and interact with the prophetic ministry. There are a variety of ways that we can function prophetically in worship. Perhaps the most common form of prophetic ministry is the spoken prophecy. Some churches move prophetically in the realm of interpretive dance. Others emphasize the use of prophetic songs. In this chapter we will devote most of our attention to the musical aspects of prophecy and their role and function in congregational worship. As we discover what prophetic worship is and how we can flow in it, we will also discover a whole new dimension in our worship relationship with God.

We need to agree on a working definition of what we mean by "moving prophetically" in worship. The following statement will serve as a broad definition: "to move prophetically in worship is to move with an awareness of the desire and leading of the Holy Spirit moment by moment, to discern the direction of the Spirit, and to lead God's people into a fuller participation of that." When moving prophetically in worship, one does not necessarily stand up and say, "Thus saith the Lord. . . ." That is a very specific application of the prophetic mantle. In this broader sense, we arc simply endeavoring to discern the way of the Spirit in the midst of the worship service and then attempting to help God's people open up to that. A worship leader may realize that something is holding back the saints in a particular service and then may sense in the Spirit what needs to be said or done to rectify the problem. By discerning the mind of

the Spirit, a worship leader can bring correction to a difficult situation, and this is the essence of flowing in a prophetic anointing.

Any church leader is willing to admit that we all encounter a lot of small difficulties in our worship services. Some
worship leaders become so threatened by these things that
they resign their post. What is necessary, however, is for
the worship leader to have a prophetic anointing in order to
gain divine insight into the various hindrances and problems that will occur. The Spirit can help the leader to
understand what the problem truly is, and then he can give
the leader supernatural wisdom to know how to deal with
the problem.

It is safe to say, then, that God intends that those in
leadership, especially musical leadership, function under a
prophetic anointing. But we need to broaden that even further to say that God intends that we all participate in prophetic worship.

PROPHETIC WORSHIP

What do we mean by "prophetic worship"? The prototype for prophetic worship is in the book of Genesis, when
the Lord God would come down to the garden of Eden in
the cool of the day to commune with Adam and Eve *(see
Genesis 3:8-9)*. Prophetic worship is, quite simply, walking
and talking with the Lord. Notice that I said *with* the Lord,
not merely *to* the Lord. Worship has always been ordained
of God to be more than a monologue of my telling him how I
feel about him. Worship is more than just my talking to God
— it is also his talking to me! Worship is an exchange — it is
two-way communication.

Worship has been called the "language of love." When
we worship, we express our love to God. But love must flow
as an exchange between two individuals. There must be
give and take, talking and listening, transmitting and
receiving. When I love my wife, I do not go on and on about

my feelings for her, nor do I occupy the conversation exclusively with my own opinion and feelings. I give her an opportunity to respond, allowing her to give expression to her own inner emotions.

Worship must contain both elements in order to be complete: it must consist of our expressions unto God, and then it must also include listening to his responses. Many of our worship services go like this: we sing and shout and praise and speak in tongues and love God and worship him — and then we hear "You may be seated." And God is waiting with bated breath to respond! Oh, how he wants to speak to us and share his heart with us! But we do not give him the opportunity; or we do not have time in our service schedule for that sort of thing, because we have a guest speaker this Sunday, or a baby dedication, or. . . . We feel fulfilled because we have given vent to our emotions, but God has not had opportunity to express himself to us. In failing to recognize the relationship between praise (us speaking) and prophecy (God speaking), we lose a very important element in our worship.

THE SCRIPTURAL LINK BETWEEN MUSIC AND PROPHECY

There is a dimension available to us in music ministry that will never be enjoyed by those who believe that the prophetic gift or anointing is no longer intended for our use today. In no way is this a disparaging word against Christians who do not believe in the fullness of the Holy Spirit as we know it (speaking in tongues, the gifts of the Spirit, and so on). But the sad truth is that these good brothers and sisters are robbing themselves of a fuller and more blessed dimension in praise and worship, and until they accept the role of prophecy in music and worship, they will never have the joy of participating in this aspect of praise and worship.

The Scriptures show us a beautiful relationship between the role of music in the church and the function of prophecy. This is not just vocal music — it is instrumental as well. First Chronicles 25 tells how David and the leadership of Israel set aside certain musical Levites specifically "for the ministry of prophesying, accompanied by harps, lyres and cymbals" (verse 1). The third verse of this chapter mentions some of these Levites by name, saying they were the ones "who prophesied, using the harp in thanking and praising the LORD." There are two ways we could interpret these verses: we could say these Levites prophesied while musical instruments were being played; we could also say that they played prophetically upon the instruments themselves. I believe that both these interpretations are correct — they prophesied while accompanied by musical instruments, and they also actually prophesied upon the instruments.

Saul had a very intriguing experience when he was anointed by Samuel to be king over Israel. After anointing Saul with oil, Samuel prophesied over Saul and began to tell him some things that were going to happen to him that day so that Saul would be assured of the Lord's calling upon him. Samuel went on to say, " 'After that you will go to Gibeah of God, where there is a Philistine outpost. As you approach the town, you will meet a procession of prophets coming down from the high place with lyres, tambourines, flutes and harps being played before them, and they will be prophesying. The Spirit of the LORD will come upon you in power, and you will prophesy with them; and you will be changed into a different person' " (1 Samuel 10:5-6).

The following verses go on to say that that is exactly what happened. Picture the scene. Down from the high place came a band of musicians who were playing their instruments, with a group of prophets who were singing and prophesying as they walked along the way. Perhaps one of the men picked up a lyre and began to strum melodiously; and as he did, the Spirit of God came on one of the prophets, who began to prophesy and praise the name of the Lord. As the musicians played, the prophetic flow was released and

Saul participated in it.

The prophet Elisha was another who recognized the close relationship between music and prophecy. He was once in a situation in which he was expected to prophesy, but he did not want to do so. He was called to appear before the kings of Israel and Judah, who had united forces against Moab. Joram, the evil king of Israel, was on one side, and Jehoshaphat, the godly king of Judah, was opposite him. Before attacking Moab, Jehoshaphat asked Joram if there was a prophet in Israel so they could hear a word from God. In response, Joram sent for Elisha.

Elisha arrived full of righteous indignation and said to the king of Israel, " 'As surely as the LORD Almighty lives, whom I serve, if I did not have respect for the presence of Jehoshaphat king of Judah, I would not look at you or even notice you' " (2 Kings 3:14). Elisha was mad! He did not like that scoundrel Joram one bit, and he did not mind saying so. So there was Elisha, with his spirit extremely agitated, and he was being called upon to prophesy. What did he do? He said, " 'But now bring me a harpist.' While the harpist was playing, the hand of the LORD came upon Elisha and he said . . ." (verses 15-16). It is very difficult to prophesy when the spirit or soul is distraught. But Elisha knew how to quiet his spirit. He called for a musician, and as the harp was being played, his spirit was calmed, he began to feel the Spirit of God stirring in his heart, and the prophetic ministry began to flow. Music can so beautifully enhance the prophetic flow by soothing our hearts so that we are more receptive to God's Spirit.

A musician can function prophetically too! By playing with sensitivity to the Spirit, a musician can do more in a few minutes to cause people's hearts to open to the Lord than three hours of preaching ever could. An anointed, prophetic song on an instrument can add much to the quality of a worship service.

THE "SONG OF THE LORD"

This does not, of course, make vocal music any less important. The Scriptures tell us that the Lord joins us in our singing. ". . . he will rejoice over you with singing" (Zephaniah 3:17). The Revised Standard Version phrases that verse uniquely: "The LORD, your God, is in your midst, a warrior who gives victory; he will rejoice over you with gladness, he will renew you in his love; he will exult over you with loud singing as on a day of festival." When we sing praises unto God, he responds by singing also. Psalm 22:22 reads, "I will declare your name to my brothers; in the congregation I will praise you." Psalm 22 is a Messianic psalm and so speaks much about the Lord Jesus. Also the writer of the book of Hebrews made it clear that Jesus was the one speaking in the first person in this passage: " '. . . in the presence of the congregation I will sing your praises' " (Hebrews 2:12). In other words, Jesus says that when we praise the Lord in the congregation, he will join us in singing praise unto the Father! So we have the song of the Father, who sings over his saints, and we have the song of the Son, who sings in the midst of the congregation. Some folks call this "the song of the Lord," and that is precisely what it is.

The term "the song of the Lord" has been used widely to refer to "prophetic song" — that is, a prophetic utterance sung either unto the Lord or unto believers. This term is taken directly from the KJV rendering of 2 Chronicles 29:27: "And when the burnt offering began, the song of the LORD began also with the trumpets, and with the instruments ordained by David king of Israel." The NASB and the RSV use the phrase "the song to the LORD"; the NIV says, "singing to the LORD began also"; the Amplified Version reads "the song of the LORD."

Exactly what was this "song of the Lord" or "song to the Lord"? Was it a prophetic song, a spontaneous utterance under the anointing of God? I would suggest that

Psalm 137:4 gives us better insight into this term. "How shall we sing the LORD'S song in a strange land?" (KJV). The NIV gives this as "the songs of the LORD." The preceding verses tell us what those songs were: "By the rivers of Babylon we sat and wept when we remembered Zion. There on the poplars we hung our harps, for there our captors asked us for songs, our tormentors demanded songs of joy; they said, 'Sing us one of the songs of Zion!' How can we sing the songs of the LORD while in a foreign land?" (Psalm 137:1-4).

These "songs of the Lord" were simply "the songs of Zion." They were the favorite praise and worship songs of the day. These songs of Zion were widely known as being particularly beautiful and delightful, so it was to be expected that Israel's Babylonian captors would desire to hear those songs and would demand that they be sung.

If the term "song of the Lord" is not a biblical term for prophetic song, then should we avoid the term? That would not be absolutely necessary, but it is my opinion that the term is somewhat misleading. Many times we will call a prophetic song "the song of the Lord" when it is simply the song of a man or woman. What term best describes these prophetic songs? Well, for one, "prophetic songs" is appropriate! But Paul's term, I believe, was "spiritual songs" (which we will examine later).

One very beautiful form that prophetic worship can take is when a singer, under the prophetic anointing of the Spirit, will sing forth the "song of the Lord," or prophetic song, so that all the saints can actually listen to and participate in that song which Jesus is singing among his people. Spoken prophecies are very meaningful and good, but there is the potential for sung prophecies to be even more beautiful and meaningful. This is simply because singing is more pleasing to the ear than just the spoken word. From the Scriptures we get the impression that even God himself prefers to listen to singing more than just to speaking. In one sense, singing is to speaking as flying is to driving. Both forms will get you there, but one is much loftier than the other. Therefore, if someone has a prophetic message to share with the body in the midst of the worship service, he or she may consider singing it to the saints.

One more verse deserves our attention in our considera- tion of music and prophecy. "King Hezekiah and his offi- cials ordered the Levites to praise the LORD with the words of David and of Asaph the seer. So they sang praises with gladness and bowed their heads and worshiped" (2 Chroni- cles 29:30). Notice that Asaph is here called a "seer." Asaph was the chief musician at the time of David — he was the "minister of music." And he was also a seer! He had a definite prophetic anointing upon his music ministry. The Lord has always intended that his "ministers of music" should have a prophetic anointing. Our churches are plagued with very capable musicians who know nothing of moving in the anointing of the Spirit. But qualifying as a "minister of music" means manifesting more than just fine musicianship; it means also displaying an ability to flow pro- phetically with the moving of the Holy Spirit in the congre- gation.

Let's go one step further. If God has called someone to a music ministry — if that person knows that he or she has been called to be a singer, or a worship leader, or a musician — let me suggest that God has also called that person to function prophetically! He would not call a man or woman to the ministry of music without also equipping that person to perform that ministry.

PSALMS, HYMNS, AND SPIRITUAL SONGS

The apostle Paul referred to an element of prophetic worship when he mentioned "psalms, hymns and spiritual songs" *(see* Ephesians 5:19; Colossians 3:16). There has been considerable difference of opinion regarding what Paul meant when he used these three terms. The following definitions deserve careful thought.

There is no doubt that when Paul spoke of *psalms,* he was referring to the singing of the Scriptures. The Psalms comprised the majority of the "hymnal" in the early church, and I am sure portions from other books were used as well, such as Isaiah, the Pentateuch, and so on. We sing "psalms" today — the Scriptures set to contemporary tunes.

A *hymn*, as Paul used the term, is nothing more than a song of human composition. The lyrics are not copied from the Scriptures but are rather composed in the mind of the poet and then set to an enhancing tune. According to this definition, the majority of songs in our "hymnals" fall under Paul's category of "hymns." But there are many "choruses" we sing today that would qualify under this category of "hymns." They are not hymns in the sense that they are found in our hymnals, but they are short songs of praise and worship that were composed by an individual who was under the creative anointing of the Holy Spirit. As such, they too can be termed "hymns."

One reason I am bringing this out is because there are those who would suggest that the short choruses we sing are in fact "spiritual songs." By saying this, such folks completely bypass the beauty of the true essence of "spiritual songs." Another reason I am emphasizing this point is because some sincere believers have used this verse of Paul's to defend the use of hymnals in church. But Paul was not talking about our modern-day hymnals! The "hymn" or "anthem" as we know it today is an art form that has emerged within the last few hundred years; "hymns" did not even exist in the days of the early church. Therefore, the Scriptures do not place a holy sanction on the "old hymns" of the church. There is nothing inherently sacred about the hymn form as we know it today. I am not against hymnals, but I am against the use of Ephesians 5:19 as a biblical premise for keeping hymnals in our churches.

Since Paul was not referring to the hymnals that many churches have used in recent years, should we then sing hymns as we have come to know and love them? Of course, but our reasons for doing so must be different from simply saying, "The Bible tells us to sing hymns to God." Some contemporary charismatic churches have completely removed their hymnals without violating Paul's injunction. If the Bible, then, does not officially endorse our hymnals, upon what basis should a church decide whether or not to use hymnals? We should ask ourselves these questions:

Do our parishioners have a particular predisposition for or an antipathy toward the old hymns of the church?

Does our budget permit us to purchase a quantity of hymnals?

Would our church be better served by projecting the words of the hymns onto a screen?

Are we in a hymn-singing rut? Would we do better to stop singing hymns for a few months, so that when we return to them we would appreciate them more?

Are we prejudiced against singing hymns? Have we been so turned off by the formalism of hymn-singing in many churches that we have "thrown the baby out with the bath water"? (I heard of one church that wrote into their constitution that they would never have a hymnal in their church.)

The historic hymns of the church cannot be supported as a sacred art form based upon Paul's use of the word "hymn." But there are good reasons why we today would choose to incorporate the beloved hymns of the church into the worship of our own local church body. Consider the following reasons:

First of all, hymnals give us a valuable link to our rich Christian heritage. Some "charismatic" churches cast a belittling eye toward those who have gone before us. They would assume that the saints of previous ages were not too spiritual, did not enjoy a very high revelation of God's truth, and simply did not live on the same spiritual plane that we enjoy today. But reading carefully through an old hymnal may quickly change that opinion! The hymnwriters of previous centuries were many times more profound in their expressions of praise and worship unto God than are many contemporary songwriters.

Second, hymns provide us with a depth of vocabulary that many of our choruses do not. Consider one little tune that many of us sing: "This is the day, this is the day that the Lord hath made, that the Lord hath made; we will rejoice. . . ." What is this chorus really saying? — just one very simple thought. It took only one verse in the Bible to say what that entire song says. Consider, on the other hand, how rich and varied are the words to many of the old songs of the church. These rich hymns will definitely require a greater use of our minds in worship, but the rewards can also be much greater.

Further, the old hymns have a much longer lifespan than many of the choruses we sing today. It is unlikely that two hundred or so years from now, anyone will have even heard of the chorus "This Is the Day." In contrast, consider Luther's hymn "A Mighty Fortress Is Our God." That hymn has survived for more than four hundred years, and it may well survive for four hundred more, should the Lord tarry. If we read the words to that hymn, we will gain some understanding of why it has survived the passing of time. The wealth and value of a song or hymn can many times be gauged by its permanence (or lack thereof).

Hymns can also, at times, be much more effective than many of our choruses as teaching tools for our children. The hymnists of past centuries were often bona fide theologians in their own right. They had a comprehensive grasp of the word of God and had a tremendous ability to express that knowledge in beautiful poetry. Our children will surely be richer if they are taught by songs with this lofty a caliber of theology.

Fifth, hymns can provide us with a much wider variety of subjects and themes for expressing ourselves. Suppose the pastor tells the worship leader that he is going to preach on "The Centrality of the Cross" and wants to close with an appropriate song following the sermon. The chorus list may not contain anything suitable. But checking the index of the hymnal reveals a number of quality hymns that address the importance of Christ's cross.

There are times when our chorus repertoire simply does not address certain subjects. If God would speak to a church about setting aside more time to seek his face, for instance, is there a chorus that would emphasize that theme as adequately as the beautiful hymn "Take Time to Be Holy"? When special events like Christmas or Easter come along, how many appropriate choruses does a church know? But most hymnals will contain at least one song, and usually many, for virtually any occasion and theme.

I understand perfectly well some of the problems that some charismatic churches have with hymnals. They tend to cause the people to bury their heads in a book rather than to lift their countenances unto the Lord. And some of the hymns are quite poor theologically. Others are gloomy and depressing. Most of these objections can be circumvented without too much difficulty by being eclectic in our choices of which hymns to use.

In many quarters a strong protest has been vocalized against the contemporary tendency to downplay or even discard hymnals in congregational worship. The debate is not a new one. A prominent American clergyman compiled the following ten reasons for opposing the new music trend of his day:

1. It's too new, like an unknown language.
2. It's not so melodious as the more established style.
3. There are so many new songs that it is impossible to learn them all.
4. This new music creates disturbances and causes people to act in an indecent and disorderly manner.
5. It places too much emphasis on instrumental music rather than on godly lyrics.
6. The lyrics are often worldly, even blasphemous.
7. It is not needed, since preceding generations have

gone to heaven without it.

8. It is a contrivance to get money.

9. It monopolizes the Christians' time and encourages them to stay out late.

10. These new musicians are young upstarts, and some of them are lewd and loose persons.

These ten reasons are adapted from a 1723 statement directed against the use of — hymns! Some of these arguments are given today, but rather than being directed against hymns, they are now levied against contemporary Scripture and praise choruses.

The following ten reasons were given in 1984 by a group of Bible college students to state why they did not support hymns:

1. Many hymns are doctrinal and instructional in nature, rather than contributing to praise and worship.

2. The music is formal, structured, and outdated, as opposed to being youthful and contemporary.

3. Many of the words are archaic.

4. Some have forsaken hymns as a part of their break with the dry deadness of their traditional background.

5. Many hymns *are* dead.

6. Many churches cannot afford hymnals.

7. Hymns represented the new move of God in their day, and choruses represent the new move of God in our day.

8. Choruses are simple and easy to concentrate on.

9. Having to hold a hymnal is a negative factor.

10. Choruses lend themselves more easily to flowing in the Spirit.

The voice of those defending hymns as a viable form of contemporary worship is very strong. Perhaps even the words of John Wesley, when he commended the *Methodist Hymnal of 1780* to his constituency, apply today: "Large enough to contain all the important truths of our most holy religion. . . . In what other publication of this time have you so full and distinct an account of scriptural Christianity?

Such a declaration of the heights and depths of religion, speculative and practical? So strong cautions against the most plausible errors? And so clear directions for making our calling and election sure: for perfecting holiness in the fear of God?"

On a contemporary note, Dan Betzer, speaker for the "Revivaltime" radio broadcast of the Assemblies of God, expressed his feelings in an article entitled "Whatever Happened to the Great Hymns?" which appeared in the February 1983 issue of *Motif* magazine. Although not maligning the use of Scripture choruses, Betzer mourned almost nostalgically the sense of loss he feels over the lack of hymns in churches today.

Another defender of hymns is James Rawlings Sydnor, author of *Hymns and Their Uses* (Carol Stream, IL: Agape, 1982). His book lists some tips for enhancing a congregation's appreciation of hymns, including teaching a "hymn of the month" to the church; educating the people in how and why hymns were written, giving the scriptural basis for each hymn and informing them about the authors and composers; encouraging the purchase of hymnals for use at home; having a hymn-writing contest; conducting a hymn survey, followed up with a hymn-sing; teaching on hymnology; and preaching sermons based upon hymns.

The third category is *spiritual songs,* which are simply "songs of the spirit" — spontaneous songs of the moment that arise from our spirits unto the Lord. Spiritual songs are sometimes spoken in our native tongue and sometimes in an unknown tongue. They are usually not premeditated or studied but are offered spontaneously to God — "off the cuff," so to speak.

The beauty of spiritual songs is in the individuality that they provide. Each worshiper is able to sing his or her own unique spiritual song to the Lord — an offering that is particularly pleasing to the Lord because it is the genuine expression of each individual. Many churches will allow for the singing of psalms and hymns, but relatively few provide for the singing of spiritual songs. This type of spontaneous song, however, can be one of the most rewarding expressions of praise and worship we give to the Lord! And it is within the context of "spiritual songs" that we can most readily enter into dimensions of prophetic worship.

The charismatic renewal has seen one very common type of spiritual song: the singing of spontaneous praise with one sustained chord. The piano and organ hold down one major chord, and the entire congregation sings, alternating notes between the first, third, and fifth notes of the scale. This type of spiritual song can be augmented by adding a rhythmic pattern on the musical instruments. By simply adding a 4/4 rhythm, we can find a new dimension in the common practice of "singing in the Spirit" to one sustained chord.

Another beautiful way to sing spiritual songs is to choose the melody of a known chorus, and rather than singing the words that everyone knows, instruct the congregation to sing the same tune but to create their own words of praise and thanksgiving unto the Lord. In this way we are able to fulfill the scriptural injunction to "sing a new song" unto the Lord, and we do not even have to learn a new tune.

I once went to a home prayer meeting where it was my responsibility to lead worship. But in preparing for the worship time, I could not think of any songs I wanted to sing. I went through the entire list; nothing seemed to "grab" me. So I decided that we would not sing any songs at all. Rather, using the melody of the simple chorus "Alleluia," we sang our own verses unto the Lord. Everyone was able to lift up his or her voice in a meaningful expression of love and appreciation to the Lord, and we did not have to learn a new tune in order to do it. There was a beautiful release in the group that night, and I learned a valuable lesson: we do not have to sing known songs in order to worship! We can sing "spiritual songs" too.

Another musical form that has gained popularity more recently is the singing of spiritual songs to a set chord progression. This musical technique can be a challenging art form to master in and of itself. (See Appendix 2 for detailed and technical information on the use of chord progressions in worship.)

Generally, there are two levels of spiritual songs. On the first level, we sing a spontaneous song to the Lord, for the exclusive enjoyment of the Lord and the individual. On the second level, we can sing a spiritual song that is for the benefit and uplifting of the entire congregation.

On the second level, there are at least four forms that spiritual songs can take. In the broadest sense, we can sing a spiritual song that constitutes nothing more than a simple praise unto the Lord, and this can be expressed in the hearing of the congregation. This type of spiritual song does not necessarily require any great "prophetic" anointing on the singer. A person may simply be overflowing with thankfulness to the Lord for his goodness and may sense that a song of thanks would be a blessing and inspiration to the entire body, and so would sing a new, spontaneous song of thankfulness unto the Lord in the hearing of the congregation — perhaps using a microphone. (The use of microphones for such singing in public contexts must be determined by the leadership of each church.) After the song is sung, the congregation can judge the appropriateness of that expression. If the general level of worship and praise crescendos because of that spontaneous spiritual song, then we can be assured it was done in the Spirit. If the opposite occurs, we need to learn from our mistakes and seek to improve the quality and content of our spiritual songs.

Second, a more precise, particular expression of a spiritual song would be what has been termed by some "the song of the Lord." In this type of expression, the singer prophetically senses the song of the Bridegroom over his people and reflects that to the congregation. Many times such songs are sung in the first person — for example, "my people, I glory in your praises." The Lord speaks to his church through a human vessel who carries a prophetic sensitivity.

A third type of spiritual song is very similar to a spoken prophecy, but rather than being spoken, it is sung. Since it is a prophetic utterance, it should follow the guidelines of 1 Corinthians 14:3 — it should either edify, exhort, or comfort God's people. In this type of spiritual song, the singer prophetically speaks a word of exhortation or comfort from the Lord to his people.

As a final consideration, a spiritual song could conceivably be a reflection of the heavenly song. Through prophetic insight a person could sing before the congregation the song that is being sung in heaven around the throne.

Effort is required to maintain a balance between psalms, hymns, and spiritual songs. If we get too imbalanced in any one area, we will soon develop our own unique rut. (And someone has said that the only difference between a rut and a grave is the depth of the hole!) Some pastors, in an attempt to incorporate hymns into their singing, will ask their worship leaders to sing at least one song from the hymnal each service. Hymns can be included in a church's repertoire even though the church has no hymnals simply by properly procuring an overhead projector transparency for the songs desired.

In seeking a balance between songs, hymns, and spiritual songs, most churches tend to neglect the last category — probably because spiritual songs require a good deal of initiative from the individual, and many people are introverted when it comes to expressing themselves before God and a company of believers! A congregation must be *trained* to respond to the Lord without looking for some stimulus from the worship leader.

THIS IS FOR EVERYONE!

Those reading these lines, particularly relative to spiritual songs, might be tempted to think, "Why, I could never do that! I don't have that kind of a prophetic anointing on my life." But I am suggesting that there is a "spirit of prophecy" that is upon all God's saints, if only they will recognize it and accept it. Revelation 19:10 says, "The testimony of Jesus is the spirit of prophecy." This suggests two things: when we testify of Jesus, the prophetic spirit rests upon us; and when we prophesy, we should testify of Jesus.

Furthermore, the Scriptures show us that God desires that *all* his people function prophetically. This thought occurred in kernel form early in the history of the nation of Israel, when the elders of Israel came apart with Moses and Joshua to seek the Lord *(see* Numbers 11). As the Spirit of God came upon these seventy elders, they all prophesied. Two elders, however, who had previous commitments could not be there, but the Spirit came on them while they were in the camp, and they too prophesied. Someone ran to report this to Moses, and Joshua spoke up, " 'Moses, my lord, stop them!' " Notice Moses' response: " 'Are you jealous for my sake? I wish that all the LORD'S people were prophets and that the LORD would put his Spirit on them!" (Numbers 11:28-29). Joel may well have had this prayer of Moses in mind when he prophesied the outpouring of the Spirit "on all people" (Joel 2:28). Moses' wish has become a reality in this day of the Holy Spirit, for since the day of Pentecost *(see* Acts 2) God's Spirit has been placed indiscriminately upon all peoples and nations.

When I first began to understand the role of prophecy in worship, I wanted to be used prophetically of the Lord, but I was not sure if it was his will to use me in that way. I asked the Lord, "Do you really want to use me prophetically?" I had not functioned prophetically before, and I had never had an experience in which someone laid hands on me and imparted to me the gift of prophecy. I had never heard a voice from heaven, nor did I feel chills up and down my spine. So how could I know? Then the Lord directed my attention to the verses that we considered earlier (1 Chronicles 25:1, 3; 1 Samuel 10:5-6; 2 Kings 3:15-16; 2 Chronicles 29:30), and I came to realize that since the Lord had called me to a music ministry and had anointed me to lead worship, he also intended that I have a prophetic mantle upon my life and ministry. In fact, I accepted from him that he had *already* given me a prophetic anointing! The only thing left for me to do was to accept that and begin to act upon it. So I did precisely that. I began to function with a prophetic anointing, and immediately I found that it was confirmed by others as genuine.

TAKING A STEP OF FAITH

A principle found in Romans 12:6 is extremely vital in unlocking the prophetic anointing in our lives: "If a man's gift is prophesying, let him use it in proportion to his faith." The prophetic gifting is unlocked by faith. The first time someone steps out to move prophetically, it will take an abundance of faith! But until we are ready to exercise our faith like that, we will never be used in a prophetic dimension. If we wait for a thunderbolt from heaven or hold back until we have a prophetic message burning so in our hearts that we cannot refrain from blurting it out, we will be waiting a long time. Once we know that God would desire that we prophesy, we must "go for it" and unlock that flow with a step of faith.

When we "go for it," though, we must be prepared to face the consequences. When we first begin to step out in the realm of the prophetic, we might get a rebuke, or a word of correction from the pastor. But if we wait until we are able to deliver a mature, perfected word, nothing will ever happen. The chances are good, however, that instead of a rebuke we will receive a beautiful confirmation of the prophetic anointing. As we take a step of faith and let that anointing find confirmation, we will be encouraged to exercise our faith again.

We might ask ourselves, "If I were to take a step of faith right now, and deliver the message that I feel in my heart, what is the worst possible thing that could happen?" The pastor might rebuke us publicly from the pulpit. The elders might kick us out of the church. Our family might be embarrassed and insist that we change churches. Once we have labeled the absolutely worst possible thing that could happen, we should then ask ourselves, "Is it worth it?" Personally, I would rather take a chance on what might happen if I am used by God than to take no chance at all and never be used by God. I am eager enough to be used by God that I am willing to chance excommunication, or anything else, if need be. All of us need to come to a similar conclusion in order to muster the courage to speak forth from our hearts.

Virtually every time we function prophetically will require the initiative of faith. No matter how much experience we might have in these areas, each time we must exert our faith anew.

"Surely the Sovereign LORD does nothing without revealing his plan to his servants the prophets" (Amos 3:7). God has much to say to his people! We thought that we have much to say to God, but how much more the greatest mind in the universe has to say to us! Let us give him opportunity to respond to us in our worship services so that our worship might truly become a beautiful dialogue between the Bridegroom and the Bride.

GUIDELINES — THINGS TO DO

We have been considering how we can use our musical abilities to enhance the prophetic flow. Now let's consider some very practical guidelines for the exercise of prophecy. These apply to all prophecies, whether spoken or sung. First let's look at some "things to do."

1. To move prophetically, one must first of all spend much intimate time in the presence of God. This time is spent cultivating spiritual sensitivity and learning the heartbeat of God. These things are gained only through time spent in prayer. The Bible says of Anna the prophetess that her ministry was chiefly that of spending countless hours

fasting and praying in the temple *(see* Luke 2:36-38). She was noted not for her prophesying but for her praying. The prophets in Antioch participated chiefly in prayer and fasting *(see* Acts 13:1-3). The Old Testament prophets, particularly Elijah and Jeremiah, were men of prayer.

Ralph Mahoney, of World M.A.P., has commented, "What I feel God wants us to see . . . is that there is a direct connection or tie between prophecy and prayer. Many people have received a prophetic word for their lives but failed to see it come to pass because they didn't play their part by birthing the divine purpose from the womb of intercession. Prophecy must be conceived, received, and birthed in prayer and intercession. Both the prophet who speaks the word and the one who receives the word have a responsibility before the Lord" *(World M.A.P. Digest,* May/June 1985).

2. We must study the Scriptures regularly. A Scripture made alive in our hearts will frequently be the basis for a prophetic word from the Lord.

3. A certain proverb reads: " 'There are three things that are too amazing for me, four that I do not understand: the way of an eagle in the sky, the way of a snake on a rock, the way of a ship on the high seas, and the way of a man with a maiden' " (Proverbs 30:18-19). Something that is even more amazing is the way of the Lord with his Bride! To function prophetically, one must understand the way the Lord deals with and entreats his church. We learn the way of the Lord chiefly through studying the Scriptures and observing God's ways in the sanctuary. One good method is to study the gift of those who have a matured prophetic voice and allow their mature gift to teach things like timing, vocal inflection, and types of messages.

4. "The words of the LORD are flawless, like silver refined in a furnace of clay, purified seven times" (Psalm 12:6). Since God's words are so pure, so ought to be the lives of those speaking the words. Otherwise, how can a bitter fountain bring forth pure water *(see* James 3:11)?

5. First Corinthians 14:32-33 tells us, "The spirits of

prophets are subject to the control of prophets. For God is not a God of disorder but of peace." This suggests at least four things. First, we can stifle the prophetic flow, and we can release it. Second, we are capable of waiting for the proper timing. Next, we are in control and thus are accountable for what we declare. We cannot hide behind excuses such as "If you don't like what I said, don't talk to me — talk to God. He's the one who said it!" Even the prophet Jeremiah, who spoke the pure word of God, had to suffer the consequences of what he spoke, because the sinful Israelites would not receive it. However, rather than suffering for delivering the pure word of God, we usually find that we are accountable because of our tendencies to misuse the prophetic flow. Finally, this verse shows us that God is concerned that the prophetic ministry operate in an orderly manner. Emotions should always be controlled. When prophecies are given, onlookers should not be inclined to term the proceedings a "fiasco."

6.   We must consider carefully that we speak only what God gives us. The prophet Micaiah knew what "prophetic restraint" was: speaking only what God had spoken, and no more (see 1 Kings 22:13-14).

7.   We must wait for our turn and be alert to the best moment to participate. Ecclesiastes 3:7 says there is "a time to keep silence and a time to speak." Timing is critical in prophecy, and sensitivity to timing can often determine the propriety of one's contribution.

8.   We need to listen for a key word that will ignite in our spirit. Sometimes a single word comes to mind, sometimes a phrase, and occasionally an entire message. This is the point at which we step out in faith, even if we have not yet received the entire message. We can learn to recognize the promptings of the Spirit and yield to him.

9.   We must learn to listen for a theme or keynote to emerge in the worship. What was the subject matter of previous prophecies in this service? At the same time, we should seek to augment, not repeat, what has already tran-

spired. We should not fall into the trap of reiterating or stating in a different way what has already been said, but we should build on what has preceded.

10.   We must also evaluate the impulse we are feeling. Is it for the entire congregation, or perhaps just for us? Should it be sung, or spoken? Is it a prophetic utterance, or an exhortation?

11.   It is important that we speak loudly and clearly. If an utterance is *inaudible,* it is *invalid.* A valid utterance edifies the entire congregation. We may have a bona fide word from God, but if we mumble it so that it is not heard by everyone, we have rendered our prophecy invalid. An inaudible mumble brings an awkward quietness in the congregation while everyone strains to hear what is being said. This is not orderly and is thus invalid. If we have a genuine word from God but do not have the vocal projection to be heard from where we stand, we should use a microphone on the platform.

12.   We must contribute but not exhaust. If a prophecy is too long, the service ebbs. We should be succinct and to the point, deliver our heart, and stop.

Amos said, "The lion has roared — who will not fear? The Sovereign LORD has spoken — who can but prophesy?" (Amos 3:8). In other words, when a lion roars, it is easy to be afraid, and when God is speaking, it is easy for us to prophesy. In some services God is speaking, and the prophetic spirit is so strong that we find it difficult to refrain from prophesying. Even so, we must be sensitive to the time when it is no longer appropriate to continue with another prophetic utterance. After such a point, an additional prophecy can be anticlimactic. The question we must ask of "run-on prophetic sessions" is "Are we really hearing anything of what God is trying to say to us?" Maybe we have so many prophecies because God is hoping that we might, perchance, truly hear just one of them. That syndrome is called "spiritual deafness."

Familiarity breeds contempt, and if we have too many

prophecies in a service it is easy to find ourselves despising them because they are too numerous. Perhaps this is why Paul seemed to confine prophetic utterances to two or three *(see* 1 Corinthians 14:27-29).

13.   If the prophecy fails to reach a peak, or our minds go blank, it's time to stop. Embarrassing situations can be healthy, if we will learn from them.

14.   We should learn to be creative. Hebrews 1:1 says God spoke to the prophets "at many times and in various ways." Let us not limit how the Holy Spirit would speak through us to his people!

15.   We must also distinguish between a true statement and a prophetic message. To say, "I love you, my children," is a true statement, but it may not carry the prophetic burden of the Lord for that occasion.

16.   We should use our own terminology when prophesying. "Thee"'s and "thou"'s are not necessary and can even give a prophecy an air of unreality.

17.   When visiting another church, we should always be more reticent to speak forth prophetically. Correction and instruction of the prophetic ministry flow out of relationship, and so the Lord will rarely give us a message for those with whom we have no acquaintance or relationship.

18.   If we question the relevancy or accuracy of our message, we should share it with those in leadership before speaking it forth.

19.   It is in order for us to seek out confirmation of our ministry. A prophetic ministry that does not submit to confirmation or correction will inevitably become imbalanced. We should not wait for someone to approach us with a word of correction. After bringing forth a prophetic utterance, we can seek out someone on the pastoral staff or in the eldership and request an evaluation.

20.   We can also practice prophesying. We can cultivate it, becoming more confident, with clearer messages. A good way to practice is to sing spiritual songs to the Lord while worshiping alone. Those trying out their "prophetic

wings" should learn and practice in small group contexts and let the more experienced minister in large congregational meetings.

21.   When we are waiting upon the prophetic spirit, it is good to pray in tongues. As we become yielded and sensitive to the Holy Spirit, we will become ready to receive God's word. Ralph Mahoney has said that when we pray in tongues we pray God's prayers, feel God's feelings, and think God's thoughts.

22.   We must keep a clear conscience. We will then have confidence to move out into ministry. Proverbs 28:1 says, "The righteous are as bold as a lion." If our conscience condemns us, our boldness to minister is eroded. We must guard the confidence that comes with a clear conscience.

23.   If we want to be used prophetically by the Lord, we must do more than just "be open to it." We must exert our wills, take a step of faith, and allow the Lord to honor that.

GUIDELINES — THINGS TO AVOID

Now that we have seen what to do, let us consider a few "don'ts."

1.   We must avoid bringing a rebuke or a harsh word. Such utterances are extremely rare and are to be reserved for those who have the proven ministry of a prophet. A prophetic word will *never* condemn. One who comes forth with a rebuke is likely to receive a rebuke. If we watch carefully, we will notice that God usually speaks softly to his people. That is because he loves us, cares for us, and shepherds us. "Let me hear the words of the LORD: are they not words of peace, peace to his people and his loyal servants and to all who turn and trust in him?" (Psalm 85:8, NEB).

2.   We must not be satisfied with platitudes. Too often we hear prophetic messages that say something like this: "I love you, my people; draw near to me. Oh, how I love you, my people. I love you so much I sent my Son to die for you. Respond to my love. . . ." There is nothing wrong with that

kind of message, because God truly does love us. But what does the message really say that we do not already know? The message is so full of cliches that it carries no punch. We may give this type of message when we are first testing our "prophetic wings," but we need to mature that ministry. We should endeavor to contribute something significant, so that when people hear us lift our voices in prophecy, they will recognize that something important is about to come forth.

3. We must avoid the temptation to embellish a prophetic message in order to impress the congregation with our oratory skills. It is tempting to want to repeat a message at a higher pitch (or volume) if we feel the message is not getting an appropriate reception.

4. We must not despise prophecies because they seem immature or full of mistakes. We are admonished, "Do not treat prophecies with contempt" (1 Thessalonians 5:20). In another place Paul reminded us that "we know in part and we prophesy in part" (1 Corinthians 13:9). Our understanding is limited, and we prophesy only as well as we can. Some prophecies may have weaknesses in them, but the message should be received without contempt. In other prophecies, only part of the message is brought forth, and it is necessary for someone else to shed further light on what God is wanting to say. Thus as we congregate and various ones share their part of what God would say, the pieces of the puzzle come together and a picture begins to emerge. If one person holds back from bringing his or her "part," a portion of the whole will be missing.

5. Neither should we treat prophecies with inattentiveness. If we soon forget the word of God delivered prophetically, that is just another way of treating prophecies with contempt. We might need to write down some thoughts in order to remember what was said. At other times, we might even find it appropriate to transcribe the prophecy from a cassette recording of the service (if one was made), as a permanent record.

6. We must not feel compelled to sing a prophetic word every time. Many churches are thrilled when they discover the added dimension of singing their prophecies, and the human temptation is then to try to sing every prophetic word that God speaks. Some prophecies are not intended by God to be sung. In fact, the impact of some prophecies can be lost if someone tries to sing them. We should be free either to speak or sing a prophecy as the instance dictates.

7. In a very general sense, there are two types of wrong prophecy: wrong ideas, and wrong timing. We struggle more in the second area, it seems. Spiritual sensitivity is required to deliver a message at the proper time. A prophetic utterance may be genuine, but if through insensitivity it is given at the wrong time, it is rendered inappropriate.

8. We must never fear failure. Those who aim for nothing will achieve nothing. We are not a failure if we try.

9. "If I have the gift of prophecy and can fathom all mysteries and all knowledge, and if I have a faith that can move mountains, but have not love, I am nothing" (1 Corinthians 13:2). Prophetic utterances not based on love are useless. We must never attempt to address a situation prophetically because we are annoyed about something. Worship is the language of love, and worship enables us to prophesy in love.

At all times let us remember that these guidelines are just that — guidelines. We must be careful not to confine God to any one of these guidelines; otherwise, we might miss him because of our preconceived ideas of what is proper. Let's remind ourselves to be sensitive to the Holy Spirit and to be prepared for some surprises!

Most of what we have covered thus far has been in the devotional realm, with only a few suggestions here and there as to practical implementation of the concepts under consideration. This is our foundation. From here, let's build upon what we have already established, and move from the "what" and "why" to the "how" as we take an in-depth look at the practical outworkings of praise and worship in action.

CHAPTER 8

THE ART
OF LEADING WORSHIP

This chapter speaks of the "art" of leading worship because it is a learned ability. Worship leaders do not spring up overnight. Just as a preacher improves in his skills of communication, and a teacher learns through experience to grow in effectiveness, so too can a worship leader expect to improve with time and practice. In this section we will explore many of the dynamics of leading worship. Suggestions and ideas will be presented which are intended to help worship leaders in the practical implementation of praise and worship.

THE NEED FOR A WORSHIP LEADER

Every situation may not call for a worship leader. In some gatherings, such as home prayer meetings, the group can feasibly have a short time of praise and worship without having an appointed worship leader. If a group is able to function without a worship leader, though, it is because of the small number of participants. Any large gathering must almost always have a designated leader, and even in small group contexts it is usually desirable to have one person responsible for directing the singing. A leader will bring focus and direction to the time of praise, whereas meetings that are completely "open" for all to initiate a song can meander without any apparent purpose or can even become disorderly.

Congregational singing demands that a worship leader be appointed. Sheep need to follow; without a leader they wander aimlessly. Proper leadership is essential for main-

153

taining unity within a group. Without leadership, congregational singing will be haphazard and will never crescendo to a zenith. When a worship leader plans a worship service, all the songs will flow together according to the thoughts of that one leader. If many people lead out in songs, with each song initiated from a different mind-set and perspective, the service will continually be shifting in emphasis and direction. By following the direction of one leader, the service is focused, and there is strength in the consequent unity within the congregation.

A worship leader also unites the musicians and congregation rhythmically. A steady and consistent rhythm is essential for a smooth flow in worship, so there must be one person who is authorized to determine and maintain the rhythm for the songs. Sometimes that can be the pianist or the drummer, but usually it is the worship leader. Also, since some songs have tempo changes from the verse to the chorus, an appointed leader establishes the new tempo. He will also indicate holds wherever they might occur. Since there are many things for which he is responsible, his position is strategic to the flow of worship in a church.

QUALIFICATIONS OF A WORSHIP LEADER

The standards and expectations for worship leaders will naturally vary from church to church. In some churches, being on the pastoral staff means being asked to lead worship. In other churches, if one is an elder or a member of the church board, one has fulfilled the sole requirement for this function. But if the effectiveness of the worship leader is indeed vital to the success of the service, then fuller consideration must be given to the qualifications that a worship leader should bring to the position. The following nine qualifications are, I believe, among the raw essentials for any worship leader.

The leader *must* be a worshiper. This requirement comes first before all others. One who is not a worshiper has no business pretending to lead others in worship. In one church I attended, the pastor wanted to make a certain newcomer feel welcome and be a part of the fellowship, so he asked the brother to lead worship on a Sunday night. Such a policy totally contradicts this first premise. I suppose the leading of worship was thought to be a good way to make someone feel involved, and no care was given to whether or not that person met the very first criterion, namely, that of being a worshiper. Others are made worship leaders because they have a nice voice or a good ear for music, or because they like to sing or even to worship. But there is a difference between liking to worship and being a worshiper. A worshiper is someone who has learned the daily discipline of submitting to the total Lordship of Christ regardless of personal emotions or circumstances of life. A worship leader must display this quality of heart and life.

The second requirement, which goes hand in hand with the first, is a deep and a proven spiritual walk. We do not need spiritual novices leading our worship services.

A leader must be familiar with the style of praise and worship of his or her particular church. Each church has its own unique style and flavor in which the worship leader must be able to flow. A leader coming to a new church should be given time and opportunity to become familiar with the church's worship style and repertoire of songs before endeavoring to lead the congregation in worship.

Next, the leader must be musically inclined to an acceptable level. Each church must determine for itself what that acceptable level is to be, and then the candidate must meet that specification. It is unlikely that someone who cannot carry a tune at all will be put into the position of worship leader. That person would probably be far more effective in another avenue of ministry.

It goes without saying that a leader must have a good reputation in the fellowship. If someone is not respected among the parishioners for his daily walk with God and his family life, he will not instantly gain the respect of the people simply by stepping behind the pulpit.

The leader must be able to function as part of a team. Some folks are so highly individualistic that they are unable to get along with others. But any worship leader must be flexible to flow with the pastor and others on the worship team.

The leader must have a proper attitude toward the church, the pastor, and church doctrine. If he has hidden resentment toward the pastor or major doctrinal differences with the church, he may not be able to stick it out for too long in that church, and it could be hurtful to have someone in a visible post like worship leader leaving under negative circumstances.

Also, the leader must be willing to commit himself to this position, sacrificing the prerogative to visit other churches or attend special events elsewhere. Some mighty evangelist might be in town conducting a crusade, but the leader should be found leading worship at his own church. Like the pastor, he must be there for every service in which he is participating, barring illness or emergency.

Finally, it is desirable for the worship leader to have an enthusiastic, friendly, warm personality. If he is not enthusiastic in his leadership, it is unlikely that the people will respond with any degree of enthusiasm. If he is not a friendly person who relates well socially to the people, he is not likely to be received well behind the pulpit. The saints will have difficulty giving their allegiance to a social introvert.

This listing of qualifications is not intended to discourage all candidates from becoming worship leaders! We must decide, though, to give serious thought to the designation of worship leaders. Most churches will want to include these nine areas as minimal requirements for worship leaders. Those who desire to become worship leaders should be challenged with the excitement of attaining these qualifications.

A distinction should be made, however, between the qualifications a worship leader must meet before taking on the position and the abilities that must be learned through time and experience. If our demands on worship leaders become too stringent, no one will be able to qualify. Most worship-leading abilities are learned through experience only, and thus they can be unreasonable qualifications for the novice. If they are willing and have the potential, worship leaders will quickly grow and develop in their effectiveness of ministry. Experience is the necessary ingredient.

The challenge continually comes to the worship leader to be the person God has called him or her to become. Leaders must continually apply themselves to living up to that calling. It is mandatory that they live a consistent lifestyle both behind and away from the pulpit — that they "walk worthy" of their calling and ministry. The leader must not be one thing behind the pulpit and another thing the rest of the time. Some people assume a "pulpit personality," an artificial and pseudo-spiritual front, in an attempt to impress people with their stage presence and flowery style. Such false fronts will not endear them to the people. The people may love that leader but will not love the "person" the leader becomes on Sundays. Any congregation will respond most gratefully to the "real thing." When one accepts a ministry, such as leading worship, there comes with that a tremendous impetus to make one's life consistent with that calling. Rather than allowing a lack of spirituality to discourage him or her from participating, the leader should allow the responsibility of leading worship to challenge and motivate his or her spiritual walk with God. Those who place themselves before the people as an example of a worshiper become much more motivated to be consistent worshipers throughout the week.

Though the "inward man" is definitely the most important element for a worship leader to consider, this does not mean that the outward man should be neglected, for it is a fact of life that man looks on the outward appearance. Worship leaders are in a very visible position, and one thing that invariably comes under scrutiny is the way they dress. The worship leader's general style of dress can either be a distraction to the people or can tastefully contribute to a low profile. The leader can have the people worshiping with him, snickering at him, or envying his wardrobe — depending upon the propriety of his clothes. It is in order to dress nicely, modestly, and appropriately and to wear well-fitting clothes, with colors and designs that match. (By the way, this is not the equivalent of spending a great deal of money or coming out in the newest trends. An impressive wardrobe is not a requisite for a worship leader!) Although one need not wear the latest in fashion, one should avoid clothes that are obviously outdated or "old-fashioned." With careful choices, one can dress tastefully and attractively on even the most modest budget.

THE LEADER'S MUSICAL EXPERTISE

The more we understand about music, the better able we are to coordinate the spiritual and musical aspects of worship. We may feel a tremendous personal anointing, but we will not get far if the orchestra is fuming in the corner, upset by our musical shenanigans and insensitivity. There are some definite things we can do to improve musically in both ability and quality.

First, we can develop our singing ability. Taking voice lessons, if at all possible, will increase our vocal projection and control. We should practice an attractive singing voice (yes, that can be developed) and strive for a lively and interesting voice quality. We can also learn to develop a pleasant vibrato, which can do much to enhance one's vocal sonority. Sight-reading ability is another valuable and learnable skill. A worship leader should be able to sight-read a melody line in order to lead the melody of new songs confidently and correctly.

The leader should always carry the melody unless there is someone else on the team to carry the melody while the leader harmonizes. Usually people will try to follow what the leader is singing. If we are harmonizing at the microphone and visitors are trying to learn the tune of the song, they could become frustrated with trying to determine which note to sing. The leader should not make a habit of "soloizing" over the microphone. Some worship leaders sound like they are singing a solo, for they deviate from the correct melody onto little harmonies of their own, thus making it difficult for people to know exactly which notes to be singing themselves. By singing the melody accurately and properly, the worship leader will help newcomers learn the songs correctly.

Sometimes a song will get started in the wrong key. Either the people are growling way down in their vocal range, or they are all straining to sing way up there somewhere. We should not feel the need to sing the entire song like that, especially when everyone knows it is way off. We should simply stop, turn to the organist or pianist, and say, "I think we are in the wrong key. Can you give us a better key, please?" And away we go.

A leader can also grow and develop in conducting abilities. Definite hand movements are an invaluable aid. It is very difficult to communicate our rhythmic intentions to someone else by our hand movements. Therefore, those hand movements must be purposeful, distinctly showing the moment of downbeat, and with a gracefulness that appears natural — no peculiar gestures or mannerisms. One way to improve the quality of hand motions is to practice before a mirror. Also, a frank and honest rapport between leader and musicians will help. Can they read our hand movements? Are our hand movements clear enough for them to follow? If we continue to have difficulty with the rhythmic stability of the music, we need to rehearse with the musicians until they are able to follow our conducting technique. It's surprising how many musical difficulties can be solved in rehearsals.

We need to be aware of how large our songleading arm movements are. If they are too large, we draw undue attention to ourselves; if they are too small, we will not properly communicate to the musicians and the people. Three factors determine the size of our hand and arm movements: the size of the audience — a larger congregation will require larger hand motions so the people in the back can see our movements; the mood of the song — if the song is quiet and smooth, large and overt motions would be out of character with the song; and the type of service being conducted — some services, because of their nature (for example, a funeral service) may not require any hand motions at all, or very small motions only.

Rhythmic stability is a must! It is amazing how quickly a wrong rhythm can destroy the effectiveness of a given song. Some songs have long gaps between lines — for example, "I love you, Lord, and I lift my voice . . . to worship you; Oh my soul, rejoice." It is very tempting to want to lead out prematurely in the next line. This could be called "anticipating the next phrase." Some worship leaders have developed a style of anticipating the next phrase frequently, as though it were necessary for them to sing the next phrase moments before the congregation does, just so the people will know who is out in front. That style will keep the people bound to watching the leader every moment, and they will never find the release that comes when all things (including the worship leader) are shut out and their attention is fully on the Lord. By maintaining rhythmic stability, we are telling our people, "I will hold every line out for its full rhythmic value. I will not anticipate the next phrase. Therefore, you do not have to worry about following my every vocal inflection. Worship God!"

It is also crucial that one learn how to initiate a correct rhythm from a full stop. When a song is first started, it can be challenging to start it off at precisely the right tempo. I remember how I learned that art. When I was growing up, I played the piano in church while my mother played the organ. When a hymn was announced, I would proceed to play an introduction at a tempo I thought was appropriate.

Then when it was time for the congregation to begin singing, my mother would press the organ pedal to the floor
and come in with a totally different tempo and rhythm,
literally drowning out my playing with her new tempo.
Naturally the worship leader would follow the tempo my
mother was setting. At first I was a bit offended and
wondered why she would "do that to me!" But then I
decided to analyze those situations and learn from them.
Why was my tempo inappropriate? What was different
about my mother's tempo? (She is a very accomplished
musician, and her tempo would invariably be the better
one!) By listening and watching, I began to learn sensitivity in initiating a tempo, in starting songs at just the right
pace.

If the tempo is just a little too slow, the people will feel
a heaviness in the singing and a lack of gusto. They will
not realize that the problem is simply a musical one — a
too-slow tempo; they will interpret the heaviness as a
spiritual "oppression" in the meeting. The discerning worship leader will correct that by speeding up the tempo.
Conversely, if the tempo is too fast, people will feel as if
they are on a locomotive that is gaining speed on a
downhill incline. They will not be able to get the words
out quite fast enough, which will make them feel as if
there is a vacuum cleaner attached to their mouths. When
people are stumbling over the words, we should slow the
song down enough so it can be sung without difficulty.

It takes practice to learn how to speed up or slow down
a tempo once the wrong tempo has already been initiated.
If we have a good drummer, the change can be made by
signaling the new tempo to the drummer and having him
pound out the new tempo on the drums. Making our hand
movements smaller and quicker will speed things up.
Another good way to increase speed is to clap out the
faster tempo. Not only does this provide a visual indication
of the new tempo, but it also gives an aural indication of
the new rhythm desired. If we are singing a fast praise

song and wish to speed up the tempo a bit, this is an ideal time to clap out the new tempo. If, on the other hand, we want to slow down the speed, then we can make our hand movements larger and wider.

If none of these techniques seems to work, then there is nothing wrong with just stopping the song and announcing, "Let's start over again, and this time speed it up (or slow it down) a bit." It's not appropriate to turn to the pianist and say, "What's wrong this morning? This sounds like a funeral dirge!" There is no need to try to place the "blame" for the wrong tempo on the piano player or anyone else. All the worship leader needs to do is simply ask for a change of tempo.

"Dancing songs" should be fast enough for dancing. Have you ever seen people try to dance to a song that was being sung too slowly? Either they forget about it and dance totally out of pace with the music, or, in an endeavor to dance with the music, they will jump higher and higher, trying to buy more time between steps. If the people are trying to dance but are struggling because the tempo is slow, it's easy to stop and say, "I see that some are wanting to dance, so let's speed it up this time. . . ."

But be careful when introducing a sudden change of tempo in the music. There are times when it is appropriate to "change gears" quickly, moving from fast to slow or slow to fast songs. But traverse those times of transition with much care. A sudden change in tempo at the wrong time can be counterproductive to the rest of the worship service. Most services have only one tempo change, usually occurring at the time when we change from "fast" songs to "slow" songs.

A leader must lead both with hands and voice. Some worship leaders seem to be afraid to move their hands to the rhythm. Perhaps they feel conspicuous or self-conscious when they do so. If we struggle with that inhibition, let's conquer it! We will be the most effective when we are free to project our voices loudly and wave our arms to the tempo without awkwardness.

These are the three most common hand movements used by choral conductors:

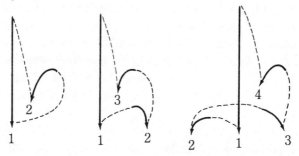

I would recommend the first hand movement above for most worship leaders. With most songs it is usually possible to conduct a clear and communicable rhythm with a simple up-down motion. There is no need to be concerned about the theoretical propriety of technique as long as we are effective in communicating our intentions to the musicians and congregation.

MUSICAL EXCELLENCE IN WORSHIP

Some folks are talking loudly these days about "excellence" in church music, and the propagators of such talk are usually so far ahead of the average worship leader that their voice is not heard. Those who crusade for "excellence" in church music, claiming we have a "stewardship mandate" to excel, in my opinion forsake the true intent of Scripture.

Obviously we want our church music to be of the highest quality our own people can produce, but for what reason? Because we have a divine mandate to do so? Truthfully, I think not. We want our church music to be the best possible not for God's sake but for human reasons.

Someone has likened our giving to God the most excellent music we can produce to the little boy who brings home a drawing from second grade. His mother tells him how wonderful it is, and after gazing proudly at his childish scribble, she posts the work on the refrigerator door to be frequently admired. Even the very best we can offer God is no more than just a "scribble" to him. Therefore, whether our music is at its best or worst is quite irrelevant from God's perspective. But to us it makes a tremendous amount of difference!

We should reach for excellence in our church music because of what it does for us. It is difficult to worship when the music is shoddy. Those who are musically inclined find this especially true. On occasion I have really struggled with this problem, because when I am in a service in which the wrong chords are being played, or the rhythm is disjointed, or the orchestra sounds like a cat fight, I simply cannot worship. I am so disturbed by the poor music that I am not able to release my heart in worship.

The better musically equipped we are, the better is our potential for increased expression in worship. To illustrate this, suppose we took our car to a mechanic who owned a pair of pliers, a hammer, and a screwdriver. How many things would he be able to service effectively on that car? Not very many! Similarly, the greater our musical expertise is, the greater will be our ability to service the needs of the congregation in worship. If we have a pianist who can play only in the key of C, then we will be very limited in what we are capable of doing in worship. Once a pianist learns to play in a variety of keys, it is like a mechanic adding an electronic tuning device to his tool bench. That pianist is better equipped to service a wider variety of needs. Therefore, we must encourage our musicians to study music further and practice their instruments more. Most areas provide access to a nearby community college or similar educational facility where music lessons can be obtained economically. Also, if they are not already able to do so, musicians need to learn to play improvisationally ("by ear"), as this ability greatly enhances congregational worship.* The musical quality of

*My brother, Sheldon Sorge, has written a text called *Piano Improvisation for the Church Pianist*. In it he outlines basic steps toward worship accompaniment and piano improvisation. He has also produced a cassette tape to be played in conjunction with reading the book, so that piano exercises are not only described in writing but are also demonstrated on cassette. The book and tape may be purchased directly from him by writing to Sheldon Sorge, 1015 Green Street, Durham, NC 27701.

tomorrow's worship is being bred in the lives of our young people today, and we must prod them on to musical expertise and achievement.

Furthermore, our standards of "excellence" in music are usually reflective of our standards in many other areas as well. If we are sloppy in our music department, we are probably also sloppy in our Sunday School department. That careless approach is reflected in all areas of church life. It we want to be an evangelistic community, we need to impress our visitors with the quality of life and ministry we display. Their first impressions when they visit our church will quickly determine how much of a rapport they feel with the congregation. Quality music has always been recognized as beneficial when there is a desire to attract visitors and newcomers.

THE LEADER'S PREPARATION

Preparation of a worship leader is both long-term and short-term; that is, there are some elements which are ongoing, and some which take place for each service. Preparation is more than making up a list of songs to sing. In the first place, we must be prepared spiritually. This begins by maintaining a regular prayer life, seeking sensitivity to the Holy Spirit. In our times of prayer, we can communicate to God our earnest desire to become more sensitive to his Spirit. We can pray in the Spirit and by faith receive a greater sensitivity and anointing upon our life and ministry as we spend time ministering to God in prayer and worship. Our ministry to God must come first before our ministry to men. When Godward ministry is our first priority, it will urge us manward.

Not only must we maintain a close relationship with the Lord throughout the week, but we must be certain that we are spiritually primed as we approach the worship service itself. We need to set aside a time on Saturday night or early Sunday morning to spend in personal praise and worship.

When we come into the sanctuary, we should be ready to go! If the praise service becomes a time for us as worship leaders to "break through," we will not be able to devote all our attention to leading the service; part of our energy will be taken in trying to get in tune with God ourselves. That ought to be the last of our concerns, and we can ensure that it is by preparing ourselves spiritually before we ever get to church.

We should be vocally primed as well when we come to the worship service. If we still have a "frog in our throat," a few moments of vocal exercises will get our vocal cords warmed up.

We should also consult in advance with the pastor or the person in charge of the service to determine the theme of the service or the thrust of the sermon. Not only will this help us, but it will also communicate our willingness to work together with the ministry team.

Some pianists and church musicians need some advance time to rehearse the songs that will be sung. If we rely heavily on a pianist who needs advance warning, we should do that person the honor of providing for his or her needs. Perhaps it will stretch our faith to ask God what songs should be sung one or two weeks from now, but he already knows and can impart that to us.

As a final point in preparation for worship, we need to avoid "hurrying" before the service. If we arrive on the platform thirty seconds before the service begins, panting, chest heaving because we had to run through the rear entrance, the worship service already has one stroke against it — namely, us! Satan will try to detain us or distract us with some irrelevant problem that will irritate our emotions. But most things can wait until later. It is extremely important at this point to be calm and in tune with the Holy Spirit. It is amazing to see what can happen to make us late for a worship service when we are the worship leader — anything from last-minute phone calls to one of the children slamming his finger in the car door. If we barely get there in time, our spirit will be in knots and our emotions will be churning. But if we get there early enough to spend some quiet time before the Lord, we will be ready to move with the gentle promptings of the Spirit.

GENERAL GUIDELINES

It is also good for every worship leader to remember some general guidelines for conducting himself or herself in that leadership position. We will benefit both ourselves and our people by keeping a few key things in mind.

Be prompt. By being on time and dependable, we are proving ourselves to be a strong asset to the pastor and the church leadership. As we have just said, we are not on time if we show up one minute before the service begins. When we are late or rushed, that communicates our level of commitment and the degree of seriousness with which we view our role as worship leader.

Be natural. We should be ourselves, without imitating another worship leader whom we respect or trying to copy the style of the pastor. Though we can observe these individuals and learn from them, we should never try to "be" them. We will be the most fulfilled, and the most effective, when we discover exactly who we are in God and are satisfied to be that before the people.

In the service, we need to stay with a theme until it is finished. When the Lord is obviously speaking to his people in a specific area (such as repentance, cleansing, rejoicing, or whatever), do not hurry on with the rest of the service until God has completed the work he wants to do. *Nothing* on the agenda of the service should be more important than meeting with God and hearing from him. Some services have been occasions for what I would term "spiritual abortions": the worship service was called to a halt before God was able to complete what he was trying to birth in the hearts of his people. If we are serious about wanting to hear all that God is saying to us, we must be willing to set aside the necessary time and let him determine what happens.

Avoid "flooding" by singing too many songs. Just as a plant can be harmed by too much water, so a worship service can be negatively affected by too many songs. We need to be sensitive to the point at which "enough is enough." Neither should we interrupt "high worship" with another song. When a congregation is experiencing high worship, they are standing before the throne of God and are fulfilling their divine calling. There is no higher end to achieve — this is truly a sacred moment, and nothing should distract or interrupt. Further songs, when used wisely, can serve to "feed" that high worship, but at the wrong time they can actually be an interruption and a detriment. Similarly, we should not seat the people in the middle of enthusiastic praise or worship. Seating the people at the height of worship is like dumping water on a fire. Standing is a most natural posture conducive to high worship.

Be "instant in season" with a chorus or hymn to fit into every situation. Worship leaders are always "on call," and pastors will take advantage of that privilege at the most unexpected times! Whatever may be transpiring, whether it is an altar call or a time of prayer, the leader should have a song ready that could fit into the situation at hand. One of my uncles who is a pastor has told me that the thing he appreciates most about a worship leader is the flexibility to have a song for the occasion at a moment's notice.

It should not take long to learn to choose appropriate songs if one is sensitive to two things: the subject matter or theme of the songs at hand, and the general mood of those songs. The theme is learned by studying the words; the mood is determined by looking at the tempo of the song and the rhythmic strength (whether smooth and fluid or militant and forceful). By carefully analyzing the theme and mood of each song, the leader can string the songs together in smooth succession.

If there are people in the congregation who are obviously unfamiliar with our style of praise and worship, the Spirit may direct us on infrequent occasions to give a short scriptural explanation to the visitors. This should not be necessary in most services and should be done only upon a special urging from the Spirit. But we should be aware that the need for some explaining does occasionally arise. Some churches have sidestepped this potential problem by preparing a short pamphlet of introduction to the church, including explanations for their forms of worship. Having a written statement in your visitor's packet is probably the smoothest way to bridge this problem.

Regarding lady worship leaders, I recommend that women try not to be too strong or overbearing, but that they remain feminine at all times. If they are gentle and sweet and natural, their leadership will be honored and appreciated.

THE WORSHIP LEADER-MUSICIAN

Many worship leaders, being musicians, play an instrument while leading worship. The most common instruments used in this way are the piano and guitar. Functioning as both a worship leader and a keyboard player or guitarist is not easy, but it does have some distinct advantages.

The leader does not need to stop and announce the next song to be sung. Since he is accompanying himself, he can change keys at will or move into a different song and thus can be very flexible in changing direction.

Second, he does not have a wide expanse between himself and the pianist or main musician. It can be difficult for a leader to communicate clearly his intentions to a musician sitting some distance away, who obviously cannot read his mind. That barrier is dissolved when the worship leader can initiate his own intentions on the instrument.

Furthermore, at times it is very pleasant to have a musical interlude in worship, when the congregation is quiet and a musician plays a worshipful tune unto the Lord.

It is difficult for the worship leader to produce that sort of spontaneous expression from a musician by commanding, "Play something prophetic!" But when the leader is an instrumentalist, he is free to initiate that type of expression himself and is not totally dependent upon others for it.

Finally, I have found that when I lead worship from the piano, people are not distracted by watching me and are able to focus on the Lord more easily. Someone standing behind a pulpit is more likely to be distracting to the worshipers, because most congregations are trained to keep a careful eye on whoever is standing at the pulpit. From the piano, I am able to provide strong leadership without being a visual obstacle.

To play and sing simultaneously is a difficult art to master and becomes even more of a feat when combined with leading the congregation in worship. Someone doing this must not only know how to play and sing at the same time but must also be in tune to the Spirit of God, discerning his guidance for the service. For a good, experienced musician, playing worship songs becomes almost second nature, and so he (or she) is free to apply mental concentration to other areas. All of this probably sounds more difficult than juggling five bowling pins, so would-be worship leader-musicians should be patient with themselves while they are learning to master these techniques, and realize that it takes time and practice.

LEADING, NOT CONTROLLING

The worship leader is a prompter, not a cheerleader at a pep rally. Being a "leader" of worship does not mean being a "conductor" or "controller" of worship. When worship leaders try to manipulate people into a certain response or expression, they are moving into this forbidden area of conducting or controlling worship. A leader does not elicit a response through manipulative means; he or she inspires a response by way of example. He leads by encouraging and inspiring the people to enter into praise, but the people have the prerogative of either responding or observing. We must never attempt to coerce the people, even if the desired goal is a noble one. Good worship leaders do not learn manipulation, but they do learn exhortation. They do not try to control, but they do seek to inspire.

Some churches learn to praise in direct proportion to the level of excitement exuded by the worship leader. If the worship leader is low-key, so is their praise. The more the worship leader shouts and dances and flails and froths, the more the people respond. This syndrome can cause worship leaders to believe that the success of the worship service is contingent upon their performance or level of excitement. Nonsense. The leader is there not to churn up the worship but rather to be used of God to positively inspire the people to open up to the Spirit and participate in worship themselves.

Many worship leaders maintain such strong control of the worship service that the congregation must remain very alert to keep up with the leader. Every move is directed from the pulpit, and the people respond almost reflexively. This type of worship leader is maintaining too high a personal profile and actually represents a distraction away from the Lord. Who needs to see Jesus when we have a one-man show to entertain us for a while? In order to be effective, a worship leader must be visible to all the people and yet must simultaneously assume a style that becomes invisible, in order that the people's attention might move from the horizontal plane to the vertical.

Many of our responsibilities as worship leaders are highly visible in and of themselves. We give visual direction to the congregation by moving our arms; we send signals and visual instructions to the musicians and worship team; we announce song names and numbers; we give exhortations, Scripture readings, and prophecies; we demonstrate praise and worship by lifting our hands, clapping, dancing, singing; and the list goes on. When all these activities are lumped together, it can become rather amusing to watch one person juggle them all at once. Because our position is so highly visible, the onus comes on us all the more to strive for a maximum degree of invisibility. The service still needs direction, so we must not relax our leadership, but we must remain as leader while maintaining the lowest profile possible.

The best way I know to become invisible is to radiate a joyful, worshipful countenance. As we lift our hands and face to the Lord with an expression of joyful expectancy, we cease being anything anyone would want to watch. Instead of looking at us, people are drawn to behold the object of our attention: the Lord.

We should avoid any quick or large movements that would draw attention to ourselves. When we are announcing songs to be sung, giving signals to the pianist, trying to get the drummer to tone down, trying to speed up the choir, directing the congregation with our arms, and singing loudly into the microphone, the obvious tendency is for everyone to be gazing with rapt attention at this one-man circus. I am not minimizing any of these activities, for we will inevitably find ourselves involved with signals and directions and microphones at various points. But it is so important *how* we handle these functions. The goal is to learn to fulfill all these necessary elements in such a way as to bring a minimal amount of attention to ourselves. A set of unobtrusive signals that are recognized by all on the worship team will be invaluable.

We can also become less visible by being no louder on the microphone than is necessary and being no more extroverted in hand motions than is necessary to provide leadership for the singing. If the people are singing the current song easily enough, we can back away from the microphone a bit so that our voice blends in with the entire congregation, and then sing strongly into the microphone when the next verse or chorus is to be introduced. Similarly, I recommend that hand motions be used sparingly. It is important to use hand motions at the right times, in order to set and reinforce the rhythm to the orchestra and congregation. But once the rhythm is set and the song is flowing along smoothly, it becomes superfluous to maintain hand motions. I operate under the guiding principle that when I am using hand motions, I am tacitly saying to my musicians, "Watch me carefully, because we have to get onto the right tempo." When I stop waving my arm, I am saying, "We're on track now, so just maintain this steady rhythm." If the pianist and drummer start to drift apart rhythmically, I will once again start motioning the rhythm with my arm, thus intimating, "Pay attention, boys. We have to get back on track."

The question has been asked if worship leaders should keep their eyes open, or closed. A combination of open and closed is necessary. I have seen worship leaders who kept their eyes closed throughout the entire service, and consequently they were completely out of tune with what was going on in the congregation. They seemed oblivious to whether or not the congregation was participating with them. On the other hand, some worship leaders are continually looking around to see how things are going in every nook and cranny. Such leaders display little personal interest in the Lord or in expressing their own hearts unto him. They become consumed with the "Martha syndrome" — serving at the expense of worshiping. An effective worship leader must look out over the congregation from time to time to see how the people are responding, but he must show that he is above all a worshiper himself. It is therefore quite appropriate for us to close our eyes at times, especially when wanting to gain new direction from the Lord. Closing our eyes helps us to focus exclusively on the Lord.

THE WORSHIP LEADER'S CHIEF DUTY

In a nutshell, the duty of the worship leader is *to provide the best opportunity possible for the people to worship.* If we have done our part in providing an excellent opportunity for the people to worship, it is then their choice to take advantage of that opportunity. It is not our responsibility or problem if they refuse to enter in. There must be a special anointing on our lives in order to create an atmosphere that is most conducive to worship, but once that opportunity to worship is there, it then becomes the people's prerogative to avail themselves of that opportunity. The unspoken thinking of the worship leader could thus be "I'm going to worship God. You are free to join me and the worship team as we enjoy God's presence, but whether or not you decide to join us, we're going to worship!" Some worship leaders get "paranoid" when the people do not join in. Never mind the people! If they decide not to worship, that is their business. Let them be, and join those who are willingly participating in offering up spiritual sacrifices to the Lord.

We must get something straight here. In the final analysis, we are not the worship leader. The Holy Spirit is the true Worship Leader — capital *W*, capital *L!* As a worship leader (small *w*, small *l)*, each of us is simply a vessel through whom he operates. He alone can inspire worship in the hearts of the people. Only he can truly lead worship! If the Holy Spirit is not birthing worship in the people's hearts, what makes us think we can? We must relinquish our control over the service and give the Holy Spirit the right to move or not move, according to his sovereign will.

The tendency of worship leaders to control worship is usually rooted in a very good and noble motivation: we are deeply desirous of leading God's people into fuller depths of praise and worship. The human tendency, though, is to try to implement our God-given vision with human energy. We frequently get impatient with the way the people are progressing in their expressions of worship, and we want them to plunge deeper into what God has for them, so we decide that God needs a little help. Since he obviously is not doing it quickly enough, we try to speed up the process a bit. And when we do that, we become guilty of striving in the flesh.

Every worship leader will doubtless find himself grappling with this propensity to strive in human energy. We can be challenged by the prophet's words " ' "Not by might, nor by power, but by my Spirit," says the LORD Almighty' " (Zechariah 4:6), and we can honestly desire to be led in the power of the Spirit, but we humans always seem to get a step or two ahead of God. We may think, "Oh, I'm forewarned! I won't fall for that one!" But we will find that the only way to cease striving is to first of all succumb to the temptation, have that illuminated to us by the Spirit, and then learn God's way to victory.

The Scriptures speak of striving in prayer *(see* Romans 15:30), and prayer is truly an exercise that requires work. But we should not strive in worship. Judson Cornwall has aptly pointed out that the priests in Moses' tabernacle wore linen garments in order to avoid sweating. Ministry before the Lord should be "no sweat." "Cease striving and know that I am God" (Psalm 46:10, NASB). And yet I will confess that sometimes after leading worship services, I have walked away with my shirt wet from perspiration. I was working so hard at leading the people that I left the platform physically drained and emotionally exhausted. Somehow this falls short of God's intention for the worship leader and for the service as well.

God may give us, as worship leaders, a vision for worship in our particular church, but then he expects us to work carefully with his Spirit in bringing that vision to pass. Worship in its essence is very simple and is not aided by any human energy. Worship is fueled by the Holy Spirit as he moves upon our hearts. We will become much more effective as worship leaders if we can learn to relax and discover how "easy" the yoke of Jesus truly is. When we attempt to plow in our own strength, we are quickly exhausted. But when we learn what it means to move in the flow of the Holy Spirit, he does the plowing, and we can rest. When we come to that point of rest, we liberate the Holy Spirit to move in great freedom according to his infinite wisdom and purpose.

Often we seek to broaden our concepts through worship seminars. They are thrilling and exciting, and I love them. But there is the danger of getting our attention on the outward expressions of worship that we see (dancers, banners, pageantry, processionals, etc.) and trying to reproduce them in our own local setting. We can become consumed with trying to start a dance troupe ministry, for instance, and thus set our affections upon the *mode* of worship rather than upon the *object* of worship. To lower one's eyes from God himself to an act of God (for instance, worship) is *idolatry*. To walk away from a worship seminar having one's affections consumed with the desire for certain physical forms of worship can be sinful! No mode of expression, be it dancing, shouting, banner-carrying, or whatever, will guarantee a greater release in worship or a higher level of worship. These various expressions can help, but there is nothing magical in their implementation. "If only we could get dance into our church — I know our worship would be so much better then!" This is an assumption based on a wrong concept. We must get our focus off outward manifestations and place our desires exclusively on God.

Our goal as worship leaders is not worship. If our goal is worship, we will fix our gaze on outward manifestations rather than on heart responses. Our only goal is God himself. We look only to Jesus Christ *(see* Hebrews 2:9; 3:1; 12:2). If he is our goal, we will most assuredly worship. There is the danger of "worshiping worship," of striving for an outward manifestation that somehow eclipses last week's experience. We seek a divine encounter with God; outward manifestations of worship are but a reflection of that encounter.

GETTING — AND LOSING — CONTROL

A good leader with a dynamic personality can arouse an elemental level of praise, but the praise will ascend no further as long as it is based on human personality. We need to be infected with the energy of God's personality! Does this mean, then, that the worship leader should do nothing to arouse praise in the people? Far from it. The worship leader's approach can be summarized with these words: *get control — then lose control.*

Get control — then lose control! (Please note that I am using "control" in the sense of "direction" or "being in charge" — *not* in the manipulative sense we have just discussed. There is a vast difference!)

It is essential for the worship leader to get control of the service at its inception. We should take control of the service in order to relax the people, to let them know that someone is in charge and that we are comfortable in that position of leading them. If we get up and say, "This is the first time I've ever led worship, and I'm scared stiff! Please pray for me, and I know God will help us through this," then we will have lost before we start. The people will empathize with us and feel sorry for us, but they will not worship. They will be continually peeking up at us to see "how the poor thing is doing." If they are to worship, they must be relaxed in knowing that the service has strong, confident leadership.

The leader must get control in order to get the service off to a good start, in a specific direction. We have spent time in prayerful preparation, and we should have confidence in how we think the service should start. If the service does not begin with strong direction, it will likely vacillate to its demise.

The leader should not be afraid to "take the bull by the horns" and attempt to arouse an elemental level of praise. People need to be encouraged and stimulated to praise, and this must be done with confidence and optimism.

The Holy Spirit commissions worship leaders to be instruments he can use to lead the people. While Jesus is the true and only Shepherd of the sheep, he has also commissioned pastors and leaders to shepherd the sheep. And while the Holy Spirit is the one and only true Worship Leader, he has called certain people to lead worship under his supervision and direction. God has purposed to use human leadership, so he does not act independently of human leaders. Therefore, if leadership is to be brought to the worship service, we must do it, worship leaders! We are not called to control, but we certainly are called to lead! We should not hesitate, look confused, appear uncertain, or feel threatened by our role as leader. Let's lead! Initiate! Lead the service with confidence and strength. We can remind ourselves that the Spirit of the Lord *is* upon us and he *has* anointed us *(see* Isaiah 61:1)! The people are eager for someone to lead because they want to follow.

Therefore, although the following paragraphs will talk about losing control, it is not because we are feeble, hesitant leaders of frail character. In actuality, we are confident leaders who purposefully determine to rescind our ability to manhandle the worship service.

With experience, novice leaders will learn to gain control of the service, and most worship leaders do learn in time how to take control effectively of the beginning part of the service. But only a few worship leaders have learned the secret of subsequently *losing control* — which is the secret to true worship.

Whereas praise can be stimulated by an enthusiastic leader, worship is a response of the human spirit to God's Spirit. No amount of stimulation from the worship leader will cause people to worship if their hearts are not right before God. God's Spirit will begin to move upon their hearts as we are willing to relinquish our control of the service and give the service to him. We must surrender our human control of the service in order for the Holy Spirit to move in freedom. If we insist upon holding a tight rein on the entire worship service, we can miss the sovereign move of the Spirit.

As long as we maintain our human leadership and control of the worship service, all we have is a man-directed service. When we surrender our control of the service to the Lord, then we will have a divinely directed worship service.

Notice that I did not say we will have a "Spirit-controlled" service. The Bible never talks about being Spirit-controlled — it speaks of being self-controlled. We are called of God to be "Spirit-led." If we are properly self-controlled, we can then purpose to be Spirit-led. A fruit of the Spirit is self-control, not Spirit-control. The Spirit enables us to keep self under control rather than permit it to control, and one of the characteristics of a self-controlled life is the ability to move in sensitivity to the gentle promptings of the Holy Spirit.

We do not "give the service over to the Spirit's control." He never attempts to control us. If the Spirit refuses to control the response of the saints, how dare we worship leaders do so? Worship leaders should initially take control of the service but not of the people. After the service is under way, however, we must relinquish our human control of the service and submit to the Spirit's leading.

Here are some ways to lose control:

1.   Back away from the microphone and get lost in God. Many worship leaders maintain control of the service by keeping the microphone one inch from their mouths. By backing away from the microphone and lifting our hands and faces to the Lord, we are tacitly saying, "I'm not going to manipulate or orchestrate what happens next. I want the Holy Spirit to take the service now." When the people "read" our posture, they will turn their attention onto the Lord, and he will take the leadership of the worship. When God takes it over, any number of things can happen. There might be a prophecy, or a spontaneous song, or a time of quiet, or whatever. It's exciting to see what God will do next when we let him!

2.   Refuse to sing another song of our human choosing. I remember an occasion on which this happened to me at Elim Bible Institute. As I was leading worship at the piano, I suddenly realized that we were in the "Elim rut" again, and the worship was not going anywhere. I sat back on the piano bench and said, "Lord, I'm not starting one more song. I'm not going to give a prophecy, an exhortation, any-

thing. It's yours, Lord. I'm not doing one more thing until I sense your Spirit in it." I have forgotten exactly what happened, but God did something — used someone to bring forth a prophecy or initiate the right song — but when I knew God had given us some direction, I was ready to sail with him! And away we went! We will usually have a song we could pull out of the bag when in a pinch, but wouldn't it be better if we refuse the human solution and wait for God's solution?

3. Go to our knees in prayer or worship. Worship leaders can do more than just stand behind the pulpit. By going to our knees, we are telling the people that we are no longer directing the service according to our preplanned list of songs but are waiting on God for his divine direction.

Morris Smith has correctly said that true worship cannot be conducted, since it is opus dei — an "act of God." Crowd control is a form of witchcraft and has no place in the approach of the worship leader. The tendency to control worship is rooted in the sad misconception that the worship leader knows where to take the people. If I think I know the end product, I will attempt to control the congregation until that end is achieved. But if I will accept the fact that I do not know all that God would do in worship, I then become reliant upon the Holy Spirit to accomplish what he alone knows and understands. Since worship is an act of God, it is as limitless in its potential as God himself. Who knows what worship holds for us? God alone knows! We must recognize that God is doing much more in the worship service than we usually ever realize through natural means. We must let God be God. We must give him the liberty to work in our worship "immeasurably more than all we ask or imagine" (Ephesians 3:20). That awareness may one day lead us to say something like this: "Let's take a little more time to enjoy the presence of God. I don't know what's happening, but I sense that God is doing a variety of things in many people's lives right now. Let's just bask in his presence a while longer, and allow him to complete that work in our hearts." Such an attitude reflects a proper understanding of our finiteness as human worship leaders.

THE ART OF EXHORTATION

We must never assume that simply because people are gathered together in one place, they are necessarily ready to worship. To all appearances they seem to be ready, but they must in fact be brought to a place of readiness. When the sheep are weary or discouraged or weighed down by sin and condemnation, it will take some time before they fully open their hearts to the Lord, and it is this time delay that works patience in the worship leader. The people do not need whipping — they have been battered by the world all week long! Rather, through loving understanding and prophetic anointing, the leader should bring them to a place of open surrender to the Holy Spirit.

It is when the people are insufficiently responsive that the worship leader learns the value of the art of exhortation. I refer to this as an "art" simply because exhortation, like preaching or teaching, is a learned ability. Some may feel it is inconsistent with their personalities to become an exhorter, but if God has called us to lead worship, he has also called us to fulfill all the dynamics of that role that are necessary in order to provide proper direction for God's people. Without the use of exhortation, our effectiveness as worship leaders will be greatly limited. There are times when an appropriate exhortation is the best way to encourage the people toward a certain response.

Exhortation is not coercion nor manipulation; it falls into the area of persuasion. Paul wrote, "Since, then, we know what it is to fear the Lord, we try to persuade men" (2 Corinthians 5:11), and he commanded Timothy, "These things teach and exhort" (1 Timothy 6:2, KJV).

When we give an exhortation, we should deliver it with firmness and confidence. "If anyone speaks, he should do it as one speaking the very words of God" (1 Peter 4:11). We should speak up so that we will be heard — not mumbling into the microphone or sounding as if we had just visited the dentist, but speaking forth resolutely so all can hear our words. How tempting it is, under the guise of "exhorting," to take out our frustrations on the people and whip them verbally with a "Thus saith the Lord!"

I guarantee that every worship leader will hit a time of being frustrated, angry, impatient, and "fed up" with the people and will fume at their lack of response, Sunday after Sunday, and their seeming oblivion to what the leader has been trying to impart to them over many months. But the leader must not show that frustration! Rather, the leader must radiate warmth and love and patience in all that is said and done. If we radiate warmth, the people will soften. Harshness will cause them to stiffen. If an exhortation is caustic, their response will tacitly say, "You're right, I'm not with it today, but now let's see if you can make me worship!" If we are sharp with our people, they will curl up into an emotional ball, and the service will be shipwrecked; but if we are compassionate and positive in our approach, we will help stimulate openness and responsiveness among the people.

Frequently I will plan an exhortation at the same time I am planning the songs to be sung. If I have a Scripture or nugget of truth already tucked in a corner of my mind, it is easily available to me during the service, and I can draw upon that Scripture or idea at any time in order to formulate a positive exhortation. I will not use the exhortation if the worship is reaching a crescendo, but if the service is waning, I will ask the Lord if it is time for me to share the exhortation I have prepared. I am usually more effective in the art of exhortation if I have something prepared, much like a preacher is more effective after preparation. I also maintain a listing of Scriptures that are especially useful when exhorting the people to increased praise or worship, and this list is a valuable resource when I need a springboard for an exhortation.

Exhortation, properly expressed, should actually function under a prophetic anointing. Many times a wisely expressed exhortation is ideal for correcting difficult situations in worship or giving direction to the worship. God's people do respond to exhortation. At times when they are not properly exercising their will to praise, a positive exhortation can help them become aware of their laziness and inspire them to renewed enthusiasm.

We must be careful, though, that we do not abuse our privilege of exhorting the people. Some worship leaders have become so "preachy" during the worship time that their pastors have forbidden them to do anything but lead in singing. Our exhortations should be kept short and to the point. We should not simply repeat the words of the song at hand but should contribute something unique that will augment what the current song is saying. This is a good place to employ an old technique: "Stand up — speak up — and shut up!"

DEALING WITH DIFFICULT TIMES IN WORSHIP

Most worship leaders are able to function well when everything is going fine. But what do we do when we encounter rough waters? How should we feel and act when nothing seems to get the worship service "off the ground," and the worship ends in what we perceive to be a failure? These times are never easy, but there are some principles that will help guide us through them, and they can contribute to our learning and development.

Worship leaders seems to be continually frustrated with those who are unresponsive in worship. People will refrain from openly worshiping with all their hearts for a variety of reasons, but one key reason is because of the natural tendency of people to be inhibited in a public gathering, unless it is socially acceptable to be enthusiastic (for example, at a sports event or a political rally). In our society, to be socially acceptable in a religious convocation, one should be very conservative and refined. Church is not thought of as a place to be enthusiastic and excited; "church" seems synonymous with "quiet and dignified."

Individuals will be even more inhibited if they do not know anyone in the church. Since many people have difficulty being open and communicative with someone as close to them as their spouse, we can expect them to be even more introverted in a public place of worship. If worship leaders do not understand these social ramifications in worship, they will become annoyed and frustrated at the people's unresponsiveness.

The challenge to the worship leaders, through the prophetic anointing of the Holy Spirit, is to help the congregation open their hearts to God's love. When we find that nothing works, our natural and immediate reaction is "What am I supposed to do??" This is the time when we must hear from God for that specific situation and not only discern what is holding back God's people but also know how to initiate a solution. It is one thing to know what the problem is; it is quite another thing to have the godly wisdom to deal with that problem. How reassuring it is to know that we can ask the Lord for a "word of knowledge" to reveal the problem and also a "word of wisdom" to know what to do about it. No amount of preparing song lists will equip us to minister effectively to these types of problems. But time spent in prayer will cultivate the sensitivity that is necessary to discern the Spirit's guidance during the worship service.

We must be sensitive to the point at which the intensity of the praise or worship begins to descend and the majority of the congregation begins to "tune us out." If this sense of decline comes too early in the service, it would be the equivalent of quitting to turn the service over to the pastor. This is the time to ask the Lord how he would have us bring correction and new vitality to the worship. We must not become intimidated by some "rough waters"; it is normal for many services to go through difficult times, and the

Lord will help us to "right the ship." Sometimes, however, when the service begins to ebb, it is an indication that we have tried to drag the worship service out too long. The solution in this event is not to prolong the service even further but to seat the people and quietly move on to another portion of the service.

When we are looking over the congregation to see how the people are participating, it can be unnerving if we see several folks who appear to be "out of it." We must not become disconcerted by the appearance of the people. I remember being part of a worship team in one service in which a certain gentleman scowled at us for the duration of the service. I was convinced he had barely tolerated the entire thing. Afterward, however, he was very warm in expressing his sincere appreciation to us. That taught me the important lesson that we cannot always "read" someone's receptivity by the expression on his or her countenance. Some people can thoroughly enjoy a worship service but look miserable throughout. If the expressions on the people's faces discourage us, let's stop looking at them! We can place our affection on the Lord, radiate his joy, and stop fretting about people's response or lack thereof.

Some churches encounter the problem of their worship style being offensive to visitors. Some people will always be "offended" by the genuine move of the Spirit, and that is similar to the offense of the cross to which Paul referred *(see* Galatians 5:11). If this is the nature of the "offense" our worship incurs, we can rejoice, for Jesus told us we would share his reproach. Genuine forms of praise and worship will not be repulsive to those whose hearts are pure before God. On the other hand, we can put others off by being overly boisterous and insensitive to culturally unacceptable forms of expression. Dance is an acceptable form of expression in our culture, but if it is executed by an obese person with no artistic form, then perhaps visitors have grounds to be "offended." Let us guard the impression we give visitors so that we might never be accused (legitimately) of behav-

ing indecently or improperly. If they stumble, may it be at
the offense of the cross and not because of carnal manifestations of emotionalism.

STANDING IN WORSHIP

We saw in chapter 1 that standing is a scriptural posture
to adopt in praise and worship. However, it can become a
problem in spite of its scriptural nature. In many
fellowships where standing is common, people complain of
getting tired, and they consequently do not enjoy the length
of the worship service. Many elderly folks simply do not
have the endurance of their youth. What should a worship
leader do when the people tend to get tired while standing
for protracted periods of time?

I do not believe the solution is to truncate the worship
time. We must learn to deal satisfactorily with this problem
without rushing the worship service. Some have tried to
solve this problem by directing the congregation to stand
and sit repeatedly throughout the worship. The leader will
cue the people with "Let's all rise and sing . . ." or "You
may be seated as we continue to sing. . . ." One pastor told
me that the people should not have to stand longer than ten
minutes at a time before the leader seats them. This particular approach of up-down-up-down has not seemed ideal
to me, because by continually directing the people to stand
or sit, we are telling them that they need not worry about initiating any responses of their own — we will engineer all
that for them. Many congregations have been conditioned
to act only upon the directives of the worship leader, and
consequently they remain introverts when it comes to expressing their own hearts unto God. Also, just about the
time we are approaching a crescendo in worship, the ten
minutes are up and it is time to seat the people again. When
we do that, we defuse what was building up, and the service
never seems to reach an apex.

The solution that has worked best for me is one I

adopted while I was director of music and chief worship leader at Elim Bible Institute. I decided that I was tired of "orchestrating" the worship — telling people when to stand, when to sit, when to lift their hands, and so on. So I determined that I would no longer tell people when to stand or sit. Instead, one Sunday morning I told the congregation that I was going to change permanently my approach to worship. I explained that I was no longer going to tell them when to stand or when to sit. Furthermore, I emphasized the importance of standing in worship and explained that nowhere in the Bible is sitting given as a proper posture in worship. I exhorted them to stand before the Lord, but to do so on their own initiative. I told them to stand when they chose because of their own spontaneous response to the Lord. They could stand when they wanted, worship a while, and if they got tired (as some older folks will) they could sit for a brief reprieve.

When we began to follow this plan, we found there were some who stood almost immediately when the service began, and many would follow. Some would wait until they felt moved upon by the Spirit, and then they would stand. There were others who would sit and pout throughout the entire service and do nothing. But, generally speaking, I found the new approach worked quite well.

Let me offer a word of caution to any who contemplate using this approach: you will have to be patient with your people, because some saints have been conditioned for so long to follow the every move of the worship leader that they will be totally uncomfortable at first with being free to use their own initiative. But stick with it, and you will be able to condition them positively in the opposite way so they will become responsive to the Holy Spirit rather than to the cues of the worship leader. It may take some time before the people begin to stand of their own initiative in praise unto the Lord, but they will soon realize that if they do not take any initiative, the entire worship service will pass them by and they will have missed out! You may find it necessary to reiterate your intentions and desires several times, because sometimes our "sheep" pretend not to understand. It will take them a while to comprehend the fact that you are serious about not "orchestrating" their praise. Be ready for some "rocky" worship services, but remember that things are always turbulent when we are jarred out of our ruts and that they will improve!

There are certain times, however, when a worship leader will sense that the people are unusually tired. Perhaps they have been coming every night to a series of meetings, and by Friday night everyone is exhausted. We can hope at such times that the Holy Spirit will infuse the people with divine energy. If nothing supernatural seems to happen in such contexts, the worship leader should be sensitive to the fact that sometimes "the spirit is willing but the flesh is weak" and should not expect the people to stand for a lengthy service under such circumstances. There are no easy answers in dealing with a tired congregation. Sometimes we can help the situation by leading a short but spirited time of praise and then progressing quickly to other aspects of the service. Not every service requires a lengthy worship time.

DEALING WITH "RUTS" IN WORSHIP

Of course, we would like to have all our worship services proceed without difficulties or hitches. Someone has said that "smooth services are often deepest spiritually." Frequently this is true, but certainly not always. When the Holy Spirit moves upon a congregation in a sovereign way and the praise and worship are vibrant, such services will be smooth and fluid because they are being "oiled" by the divine guidance of the Spirit. But not all services glide that smoothly and easily. Sometimes it feels as though the Holy Spirit is on vacation, and we are left behind to fend for ourselves. What do we do then?

Our handling of these situations will improve if we will

understand that sometimes God purposefully takes us through some "rocky" times in our worship services. He does not do it to antagonize us or to watch us dangle helplessly, but because he would lead us into newer and fuller dimensions in him. Occasionally God will deliberately engineer a "terrible" worship service. We may fast and pray all week, spend hours in preparation, and have the entire worship team at the church for an hour of pre-service prayer, but that day God has purposed that we have a "blah" worship service. He does it to keep us dependent upon him. It is all too easy for worship leaders to get overly confident in their expertise, and it is equally easy for the congregation to grow relaxed and contented with their current level of relationship with God in worship. Sometimes God stops us short and shows us that worship will not happen through the abilities or customs of people but comes "by my Spirit" (Zechariah 4:6). It is so easy to get into ruts in worship, and ruts are very smooth. If a worship service is flowing smoothly, it could mean that the Holy Spirit is doing a deep work, but it could also mean that we are cruising in our old rut one more time. If we will be open to it, God will help us get out of that rut. It will be a jarring, jolting experience, but afterward there will come a fresh flow and vitality in worship.

Ruts are usually vacated by taking a large jump in a new direction. Such a jump should be initiated soberly, with a genuine sense of the leading of the Spirit. It will likely involve the people in a way to which they are unaccustomed, which may be a threatening experience for them. We must be prepared for some awkward times and love the people as we lead them in God's way. Many worship leaders will shy away from "rocking the boat" because it can be very intimidating to move away from the familiarity of the old-time rut. When we are in the rut, we know where we are going; when outside the rut, the worship leader feels like holding up the popular bumper sticker that says, "Don't follow me — I'm lost." We worship leaders hate to feel out of control!

And yet that is precisely where God wants us, so that instead of depending upon our preconceived notions, we will rely more fully upon the guidance of the Holy Spirit.

Nobody — worship leader and church member alike — enjoys awkward feelings of uncertainty in the middle of a worship service, but these can be some of the most fruitful times we will ever have. Awkward worship times are characterized by one of two general problems. On the one hand, the worship leader may not be prepared sufficiently and is consequently floundering, uncertain as to which direction to take next. This is a very real problem and can be deadly to the remainder of the service. When the leadership is indecisive due to a lack of preparation, the door is open for multitudinous problems such as "off-the-wall" prophecies, untimely exhortations, and uncomfortable silences. This type of awkwardness is not commendable. On the other hand, there is a different kind of awkwardness in which the worship leader is well prepared but comes to the point of not knowing what God wants to do next. When this happens (notice that's *when* — not *if)*, we can take comfort in the fact that God is very near to walk us through these hard times.

It may be we will recognize that the service is flowing smoothly in the good old "Faith Chapel rut." It would be much easier to stay in the rut and sing the expected song that will effectively glaze over the problem, and the church can once again coast smoothly past a confrontation with God. But perhaps God has brought us to that point where we are weary of "sugarcoating" the problem with another little chorus and instead are desirous of having a genuine move of the Spirit. Such a situation will know an awkward time of transition. Someone will doubtless try to take control at one of these times, or lead out in a song or a prayer, but the people should be encouraged to wait quietly upon the Lord for clear direction.

Such times of quietness are extremely threatening to most churches, as they imply that the leadership does not know what to do next. The fact is, that is exactly true! We could come forth with a song of our human choosing and demonstrate our ability to control the service (and most will choose that option), but when we decide to wait upon God, we must be willing to weather the hard times in order to hear the voice of the Spirit. Sometimes we go zipping along so well in our worship groove that we do not stop to hear what "the Spirit says to the church." It takes a lot of honesty and humility to admit to the congregation that although we are having a "smooth" worship service, we are not moving in the power of the Spirit. Most leaders are not willing to admit that their worship rut is helping them cruise right past God. If we will be brave enough to stop the rut and sincere enough to call out to God, he will meet us in a new and divine way! The Spirit might direct us to change the climate of the service altogether, perhaps by calling the people to their knees in prayer. If it does nothing else, it will at least wake them up! The value of an awkward time such as this is that it will bring everyone to an awareness of the rut and of each one's need for God.

Most worship leaders tend to be far more concerned with the general feeling of the congregation toward the worship service than with God's feelings about it. If the people arrive at some sort of spiritual or emotional "high" and walk away satisfied, most worship leaders accept that as success. We rarely stop to ask God if he felt the worship service was a success. Is it possible that we can master the art of bringing the people into a state of spiritual euphoria, and all the while sidestep a truly revolutionary encounter with God? We must avoid the temptation to be happy merely when the people are happy, but must be satisfied only when God is pleased with our worship.

Just as it is occasionally appropriate to do something "revolutionary" in worship, it is equally appropriate on other occasions to avoid any sharp changes in the service. When the Holy Spirit is leading the meeting, it will be smooth and flowing. We may have some rough times initially, but once the Spirit is in charge, the worship service will progress smoothly in beautiful harmony and order. In Scripture, the Holy Spirit is likened to wind, water, and oil. These metaphors are appropriate because the Spirit flows very smoothly and gently. There are no sharp turns, no quick starts, no screeching halts. The Holy Spirit is not fast-slow-fast-slow, stop-go-stop-go, up-down-up-down, left-right-left-right. And neither should our worship services be characterized by these jerky movements. We should, and can, learn to flow smoothly and easily with the Holy Spirit.

Have you ever seen an eagle or hawk spread its wings and ascend without flapping its wings at all? It can do this by finding a "thermal" — an updraft of warm, rising air that enables it to soar. Many of our worship services seem to catch a "spiritual thermal" wherein we ascend in worship seemingly without effort. At other times, it seems we exert tremendous amounts of energy in an attempt to enter into worship. I would suggest that the reasons for this may be more emotional than spiritual in nature. God is not fickle; he is not "up" in one service and "down" in the next, nor is the Spirit excited one week and nonchalant the next week about enabling our worship. God does not play "spiritual hide-and-seek" with us. *We* are the ones who are up and down, excited one Sunday and indifferent the next. This is basically a problem with our highly fluctuating emotions.

There certainly can be some spiritual ramifications involved in some instances, and worship leaders need to be led of the Spirit to discern whether any hindrances have spiritual causes. Some services "take off" immediately, often because the people are emotionally "up" and prepared to enter in. Other services are very sluggish, and this is usually because the people are emotionally "down" and are not in the mood to praise or worship. When the people are emotionally deflated, the solution is straightforward: they need to exert their mind and will and determine to praise the Lord. God will honor their obedience and respond with his glory.

But often it isn't easy to get the people to exert their mind and will and determine to praise the Lord. Sometimes a prophecy will come forth to stir up the people to a response, but that is God-directed — we have no control over that. Is there anything worship leaders can do to stimulate the people?

The answer is twofold: through teaching and through exhortation. If the people are taught their responsibilities as worshipers, they will be better prepared to respond accordingly. A worship leader may need to become quite creative in finding ways to educate the people to their responsibilities to be self-motivated in praise and worship. An anointed exhortation can also be very effective in stirring up the people from their lethargy.

Although God is not "up" at one time and "down" at another, it is true that there are times and seasons in God. Churches go through times when the worship is vibrant and meaningful, and then they seem to go through "winters" in worship when the plowing is hard. At such times God is working deep things within, and it will probably take some time before that deep work becomes evident to us. It is during winter that trees send their roots down deeper, and this is their true growth. In the spring and summer the foliage and fruit give witness to that deeper growth. Winters in worship are not to be despised, for they will be followed by a new depth of expression.

SETTING GOALS FOR WORSHIP

It is critical that we have a vision for worship in our churches. Some worship leaders have a vision for only one service at a time, but if they lack a long-term vision, the worship of the church will stagnate. Each of us must be a progressive worship leader with progressive goals! We must not settle for the status quo or old forms and ruts; we must be visionary, and let our enthusiasm be contagious! Our vision must be progressive, for when established goals

are reached, we must reach for higher goals. Before old
goals are reached, new goals should be set so that we never
come to a point of feeling we have "arrived."

Some worship leaders have a tremendous vision for worship in their church, but then they ruin it by trying to manipulate it into existence in their own strength. Sometimes God
gives us a vision and then requires us to lay it aside and let it
die, in order that he might resurrect it in his time. He wants
us to be patient and trust him to work in the people according to his purposes and timetable.

We frequently need help in setting goals for ourselves.
Here are some guidelines which I have found useful.

Goals must be *tangible.* Our goals for worship must not
be abstract or ethereal, worded so vaguely that no one
knows when we have attained them. The goal of some
churches could be summed up as follows: "Our goal in this
church is for better worship." But what is "better
worship"? Is it longer worship, or faster worship, or louder
worship, or better-performed music in worship? Our goals
must be precise and succinct so that there is no question in
anyone's mind as to what the intended destination is — and
when we have reached it.

Goals must be *communicable.* Translate those goals into
English and put them on paper. Goals that are not actually
written down are seldom achieved. Formulate goals into
clear thoughts that can be communicated easily to others.
People will gladly follow our leadership when they understand where we are going.

Goals must be *achievable.* We should not set goals that
are so far off that our people become discouraged. Long-
term goals should be cushioned with short-term goals that
make the long-term goals seem achievable. If a goal can be
measured quantitatively, then articulate the desired amount
— for example, specify that the goal is to have eight singers
on the worship team within six months (not merely "to have
more singers").

Goals must be *definitive.* We should lay out our goals in a clear manner, showing step by step how we expect to achieve them. We should also limit the number of immediate goals; having too many simultaneous goals means that none will be fully accomplished. Outline what action is necessary to reach the goals at each stage. Setting deadlines pushes us toward accomplishment.

Here is a sample of how some concrete goals for worship could be expressed:

1. We want the people to get their eyes off the worship leader and onto the Lord. (This goal can take quite a while to achieve, as many congregations must be conditioned all over again.)

2. We purpose to sing in meaningful worship with hymns. (Since some charismatics have excluded hymns from their worship, it would be a true challenge to make hymns a meaningful part of their worship again.)

3. We purpose to sing in the Spirit to chordal patterns rather than to just one sustained chord.

4. We want to develop a system for teaching new choruses more efficiently.

Every worship leader should have as a goal the reproduction of worshipers in the congregation. Our goal as worship leaders is not simply to have vibrant worship on Sunday, but also to see our people become worshipers throughout the week. We must never be satisfied until God fills us with his love and compassion for his flock. Despite our many shortcomings, they need to know we love them.

Although we must have goals in worship, we must be careful, at the same time, that we do not become inordinately dissatisfied with our current level of worship. If God is the object of our worship, and we are dissatisfied with our expressions of worship, we could in effect be saying, "God, I'm not happy with just being in your presence. To simply be with you is not good enough. I want more." Our attitude should reflect the quip "I'm satisfied with a dissatisfied satisfaction." We must learn the blessed contentment of simply basking in his presence and enjoying the depth of worship the Holy Spirit is currently inspiring, while simultaneously praying, "More about Jesus would I know."

The apostle Paul talked about finding this balance. He said, "I have learned the secret of being content in any and every situation" (Philippians 4:12), but in the same epistle he also said, "Forgetting what is behind and straining toward what is ahead, I press on toward the goal to win the prize for which God has called me heavenward in Christ Jesus" (Philippians 3:13-14). Our attitude should be like that of Paul, who was content in his life situation, and yet he vigorously moved ahead toward the divine goal for his life.

When we lose our vision for worship, we can become disillusioned or despairing. Some worship leaders have given up completely, feeling their ministry to be completely insignificant. But I have good news for every worship leader. That role is very significant, both in the local church and in the body of Christ as a whole. God is seeking worshipers and is raising up worship leaders who have a sense of God's heartbeat. We are a part of God's great plan for these last days! Let's be excited and be fulfilled — we are playing a strategic role in the kingdom of God!

God has not intended that in our role of worship leader we "go it alone." We don't do it without him, or even without others. A worship team provides a beautiful context of "workers together" for the enhancing and strengthening of the ministry of worship and the fulfilling of God's purposes for us in worship.

CHAPTER 9

THE WORSHIP-LEADING TEAM

Traditionally in pentecostal and charismatic churches, worship has been led by one person who directs the singing from the pulpit or platform area. Support may be given by the choir and/or orchestra, but the actual responsibility of leading the worship has fallen exclusively on the shoulders of the worship leader (or "songleader," as he has often been called). In recent years, however, a new approach has come to the fore, wherein the worship leader joins together with a "team" to lead the worship unitedly. This is not another brand of "plurality of leadership," where all those on the team are co-equal in terms of responsibility and activity. One person continues to function as the leader but is now surrounded by a team that shares a common vision and purpose.

THE BENEFITS OF TEAM MINISTRY

There are two general ways in which a team enhances the effectiveness of one leader.

First, with a team there is safety and help. I traveled with a worship team for a few years, and through the services we conducted in many churches I learned the blessings of having a team for support. This may sound like a carnal confession, but I find that I do not flow in the fullest anointing of the Spirit 100 percent of the time. Sometimes I seem to move in a greater sensitivity to God's Spirit than at other times, and it is in my weaker moments that I need the support and strength that others can share. Many were the services when I thanked God in my heart for the others on my worship team, because when I was weak, they were strong; when they knew I was "down," they would rally and pick up the slack.

With a team there is power and unity. One leader may have a good ministry in worship, but the effectiveness of that ministry will be multiplied and enhanced through the joint efforts of a team functioning in unity under that leadership. We need more than individuals who have a unique anointing upon their lives; we need those leaders to be supported by a team in order that the effectiveness of their ministry might increase.

Ralph Mahoney, of World Missionary Assistance Plan, made some valid points on this subject when he said, "A 'lone ranger' will not get much done in this world. But a man who can organize others to work for a common vision, a man who can build a team, can do a significant work for the Lord's kingdom. The Bible speaks of one putting a thousand to flight and two putting ten thousand to flight. That's quite a jump! What about three or four or fifty all working together in common vision? Perhaps they could put millions to flight and win mighty victories in the name of the Lord. A vision that can be clearly communicated is the critical thing in rallying men and resources for achieving the work the Lord wants done. When you are able to communicate clearly where you are going, many will be ready and willing to help you get there. The resources will come in. The problem is not money; the problem is that we don't communicate vision and goals."

The worship-leading team is comprised of three general classifications: the worship leader; the orchestra (musicians); and the singers (which may include all or part of the choir). Some churches may also have a dance troupe as a part of their worship team. The sound system operator and the projectionist (assuming an overhead or slide projector is used for songs) can also be considered a part of the team.

We will be working from the following diagram in our discussion of the worship team:

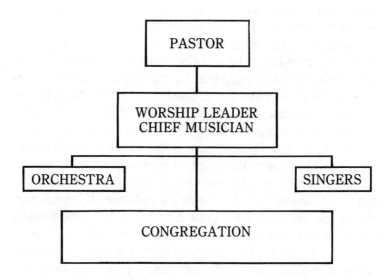

But before we look at each of these segments of the team, we must start with the one person who is most critical to the team: the pastor.

THE ROLE OF THE PASTOR

Since the pastor is the one who is ultimately responsible to God for church affairs, the worship team comes under his pastoral oversight. He is the one who provides the group with vision and motivation. He must know the general direction for each worship service, ensuring that the team flows with him. He should share his goals and philosophy for worship with the team and then work closely with them to see those goals accomplished.

Many pastors will not be involved in the "nitty-gritty" operations of the team — for instance, they should not be expected to always be present at team rehearsals — but they do provide the guiding force for the ministry of the team as a whole. If the pastor does little else, however, he can make a tremendous contribution to the worship team by teaching them how to pray. Pastors are forced to learn how to pray effectually, and worship leaders frequently need an impartation in this area.

The pastor is the key to the worship ministry. He has one major role in worship that far outweighs any other: first and foremost, he must be an example of a worshiper before the congregation. A worshiping pastor will birth a worshiping church; a non-worshiping pastor will never have a worshiping church, no matter how talented the worship leader may be. The pastor leads much more by example in this area than by preaching. He can preach about worship but see no response if he is not a living example. If he is a worshiper, he need not even preach about worship very much — the people will become worshipers anyway!

When a pastor begins to realize how much influence he holds over his congregation, the magnitude of his responsibility becomes most sobering. Supposing a visiting preacher comes to church and begins to propagate some controversial views. What is the first thing the people do? They look over to the pastor to see what he thinks. By seeing his expression, the people are able to determine exactly what their response to this visitor should be. Something similar happens in the worship service. As the service is in progress and the worship leader initiates a new direction, the people will frequently glance at the pastor to see how he is responding to the new turn of events. Is he dancing, now that the worship leader encouraged us to dance? Is he shouting, after the worship leader has exhorted us to "shout unto God with the voice of triumph"? Is the pastor supporting the worship leader by being a foremost example of worship? By his responsiveness to the Lord in worship (or his lack thereof), the pastor can do more to influence the participation of the congregation than can the orchestra, choir, and worship leader combined!

In many churches, the pastor is given a highly visible seat on the platform, together with other dignitaries and guests. This array of spiritual eminence on the elevated platform can intimidate the most humble of saints. It is natural for our folk to emulate the attitude displayed by "the ministry" on stage. It does not matter if the worship leader is dancing, the orchestra is swaying, and the choir is swinging from the chandeliers — if the pastor is standing with folded arms and wrinkled brow, the people are not going to respond. They will wait for some sign that shows the pastor's approval of the proceedings.

I do not know the derivation of the contemporary custom of seating the pastoral staff and guest ministry on the platform, and no doubt there are good reasons for this practice, but let me suggest that we need to rethink our policy in this regard. Just because someone is a pastor does not mean he looks pleasant when worshiping. Some people scowl when they worship, even though they feel elated inside. Others radiate when they worship, regardless of how they feel. If a pastor is a "scowler," my advice to him is to get off the platform and stand someplace where his face is less visible, so that those on the worship team who do radiate are seen by the people. If the people see folks on stage who radiate as examples of worship, they will be inspired to open their hearts in worship.

The worship service is not the time for the pastor to be "counting heads," or checking to see if Sister So-and-So did in fact make it to church. Nor is it the time to be brushing up on his sermon notes or discussing the order of service with his associates on the platform. It is time to be worshiping! If the pastor is too casual, he can communicate through body language that the worship time is not too terribly important, and if we can all hang in there a little longer, it will soon be over. Conversely, the pastor can show, through his posture of worship, that nothing is more important at that moment than ministering unto the Lord.

Some pastors give the impression that they are too mature to be very concerned about worship. Worship is necessary for the sheep, but the pastor has better things to do during the worship service. But the Bible makes it clear that we are never too spiritual to bless the Lord in worship. Psalm 107:32 reads, "Let them exalt him in the assembly of the people and praise him in the council of the elders." Throughout the book of Revelation, the elders are the ones leading heaven's throng in worship by falling prostrate before the King of kings. Readiness to respond in worship does not denote immaturity or youthful zeal, but rather is a mark of maturity and spirituality.

King David can be a good model for pastors to emulate, because David was in a very real sense the "pastor" of the nation of Israel. David purposefully made himself an example of worship before the entire nation. He donned a linen ephod and danced before the Lord with all his might as the ark was brought to Zion. David was the king, the leader, the "pastor" of the Israelites, and yet he considered it his proper place to be the most exuberant and expressive in his praise and worship to God. When derided by Michal for his open display of worship, he responded by saying, " 'It was before the LORD, who chose me rather than your father or anyone from his house when he appointed me ruler over the LORD's people Israel — I will celebrate before the LORD. I will become even more undignified than this, and I will be humiliated in my own eyes. But by these slave girls you spoke of, I will be held in honor' " (2 Samuel 6:21-22). It is the pastor's responsibility to cast aside personal pride and lead God's people forth in exultant praise and worship.

In addition to his influence in worship, the pastor holds the key to a successful music program. The level of music ministry in a local assembly will never exceed the pastor's vision. Not only must the pastor be available to provide vision and direction to the music department, but he must also support it by giving public approval and encouragement to those who are involved. How important it is that he affirm those who minister in music and worship, continually showing appreciation and understanding.

The pastor will unavoidably be involved in music ministry to some degree. Even if he would tend to shun it, he will inevitably end up leading worship from time to time, and he will also be required to make many decisions that affect the musical climate of the church. Between 20 and 50 percent of most services is given over to music, and the pastor plays a vital role in determining and shaping the nature of that musical involvement.

A pastor should be able to relate theology to the goals and uses of music in the church. Why do we place so much emphasis on music and worship? What is the desired end of all music in our church? A pastor must be able to answer these and other similar questions with well-considered, theologically sound answers.

Church music should have a definitive role of its own. For some, the song service has become a traditional — and therefore necessary — routine. Others have called this portion of the service "the preliminaries," with the implication that all these activities prepare for the only significant event in the service: the sermon. Some have emphasized the place of music in the church as a means for growth, knowing that good musical entertainment will attract a large crowd. And how often music has been used as a time-filler! Songs are used to give people a break from standing or sitting a long time, so they do not get cramped in one position: "We've been sitting for a while, so let's stand and sing 'This Is the Day.' " And what about this one: "While the ushers are counting the offering, let's sing 'Bringing in the Sheaves.' " Songs are used to signal transitions in a service: "While the children are going out for children's church, let's stand and sing 'I'll Fly Away.' " Or, "To let the people in the foyer know that the service is starting, let's sing 'Count Your Blessings.' " When worship songs are used in this manner, they are stripped of their meaning and assigned a disparaging connotation. The story is told of a certain organist who was asked by the pastor to "just play something" to cover a moment of delay in the course of the service. He is reported to have whispered back, "Why don't you just mumble something?'' Pastors must give careful thought to the role of music and worship in the church.

Sadly enough, relatively few schools or seminaries are adquately preparing pastors for the musical responsibilities they are certain to encounter in a pastorate. Though music programs are available in most Bible schools, they are not considered to be essential in the training of ministerial students — despite the fact that many churches, when evaluating ministerial candidates, often give serious consideration to the candidate's ability to lead worship! It is often assumed that if someone cannot lead worship well, then he probably cannot do anything else, either (the obvious implication being that leading worship is a cinch — though nothing could be further from reality!). How worthwhile it would be for Bible schools to incorporate classes on worship and worship-leading into their ministerial programs, considering such training essential in the equipping of pastors and indeed all Christian workers.

THE ROLE OF THE WORSHIP LEADER

The worship leader provides overall leadership for the congregation, instrumentalists, and singers. The worship leader's attention is divided between two general areas of concern: the musical aspects of the service, which involve the musicians and singers in particular; and the spiritual aspects of the service, which basically involve the congregation.

Second, the worship leader selects and initiates most of the songs to be sung. Some churches will allow songs to be initiated by folks in the choir or congregation, whereas others discourage that sort of thing, wanting all the leadership to come from the pulpit. All those concerned simply need to know the modus operandi of that particular church. What we do not want is a multi-headed monster. We must have one person who is ultimately responsible for the songs that are selected.

The role of the worship leader has already been presented at length in the preceding chapter, but it bears repeating that the worship leader should always be an example of a worshiper. His attention is divided among many areas, and it is easy for him to forget to worship. People will worship as they follow his example. When all else fails, try worshiping!

One thing that does need to be emphasized is the need for the training of new worship leaders. I have been asked, "What do you do when you want to involve others in the leading of worship, but when they are given a service, they do not perform adequately?" The best way for a leader to produce new leaders in a fellowship is to train them — disciple them — reproduce himself in them. We often fall short, however, in our approach to raising up new worship leaders.

One reason the worship team exists is to raise up worship leaders. This is the context we need in order to train potential leaders for the ministry of worship. The first step in the training process is to incorporate the candidate onto the team as a singer. That person's sole responsibility as a singer is to learn how to inspire others to worship by his or her example. Responsibilities can be increased slowly until he or she is given a worship service to lead. With proper post-service evaluations, the trainee can know what mistakes and weaknesses need attention. The worship team can thus be a spiritual greenhouse where new leadership is provided a safe and healthy context in which to grow and mature.

Rehearsals are a time for the trainee to catch the leader's vision, hear his heartbeat, and receive of his spirit. The anointing that is on the life and ministry of the worship leader can be imparted to each one on the team. When an aspiring worship leader receives that impartation, he or she will begin to flow in unity with the team. Then, when given opportunity to lead worship, that person will manifest a quality of ministry that will evidence the leader's input and influence.

No worship leader or pastor should be satisfied with anything less than the discipling of other leaders for the work of the ministry. The singers and musicians on the team should be encouraged to expand in their ministries. I would suggest, however, that only a few worship leaders function within a fellowship at any one given time. Some churches seem to operate all right with a large number of worship leaders that minister on a rotating basis, but I think they would meet with better success by using from one to three good leaders in major services. Others can be in training, but they should lead in other services of fewer participants. It is important that people get accustomed to the style of a worship leader so they can learn to flow easily with him or her. Worshipers can relax when they become familiar with a leader's style and know what to expect from that person in the context of the worship service.

THE PASTOR/WORSHIP LEADER
RELATIONSHIP

God intends that a mutually cooperative unity prevail between the pastor and the worship leader. These two are not vying for the limelight. Too many worship leaders wish they were the preacher (and even use the worship time to demonstrate their eloquence), while too many preachers wish they were better at leading worship. God has blessed each of us with abilities that are uniquely our own, and we must be content with his gifts. If all were preachers, who would listen? If all led worship, who would follow? If one man did everything, where would be the body ministry? The pastor and worship leader, then, are not in competition; each is able to contribute in areas that make the ministry of the other more effective.

A pastor/worship leader team that is united in spirit is an unbeatable combination! God has told us that with the combination of high praises and the sword of the Spirit (the word of God), we will take our inheritance in the nations *(see* Psalm 149:6-9). A praising church without a strong ministry in the word will flap around in circles like a one-winged bird. But a praising church with a strong pulpit ministry will thrive. The pastor needs a sharp, anointed worship leader; the worship leader needs a capable, anointed preacher. When oxygen unites with gas, watch out for combustion!

Three ingredients are vital to the maintenance of a solid, healthy relationship between the pastor and worship leader: *respect, consideration,* and *communication.*

Ideally, there will be a bonding of spirit and a mutual empathy and *respect* between pastor and leader. If the worship leader has insufficient respect for the pastor, that leader will find himself moving at variance with the wishes of the pastor and even questioning his decisions and methods. It is easy for the leader to insidiously show disrespect for the pastor by taking twenty-five minutes for worship when allotted only twenty minutes. Conversely, if the pastor does not respect and trust a worship leader in regard to spiritual stature, he will be continually interrupting, vetoing, or preempting the leader's desires and methods. Through respect, a strong bond of mutual dependence can be established.

If a pastor does not respect the spirituality and sensitivity of a worship leader, he should not appoint that person to the position. It is unfair to assign someone to a worship-leading ministry and then through lack of trust proceed to interrupt or override the intentions of the leader. If it is mutually understood that the worship leader is in training, then the leader should be given enough latitude to make some mistakes and thereby develop and grow.

A pastor and worship leader must be *considerate* of one another. At times the pastor will feel that he should lead in a direction different from that which the worship leader has prepared. Who is right? Who has the mind of the Lord, the pastor or the worship leader?

Perhaps an answer can be found in the writings of

Amos: "The lion has roared — who will not fear? The Sovereign LORD has spoken — who can but prophesy?" (Amos 3:8). When the spirit of prophecy rests on a congregation, it seems like almost everyone wants to prophesy! Similarly, in the context of the worship service, when the Spirit of God is moving, it is easy for a number of folks to gain insight into what they think the direction of the service should be. At such times, the pastor also finds his heart being stirred, and perhaps because of his position he is much more inclined than anyone else to take the control of the service from the worship leader and go with his own ideas. It is not that the worship leader is wrong and pastor is right — for either direction would probably work fine — it is just that the pastor easily feels the liberty to initiate what he thinks is best. Being preempted in this fashion can often hurt the feelings of the worship leader, whether or not the worship leader is justified in that reaction. The pastor's action intimates, "God wanted to do something, and you were not sensitive enough to pick up on it, so I decided to initiate it!" or "The worship service was going down fast, and so I stepped in to save the service from your incompetence." The pastor will ultimately gain nothing by running roughshod over the worship leader. If the problem is the worship leader's lack of experience, the pastor should spend quality time instructing him or her, not with a spirit of criticism but with an attitude of loving guidance.

When the pastor does preempt the worship leader by taking control of the service, the leader must not allow himself the luxury of getting his feelings hurt or embarking upon a pity party. The goal of ministry is to bless God's people, regardless of what channel God uses. The leader should carefully study the new idea or approach that the pastor introduced into the service, to see what he did that the leader was not doing, or in what different way the pastor was tuned into the Spirit. Many times the differences in approach or style between pastor and leader are simply human rather than spiritual. It may not be that the pastor's approach was superior to that of the leader (although it sometimes is), but it was a matter of preference — he simply wanted the service to take a slightly different direction. The leader can let this be a challenge to grow in sensitivity and ability to lead until he comes to a point where the pastor would rather have him take the entire thing!

When the pastor and worship leader have different ideas about what direction the service should take, each must have consideration for the other. The worship leader should be considerate of the pastor, respecting his expertise and experience. And the pastor should be considerate of the worship leader, at times keeping quiet even though he feels he has something good to contribute. Often (though not always) the pastor could do the job better than the worship leader, but the pastor is not there to do everything — he is there to see others trained in the work of the ministry *(see* Ephesians 4:11-12). By keeping a low profile in consideration of the worship leader, the pastor can help contribute to the health of their relationship.

Communication is also an essential element in this relationship. "Can two walk together, except they be agreed?" (Amos 3:3, KJV). Nothing will cause this relationship to disintegrate more quickly than a lack of open communication. If the pastor is disturbed by the worship leader's apparent insensitivity, that annoyance will bring an irreparable cleavage between the two unless it is discussed and resolved. If the worship leader is frustrated with the pastor's expectations, the only solution will be found in honest, loving communication.

How easily we make false assumptions or avoid a matter because of our fear of confrontation. It is especially easy for worship leaders to form false assumptions, because most worship leaders are highly intimidated with the prospect of approaching their pastor with a frustration. Because of the lack of communication, barriers begin to form — not from the pastor's perspective but from the worship leader's. If these barriers continue to build, the worship leader may eventually leave the church, much to the consternation of the pastor.

A pastor may assume that when things are going well, everyone else is also thoroughly delighted with the worship. It does not occur to him that although he is really enjoying the services, the worship leader is laboring under a burden. So the pastor must occasionally ask his worship leader such questions as "How do you feel about our worship lately?" "Have you been enjoying leading the worship?" "How do you think we've been working together?" "Are you fulfilled in your ministry?"

There are many ways in which the pastor and worship leader can complement one another. When a difficulty or new situation arises, both may have unique insight into the solution, or they may gain experience by seeing the problem from the other's perspective. A pastor needs to learn to depend on his worship leader. At various points throughout the service, for instance, the pastor can take the freedom to call on the worship leader for an appropriate song. And the worship leader needs to lean on the pastor. He can always fall back on the pastor's experience, turning the service over to him when the leader becomes frustrated or no longer knows where to take the service. If the lines of communication are open, a quick glance at the pastor can say, "I really don't know what to do next . . . got any ideas?" And similarly, rather than taking the microphone from the hand of a struggling worship leader, the pastor can reassuringly whisper, "I'm here to help if you need me."

The pastor should not be too restrictive in what he allows the worship leader to do. If worship leaders are permitted to do nothing but lead songs, they are sure to become frustrated. Leading worship is very much a pastoral role — worship leaders must have a pastor's heart for the sheep and endeavor to lead them effectively to green pastures and still waters. Because of the pastoral dynamics of leading worship, if worship leaders can do nothing more than lead songs, they will become frustrated with their inability to lead the sheep where they need to go. Songs can take a worship service only so far. Sometimes a service needs a time of prayer, or repentance, or an altar call, or a healing line. If a pastor will allow his worship leaders to step out in these areas, they will be much more challenged and fulfilled, and the tenor of the services will reflect that freedom.

A wise pastor will express his appreciation for the support of the worship leader upon whom he heavily relies. But a worship leader must guard his heart against negative attitudes that could terminate his effectiveness in ministry, especially when the pastor fails to show appreciation. "The pastor doesn't understand and properly appreciate me and my ministry. I think I'll go somewhere else where they will!" Such attitudes of pride can culminate in removal from ministry altogether. If there is a great rift between leader and pastor, so that the leader feels his ministry is not being received, and no amount of communication brings reconciliation, some leaders have taken careful inventory of their heart motivations, and then have departed only upon the counsel of respected brethren in God. How much better it is, though, when a spirit of communication, patience, and understanding prevails!

The worship leader must learn some specific things from the pastor. He must see and embrace the vision of his particular church. He must know how his ministry is to be expressed in relationship to the church structure. He must know his anointing and be aware of the perimeters permissible to him, and then function in that.

The worship leader must guard against visions of grandeur. His position is highly visible, and compliments must be taken in stride. Neither should a leader become a sounding board for those who are discontented with the pastor, nor should he get hung up on a title or position; rather, he should be a servant, a minister, a helper.

THE CHIEF MUSICIAN

The role of "chief musician" on the worship team also needs to be considered. Though the worship leader and chief musician are often one and the same person, that need not necessarily be the case. If the worship leader and chief musician are two different people, some particular points need to be remembered.

First of all, the worship leader is usually chosen because of spiritual sensitivity, and the chief musician is selected because of musical expertise. Some competent musicians have the technical ability to run circles around any worship leader when it comes to musical expertise, but just because one is capable musically does not mean that one has the spiritual sensitivity necessary to lead worship. Many worship leaders, on the other hand, lack the ability to make the musical end of things work smoothly, and so they depend heavily upon their chief musician to make the music happen. These two need not conflict in any way, but as members of the same team they should strive to complement one another's ministry.

Second, if we have both a worship leader and a chief musician, we must remember that congregational meetings demand leadership, so one leader must be affirmed. The worship leader, then, would take precedence over the chief musician as the leader of the worship service. It becomes the chief musician's duty to flow as well as possible with the intentions and desires of the worship leader. The worship leader can transmit his or her desires to the chief musician, who can in turn direct the musicians and singers.

Leading worship (contrary to public assumption) is not at all easy. And neither is playing a musical instrument. If the chief musician is a pianist, he must think about the key of the song, the melody line, the progression of chords, the tempo (how fast or slow it should be), where the other instrumentalists are musically in relationship to the piano, whether the worship leader wants to sing the same chorus over again or go to another song altogether . . . and on it goes. All these factors are usually more than enough for most individuals to handle. It can become an awesome task if the chief musician must also be concerned about what song to sing next and what the Spirit might be trying to say in the service as a whole. The chief musician must be an excellent musician in order to play an instrument, direct the orchestra, and then also lead the congregational worship. It takes a good musician to give thorough musical direction to a group of musicians and singers, all the while maintaining sensitivity to the Holy Spirit's guidance of the meeting. This is a very valid reason for having two different individuals to fill the roles of worship leader and chief musician.

Neither position is more important or necessary than the other. Without the spiritual guidance of the worship leader, the service would be dry and perfunctory. Without the musical expertise of the chief musician, the service would be a disaster. Every church desperately needs a chief musician! I have had pastors ask me what they could do to improve their worship services, because they have no one who plays the piano, and their guitar player would make a better fruit-picker. What can they do? Not much, without a chief musician! First and foremost, that church should look for someone to fill that role. One way to find a chief musician would be to contact a large church and ask if they have any good musicians who would like to take over another church's music ministry. Large churches sometimes have many musical people who are frustrated because they desire a more meaningful outlet for their abilities, but there is no room for them in the larger church.

I would rather tolerate a church that had no worship leader than to try to work with a situation where there were no qualified musicians. Hopefully, a church can have both (whether that means one person filling both roles or two individuals working together). The wise worship leader will lean heavily on the chief musician and will cultivate a close and meaningful relationship. Obviously, the selection of a chief musician should be considered as carefully as that of a worship leader.

THE MUSICIANS

If worship leaders of the past did not have a team to support them, then what were the roles of their orchestras and choirs? Musicians have usually been referred to as "accompanists," a term that attaches certain undesirable connotations to the role of musicians. An "accompanist" could be thought of as someone who "plays along with" the worship. A musician's function is thus intimated to be as critical to the worship service as an icemaker is to the operation of a refrigerator — nice to have, but not fundamentally necessary. But an honest appraisal of the role of musicians in worship will quickly reveal that our worship is predominantly dependent upon them.

David was very serious in his approach to the ministry of music in his tabernacle, as we see in 1 Chronicles. "David told the leaders of the Levites to appoint their brothers as singers to sing joyful songs, accompanied by musical instruments: lyres, harps and cymbals" (1 Chronicles 15:16). Furthermore, "Heman and Jeduthan were responsible for the sounding of the trumpets and cymbals and for the playing of the other instruments for sacred song" (1 Chronicles 16:42). Notice the use of "appoint," "responsible," "designated," and "chosen" in these and similar passages. The ministry of praise and music was considered so critical to the functions of the priesthood that men were carefully selected and consecrated to that ministry. They did not merely engage in a few moments of slipshod rehearsal! These brethren were appointed, full time, to fulfill their ministry of praise unto the Lord.

Do we have a similar seriousness about our approach to music in the church today? Too often, the only requirement for being a Levite in the house of the Lord is to be a capable musician. But we must begin to appreciate the importance of musical ministry, and people should be appointed to these ministries after serious thought, prayer, and consultation.

Those who function in music play very influential roles in the life of the church. We devote a considerable amount of time to worship in our services, and our musicians and worship leaders fulfill a strategic place in that function. They directly affect the spiritual life of the congregation in a very vital area.

Today God is raising up musicians who will not simply "play for" or "play along with" worship but who will themselves worship on their instruments. Musicians are called to be no longer merely accompanists, but rather *initiators* — worshipers on their instruments who can prophetically lead and inspire worship in the congregation. For too long musicians have thought they are exempt from worshiping because they are distracted with the business of playing their instruments. God does not ask us to put the instruments away but to learn to worship on and through the instruments. The playing of an instrument should be in and of itself an act of worship unto the Lord, regardless of whether anyone else is present to hear the instrument being played.

This means, of course, that we must determine some minimal standards for those who function in our "worshiping orchestra." Above all else, each musician must first of all be a worshiper. The playing of a non-worshiper is likely to be insensitive, self-promoting, and devoid of spirit. I am told that some churches, when putting on special musicals and Christmas performances, will actually hire unsaved musicians to augment their orchestral sound. But there is a vast difference between a "performing orchestra" and a "worshiping orchestra." Performances have their place, but that place is not the worship service. We are speaking of musicians who serve to prophetically inspire the worship of the congregation. Musicians do not join a worshiping orchestra to learn how to worship. They first of all should learn to worship in the congregation, and only after they have manifested the heart of a worshiper in the congregation should they be considered for the orchestra (provided they meet the other criteria). It is unlikely that a musician in a worshiping orchestra will become a worshiper by "osmosis"; he must be a worshiper before he comes into the orchestra.

Each musician, further, must be a worshiper on his or her instrument. It is one thing to be a worshiper — it is another to pick up an instrument and still maintain a heart of worship. Too many instrumentalists are appointed to our orchestras because they are good musicians. Many churches are so desperate for good musicians that when some come along, no care is given to whether or not they are worshipers — they are immediately welcomed into the ranks. Such policies indicate a need to rethink our priorities. What is more important: to have a larger group with "hotshot" musicians, or a smaller group with sincere, spiritual worshipers? It is time to begin setting standards that are commensurate with the seriousness of the Levitical ministry which our musicians perform. We set very high standards for the pastor because of the Levitical nature of his ministry; why, then, are we so lax in setting spiritual standards for the musicians who are responsible for leading God's people in praise and worship?

The musician must also have a heart after God and must demonstrate a consistent Christian life. Like it or not, these musicians hold a prominent place in our assemblies and so are esteemed by our people as examples of spirituality. If a brother or sister is known to be struggling with commitment to Christ and his demands of discipleship, that person should not be given a place in a public ministry such as the orchestra or choir.

Any instrumentalist should have a desire and divine calling to lead others in worship. Some folks simply have the desire without the calling. Just because they "have the itch to play" does not necessarily mean they are called of God to do so, at least for the present. We do not need musicians functioning in our worship services unless they know they are ministering according to God's calling and will.

Furthermore, there should be a recognition by the pastoral leadership that this is indeed a divine calling on the musician's life and that this is the right time for this individual to function in this fashion. The appointment of musicians and singers in the Old Testament *(see* 1 Chronicles 25) meant that demands were placed upon them to fulfill their ministry. The fact that they were set apart to that ministry indicates the seriousness of the commitment involved.

We have said that church musicians function as spiritual Levites. "Levi" means "joined," and musicians must be "joined" in heart and spirit to a local church before taking on a public ministry. People should not be involved in music ministry so that they will feel they are a part of the church. Music ministry is not the right of the talented, but is rather the privilege extended to the committed.

As a final consideration, musicians should pass a test of musical proficiency. "So the number of them, with their brethren who were instructed in the songs of the Lord, all who were skillful, was two hundred and eighty-eight" (1 Chronicles 25:7, NKJV). I have placed this qualification of musical proficiency last, but too many churches have made this the first priority. We need to renew our concern for spirituality in the lives of those performing these important Levitical ministries. Once that priority is in place, we can strive for musical proficiency, until it can be said of our music department that those who function are both trained and skillful.

Some church musicians feel they can use their talents for the Lord and then also use them in the world for such "profane" purposes as playing in nightclubs. I would never attempt to judge these brethren, but I believe it is pleasing to God that musicians use their gifting exclusively for the ministry. I see scriptural substantiation for this in the Davidic pattern: "The priests took their positions, as did the Levites with the *LORD'S* musical instruments, which

King David had made for praising the LORD and which were used when he gave thanks, saying, 'His love endures forever' " (2 Chronicles 7:6); "the Israelites who were present in Jerusalem celebrated the Feast of Unleavened Bread for seven days with great rejoicing, while the Levites and priests sang to the LORD every day, accompanied by the *LORD'S* instruments of praise" (2 Chronicles 30:21).

The instruments used in David's tabernacle belonged exclusively to the Lord! They were not used for ordinary or "secular" purposes; they were employed entirely in the giving of thanks and praise unto the Lord in the tabernacle.

WHAT IS EXPECTED OF TEAM MEMBERS

Qualifications for musicians must be followed by expectations regarding those musicians. (Actually, most of these could apply to all who make up the worship-leading team.) To begin with, attendance at rehearsals is very important to all concerned. This rehearsal time is much more than just a musical event. The primary reason for a rehearsal is to provide time for the team to spend together, developing a unity of heart and spirit. The practicing of music is a necessary but secondary function.

A typical rehearsal would probably include some of the following activities:

1. Praise and worship. Much of the rehearsal time should be spent in worshiping together, particularly when the team is newly formed and seeking a common vision. As the team spends time together in the presence of God, ministering unitedly before him, a unity of heart will be developed. This spiritual unity is to be coveted far more than musical togetherness. Through this type of unity come power and effective spiritual service.

2. Teaching and Bible study. The team should be taught biblical concepts of music ministry.

3. Discussion. There should be an open sharing of the vision for worship and an opportunity for the team members

to hear each other's heartbeat. Discussions of this nature will bring an awareness of common goals and concepts.

4. Prayer. The group will never transcend the level of "average" unless they become a praying team.

5. Musical rehearsal. Though this element is placed last, its importance should not be diminished. The story in 2 Chronicles 5 clearly reveals how the glory of God filled Solomon's temple when the singers and musicians united to lift high God's praises — 120 trumpeters alone, not counting the many other musicians and the mass choir who together heralded the event. "All the Levites who were musicians . . . stood on the east side of the altar, dressed in fine linen and playing cymbals, harps and lyres. They were accompanied by 120 priests sounding trumpets. The trumpeters and singers joined in unison, as with one voice, to give praise and thanks to the LORD" (verses 12-13).

The record goes on to say that when "the trumpeters and singers joined in unison, as with one voice, to give praise and thanks to the LORD . . . the temple of the LORD was filled with a cloud, and the priests could not perform their service because of the cloud, for the glory of the LORD filled the temple of God" (verses 13-14). As the musicians and singers were in unity — both musically and spiritually — the glory of God descended upon the priests. How do you suppose they arrived at that level of musical and spiritual unity? Through happenstance? By "the anointing"? By saying, "Now, you men in the back sing bass, and you fellows on this side sing tenor, and all the ladies who sing soprano, raise your hands — let's see now, how many musicians do we have? . . ."? No, they were unified through rehearsal. They practiced . . . and practiced . . . and practiced! Solomon wanted this august occasion to be accompanied by pomp, regalia, organization, and precision. So the musicians were well rehearsed in advance. When the glory of God appeared, they reaped the fruit of their dedicated rehearsal. One thing this story certainly shows us is that God is not adverse to organization, planning, and precision! He is a

God of order, and he responds to orderly worship.

Team members should also participate in pre-service prayer. The length of these prayer times may vary from church to church, but it is so important for the musicians and singers to be united in spirit before the service begins. This will also ensure that they get to the meeting in good time. Pre-service prayer gives each team member opportunity to "tune in" to the Holy Spirit, preparing personally for the service. It unites the team in spirit and purpose, and it provides opportunity for united intercession in behalf of the meeting.

There must be a firm commitment to the team ministry. The extent of this commitment may not be the same in each church, but if this ministry is viewed from a right perspective, the commitment of each member will be made seriously and sincerely.

An attitude of enthusiasm and cooperation is required. Not only must team members be cooperative, but they must cooperate enthusiastically with the leadership if the success of the team is to be maintained.

Team members must also sustain an openness to receive correction and instruction. How we value a "teachable spirit"!

Finally, each musician must be flexible musically, willing to change personal styles to accommodate the entire team. This is a touchy area because addressing a musician's style of playing is usually taken as a personal jab. Musicians are very sensitive in this area, for they see their style as springing out of their personality. Critiquing their style is interpreted as criticizing their personality. It is imperative, therefore, that there be a strong understanding from the beginning that all must be willing to be flexible in their musical style. If there is a good understanding about this from the outset, it will be much easier later on to address problems of individual styles. Each one must be willing to relinquish his or her musical "quirks" for the sake of unity within the group.

Musicians will begin to flow in unity and sensitivity after proper instruction on how to be aware of the sounds around them and how to balance with the other instruments. It is very possible for a certain section (for example, the trumpet section) to play together spontaneously and prophetically.

Sunday morning is not the time for musicians to show off their improvisational abilities. Their intent should not be to play every song with the greatest amount of flourish and pizzazz they can muster. A worshiping musician is not concerned with "grandstanding" his or her ability but instead is preoccupied with contributing meaningfully to the flow of worship. The musicians should feel the freedom *not* to play occasionally, in order to stand and worship with hands upraised. If musicians have "the itch" to play an instrument, they should "scratch the itch" on Saturday so that when they come on Sunday to lead on the team, they are able to participate or refrain according to the promptings of the Spirit.

THE SINGERS

The main function of the singers on the worship team is to stand before the congregation as a visual inspiration to worship. Everything about their countenance should say, "The river of God's Spirit is so gentle and refreshing today — jump in!" Their main duty is to radiate the joy and peace of Christ; vocal abilities are secondary.

Singers should be appointed to the team. This is a highly visible ministry and should not be opened to volunteers. Too often, singers are assigned to the worship team because they have a pleasant voice, or are able to harmonize nicely. The chances are that these people will be the hardest of all with whom to work, because they will think they are doing the church and God a favor by being on the team. The first consideration again must be: are they worshipers? Second, do they radiate? Some people are true worshipers, but when they worship they look as though they are in pain. They do not present a positive visual image, even though they are truly enjoying the presence of God. And then there are others who simply shine when they worship. They smile without effort during their worship; their countenance glows. We need this type of individual on the team. I would recommend four or more singers on the team, but I would settle for two that know how to shine!

The singers should also be free in their praise and worship, with the liberty to raise their hands, to dance, to kneel, or to express other forms of worship. They serve as examples of worship, and their example will be followed. I would rather have two people who are free to praise and who radiate while worshiping than to have ten individuals with excellent voices but no spiritual liberty.

Although vocal abilities are secondary, they are nonetheless a consideration. It is very effective when the singers can sing harmonies (particularly alto and tenor) in the context of the worship service, particularly if those harmonies are amplified by use of a microphone. When new songs are taught to the congregation, the people often enthusiastically learn a song that is presented in three-part harmony as opposed to a simple unison. Harmonies add another dimension to the singing — a certain spice that can spoil a congregation very quickly to anything less. Ideally, we want to choose singers who can both radiate and harmonize.

Several times we've mentioned the use of microphones. There are some excellent reasons for microphone use by singers:

1. For security. A person feels more secure standing behind a microphone than just standing right out in the open. Singers will be able to relax more easily with a microphone before them.

2. For validity. When someone is given a microphone, everyone easily recognizes that he or she has a valid, credible position on the worship team. With a microphone comes immediate authority.

3. For prophetic songs. If anyone on the team sings

forth a prophetic song, it can be heard much more easily by everyone if the singer's voice is amplified.

4. For sound reinforcement. The singers can support the worship leader in singing forth the melody clearly or in singing harmonies that are soothing and inspiring. If there is someone on the team who has been chosen because he or she radiates the joy of the Lord but who "cannot carry a tune in a bucket," the solution is simple: give that person a microphone — but just turn it off! The congregation will be blessed by the fact that the "singer" is a worshiper and will likely never realize that, in fact, the person cannot sing!

The singers should not be heard too loudly over the sound system. If the system is turned up too high, it is possible for the singers to drown out any sense of "congregational sound." We do not want to replace the sound of the congregation with the amplified voices of a chosen few. The singers are there only to support and encourage the congregation, inspiring the people to release their hearts and voices unto the Lord. People will be reticent to sing enthusiastically if they feel they are the only ones in the whole place who are singing. By amplifying the singers to the right level, we provide a sense of atmosphere, creating the feeling that we are surrounded with the sounds of praise. In that atmosphere, the people will be released and the praise will crescendo.

OTHER TEAM MEMBERS

A dance troupe in a church should be considered a part of the worship team. They should participate in rehearsals and share the common vision of the group. What applies to musicians and singers in regard to spiritual life, motivations, and attitudes applies to dancers as well. It should never be forgotten that in the context of the worship service, dance is a *ministry* — not a performing art.

Though it may seem strange, it is true that the public address (sound system) operator is an important member of the worship team. Although the P.A. operator may not need to be at every rehearsal, he or she should come to enough rehearsals to establish a strong understanding and working relationship with all the musicians and singers.

When the operator does attend rehearsals, he should adjust the controls as though an actual service were in progress. Many "bugs" in a sound system can thus be worked out during the rehearsal rather than during the Sunday morning worship.

The operator should be sure that all microphones are set up well in advance of every service (since some churches disassemble their microphones after each service to guard against theft). Also, getting a "sound check" before each service is an excellent idea.

The operator must be sure to remain alert throughout the service. The pastor might decide, without advance warning, to use a microphone that is not turned on. Or a prophetic utterance might come from an unexpected quarter, and a different microphone would need to be turned up. All we need is five seconds of earsplitting feedback during a high point in the worship to appreciate the vital role the P.A. operator fulfills on the team!

Another important member of the team is the person who operates the overhead or slide projector (if the church uses one). The capability of this person is critical if distractions are to be kept to a minimum. The operator must be willing to sacrifice extra time in order to keep the songs organized and updated. In many churches, most of the musically-oriented people are involved in the choir or orchestra, so a non-musical person is asked to operate the projector. In my experience, non-musical people who attempt to operate the overheads for the worship service usually encounter frustrations, simply because this is actually a musical position. The projectionist should be able to carry a tune and should have a working knowledge of the church's repertoire of songs so that he or she can quickly recognize them. The projectionist may not need to attend rehearsals, but since he or she works so closely with the worship leader, the position should be considered to be a part of the worship-leading team.

A PERSPECTIVE ON TEAM MINISTRY

Worship is not a performance, nor is it successful when only those on the platform experience a release in their own worship. A worship service is not successful until the entire congregation has known a release in the presence of God. The worship-leading team must constantly keep the right perspective of their role in the service and realize that they are there simply to inspire and lead the people in lifting high God's praises — not to monopolize the worship service.

The team must take care to bring the people with them. Though the team may be "all fired up" and ready to worship, the congregation as a whole probably has not been prepared to the same degree for worship. The team must start where the people are and bring them "up to the mountain of the Lord." The team does not "do its own thing" but reaches out to identify with the people, and then reaches out to the Lord, and by God's grace brings the two together.

The worship team is called of God to lead His people through the "gates of praise" (Isaiah 60:18) and into His presence. The team pioneers the way, and the people follow. " 'One who breaks open the way will go up before them; they will break through the gate [praise] and go out. Their king will pass through before them, the LORD at their head' " (Micah 2:13). This verse can be said to describe the function of the worship team, as it "breaks open the way" for the people to follow, with "the Lord at their head."

This does not "just happen." Thought and planning must go into each worship service to make it a time when people *do* move into the presence of God — which is the reason why we have a service in the first place. Planning a worship service is, therefore, an activity which cannot be emphasized too greatly.

CHAPTER 10

PLANNING THE WORSHIP SERVICE

The worship team will be successful only as all involved approach that ministry with seriousness. An equal amount of seriousness and diligence must go into the planning of a worship service. Without careful planning, our goals for congregational worship are not likely to be realized.

THE NEED FOR PLANNING

Most pastors spend many hours in preparing sermons each week, but give relatively little time to preparing the worship service. Churches that follow a liturgy supplied by their denomination may find themselves devoting very little time to the planning of worship, since the service is pre-planned for them. "Free" churches can also neglect the preparation of worship with the unspoken thought "I think we can 'wing it' again this Sunday just like we did last week." But if worship truly plays a highly strategic role in our services, we should place a commensurate amount of effort into its planning.

A certain tension exists between the poles of over-planning and under-planning. Both extremes are dangerous and are to be avoided. First among the pitfalls of over-planning is the tendency to become too bound to one's preplanned program. Should anything unexpected happen to introduce a complication into the direction of the service, we become very nervous because we are not prepared to change course. Suppose a prophecy about rejoicing comes forth when we had planned all our songs around the theme of repentance. Or suppose the pastor asks us to begin the service with a song that is totally out of keeping with our prepared list of songs. What would we do? If we are bound to our planning, situations like this can be very unsettling.

On one occasion I came to a worship service after spending a good deal of time in preparation, only to find that the pastor wanted to take the service in a totally different direction. It was necessary for me to be flexible enough to lay aside my preparation and flow with the desires of the pastoral leadership.

When we over-plan worship, we can easily become threatened by any change of direction initiated by the Holy Spirit. It is very easy to become so involved in one's program that no consideration whatsoever is given to whether the Spirit might want to interject an alternate course. Our list of songs can become a job description for the Holy Spirit: "You have the freedom to move sovereignly, Lord, in accordance with my agenda of songs." The Spirit-led worship leader must be prepared to mentally discard his song list and flow extemporaneously if the Spirit begins to move in the congregation. Services of human invention can easily become stereotyped and predictable. If too predictable, worship can become rote and meaningless.

Further, if worship is over-planned, we can place too much confidence in our preparation. We begin to believe that if we have spent enough time in the formulation of a song list, our preparation is adequate and complete. But the preparation of the worship leader has only begun once the song list is compiled. The most important aspect of our preparation involves prayer and the cultivation of a sensitivity to the Spirit. The first priority of the worship leader, and the most demanding, is spending time in personal prayer, praise, and worship.

If we do not properly understand our responsibility in worship, we can end up with over-planned worship. We tend to claim complete responsibility for the worship time, forgetting that our worship is completely dependent upon the Holy Spirit. We over-plan worship as though it were necessary to orchestrate a love session with God. The success of the worship service is not so dependent upon our clever planning as upon the moving of the Holy Spirit. If we truly understand that, we may spend less time planning worship and more time seeking God.

On the other hand, many worship leaders have been guilty of under-planning worship, shrugging off their laziness with platitudes such as "We just want to let the Lord have his way." The dangers of under-planning are readily evident. First of all, the service is likely to be aimless, without direction or purpose. When worship leaders have little advance direction, they are frequently prone to "go fishing" to find out what song the "fish" will "bite." Songs are thus introduced in a random and somewhat desperate manner in an attempt to find the song that will get the service off the ground. When several songs fall flat, the worship leader will likely resort to the number one song on the list of the recent "top ten" for that church. (Most worship leaders keep a mental note of the songs that are most likely to evince a positive response when the service begins to droop.) When that song in turn falls flat, the worship leader knows he is in trouble. It is time to pull back and "punt" (i.e., turn the service over to the pastor with a whispered gasp for help).

A second problem associated with under-planning is the tendency for the service to become disjointed or too informal. Too much informality can become distracting and disorderly, countercurrent to the biblical injunction that all things in worship be done "in a fitting and orderly way" (1 Corinthians 14:40). Another pitfall attending under-planning has become a veritable syndrome among worship leaders: without a written list of songs before him, a leader can get nervous and have his mind go blank. How terrifying it is when everything goes blank and the only song that comes to mind is "This Is the Day." Unplanned worship services are usually characterized not by a special sense of following the Spirit's direction but by unanointed, disjointed ramblings.

FINDING A BALANCE

We need a balance between preparation on the one hand and a continual sensitivity to the direction of the Spirit on the other. It is not uncommon for worship leaders to feel uncertain frequently about what direction to take the people during a worship time. They know the frustration of spending hours in prayerful preparation, only to find that they cannot seem to discern God's direction in the middle of worship. Worship leaders should be comforted to know that they are not alone in feeling this uncertainty, and that the problem is not always with them. It is not necessarily because they did not spend enough time in prayer or preparation — it is because God will purposefully keep them entirely dependent upon him.

Sometimes we feel like we are on the back of our heels, arms flailing, and we don't know whether to fall back or stand squarely with both feet firmly planted. God will repeatedly put us back on our heels so that we can be influenced one way or the other with a gentle breath of God's Spirit. If our feet are planted squarely and we know exactly where we are going in worship, chances are that we will plow ahead with our program and miss God. A sincere worship leader will frequently experience that sense of uncertainty, which is designed by God to keep us totally dependent upon him. When we lose that sense of total dependence upon the Lord and begin to get overly confident in our own abilities, God will bring along a "bad" worship service. He will sit in his holy heaven and design a divine disaster with our names on it, in order to keep us completely dependent upon him.

If this sounds too threatening — if we would rather know exactly where God is taking us every step of the way — then we should find a vocation other than worship-leading. Our churches are already loaded with enough songleaders who remain insensitive to the gentle voice of the Spirit. What we now need are worship leaders who are willing to forsake their human institutions of worship for the sake of following the Spirit of God.

A worship leader must come to the service prepared but then should remain open to any changes inspired by the Holy Spirit while the service is in progress. The changes the Holy Spirit would initiate, however, do not always include an alteration of the songs being sung. Worship leaders must be open to more than simply singing songs different from those that were preplanned. They must also be sensitive to discerning God's will in terms of the exercising of spiritual gifts. Does the Spirit want to bring forth a prophecy, or a word of knowledge, or an exhortation? Is it time to change gears and move into a season of prayer or of quiet contemplation? These sorts of activities cannot always be easily anticipated in advance of the service, and yet they are critical elements in the success of the worship service.

It is crucial that the worship leader be adequately prepared, and this should include the preparation of a list of possible songs to sing. But far more important than being prepared musically is being prepared spiritually. This preparation comes through time spent on our knees, through worship and prayer. The tendency of some is to spend thirty minutes selecting songs and five minutes asking God to bless that selection. We may need thirty minutes or more to choose our songs, but we should spend far more time than that in spiritual preparation. The spiritual preparation of the worship leader is much more than a Saturday evening or early Sunday morning phenomenon. The worship leader, like any pastor, must learn to cultivate a daily prayer life. Worship leaders need a level of spiritual sensitivity that comes only through a disciplined, daily devotional life.

GOD USES HUMAN LEADERSHIP

Finding — and maintaining — this balance should not be intimidating, for it is within the reach of every worship leader. It is God's design. He has chosen to move through human leadership. When God appoints a person to a ministry, he honors that by giving that person divine guidance. If God has called us to minister in leading worship, we should expect him to guide and help us.

We sometimes become distracted with such thoughts as "Maybe that was my own carnal thought just now — maybe that wasn't the mind of God at all. Am I really being led by the Spirit, or am I following human impulses?" I do not allow those kinds of thoughts to disturb me during the worship service. When I have an impulse to go a certain direction, I accept by faith that it is from God, and I act upon it with certainty. If I later realize it was not from God, I will then analyze my heart and motivations. But in the context of the worship service, by faith I act with certainty, knowing that God honors leaders and divinely directs them.

God honors human leadership to such an extent that we can make a big blunder and God will still honor our effort. God will not give a "word" to someone in the congregation to say that the leadership is missing God and we must take a different direction. Even if someone in leadership does need correction, that should be done in private, not in the context of the congregation. God does not embarrass his leaders. Even if someone had the sensitivity to know the leadership had missed God in the worship service, God would still expect that person to love and support and submit to the leadership. So worship leaders can relax — God will not "zap" them if they miss his direction. To the contrary, he will honor that leadership and give understanding so they can learn from their mistakes.

Leaders may tend to accommodate certain items in the agenda of the worship service because "the people expect (or like) it." It's not wrong to plan to include such elements in a service, but they can divert our hearts away from a posture of worship. Prayer and prayer requests can kill the anointing of a service if they are offered perfunctorily, out of habit. Testimonies can also break the flow of worship if we must fit in a few for the sake of custom. Special music can be anything but worship if we lower this activity to the level of entertainment or make it a time-filler. In many churches, the announcements and offering usually signal the people that the worship service is over and it is time for a change of position and pace. If announcements are habitually a distraction from worship, perhaps they can be given near the outset of the service. It may be that the items noted in the bulletin really do not need to be mentioned from the pulpit at all. Folks will get in the habit of reading the church bulletin if they realize that the notices listed in it will not be repeated from the pulpit and that if they don't read the bulletin, they simply will not be informed!

This is another facet of balance in planning — weighing out our activities for their value and contribution to the worship service. Each aspect of the worship service should be continually scrutinized, to assess the viability of maintaining that function. We must be careful that activities in the service do not come as interruptions to the worship but that if they are used, they are incorporated as further expressions of worship. We do them not for their own sake but for what they can add to the primary goal, which is to worship God.

A THEME FOR THE SERVICE

We have said much about preparation and sensitivity and balance in regard to the worship service. We know that there is no one right approach for each service, no formula that we can employ every time to produce what we want in that service. My preparation may be good and workable, but events may transpire in such a way that my preparation is not fitting for the moment. To illustrate, suppose a pastor would ask five excellent, experienced worship leaders to fast and pray all day before a service and come up with a worship format under the inspiration of the Spirit. I would venture to guess that there would be five completely different approaches, with different songs chosen, and a different theme in each approach. I would also guess that any one of those five approaches could be used for the service and it would work. Why? Because God is not so concerned about what songs we sing or the order in which we sing them — he is concerned about how and why we sing those songs, regardless of what they may be or how many of them we use.

While preparing for worship, perhaps some worship leaders have cried, "Oh, God, what's your will for Sunday morning? Should we start with 'Come and Let Us Go' or maybe 'Horse and Rider,' or should we try something slow? Or how about an anthem? Please, God, reveal to me your divine plan for this service!" God's answer to that prayer is "I really don't care *what* song you use — but whatever one you choose, open up your hearts to me! Rejoice before me! Let's enjoy one another!"

God is not that concerned whether we sing one song or twenty songs. What he desires is that we enter into the beautiful communion of worship, regardless of the song at hand. Sometimes we miss God by singing another song. God knows that at certain times we will not open up to him unless we get out of our rut of just singing one song after another. Even Scripture choruses can hinder us from opening up to God if they are sung just for the sake of maintaining a song service. Some worship leaders have the mistaken idea that the solution to any problem in worship is the right song. Not necessarily so! Sometimes the last thing we need is another song. If we insist on singing another song, God will allow us to go ahead, but his blessing and power will not be in it.

The worship leader should prayerfully prepare a list of songs for the service, but he should also remember that that list is not sacred, nor is that order of songs engraved in heaven. If a different direction emerges, go with it! But usually the leader ends up following his prepared list of songs fairly closely. There is nothing super-spiritual about the leader deviating from his list every week. In fact, such a tendency would not indicate spirituality on his part but rather an insensitivity to the Holy Spirit during the planning process. If he finds himself forsaking his prepared list on a regular basis, either God is fickle or the leader needs to develop spiritual sensitivity. And since the leader does depend upon the list, he needs to put substantial thought and prayer into its preparation.

PREPARING A SONG LIST

Before preparing a list of possible songs to sing in a service, I recommend that a leader first of all complete a master list of all the songs his church knows. This master list is an invaluable aid to planning worship. (Appendix 3 shows how to make a master list of songs.)

After a master list of songs is made, a leader must put together a list of songs for each individual service. Here is an approach to making a list of songs that I have used frequently with good success. I divide my list of possible songs into three categories: hymns, fast songs, and slow songs. The order in which these occur on my list will vary with each service.

I usually start my song selection by looking through the list of hymns we know, and I note one or two hymns that "jump out at me." Then I will turn to my master song list and write down the names of choruses (and their keys) that catch my attention, dividing them into fast and slow songs. I now have a skeleton of hymns and choruses that seem especially appropriate to me, and I will proceed to add some "meat to the bones."

If I have an urge to sing a song that is in the key of F, for instance, I will then scan the names of all the choruses in the key of F for other possibilities, writing those chosen below the first song selected. This procedure will be followed for each of the songs that first caught my attention, so that under each key selected I have several songs I can sing without having to stop and announce a key change to the musicians. Although this is the approach I usually follow, each leader must develop his or her own way of preparing a possible list of songs to sing.

Most leaders start the service with a fast chorus or hymn, although there are exceptions, of course. One thing to remember is to avoid a chorus-hymn-chorus-hymn format but to aim instead for choruses-hymns, or hymns-choruses, or sometimes hymn-choruses-hymn. The chorus-hymn-chorus-hymn pattern becomes a problem when people are using a hymnal and they set the hymnal down, only to pick it up, only to set it down again. That can disturb the flow of worship. (Some churches avoid that problem by displaying hymns on overhead transparencies.)

When planning worship, the leader should give consideration each time to new songs to be taught or songs that were introduced recently to the church. New songs are learned through repetition, so it is important to reinforce this week the song that was taught last week. The teaching of new songs should be planned strategically, along with the reinforcing of those just taught.

Once a song list for the service has been compiled, a copy should be given to those who need one, such as the musicians and the projectionist.

"How many songs?" is a good question. In most cases I operate by the philosophy of preparing more songs than I will ever need or use in one service. That gives me the flexibility of having several options at my disposal as the service progresses. I can either stay in the key at hand and sing one of several songs listed in that key and mood (fast or slow), or I can switch to another key and have several songs at my disposal in that particular key. However, "shifting gears" to another key can sometimes be a little awkward, so if the worship service is experiencing some rough waters, it can be helpful to stay in one key for a protracted period of time.

By preparing extra songs, I find that it is possible to plan two entirely different themes within the one song list. I might thus decide just before the service begins which of the two themes to use, or I may even change themes after the service has started if I perceive the need to do so.

A theme for the service is sometimes established in advance; for instance, on special occasions such as Christmas, Easter, or Thanksgiving, the theme is obvious ahead of time. But at other times the worship leader may not have any direction from the Spirit as to a certain theme or keynote prior to the service. At those times, a theme may begin to emerge in the context of the service as songs of similar focus are sung together, or as a prophetic utterance gives clear direction to the service, or as the Spirit gently speaks something to the leader's heart. If a theme begins to resound throughout the worship, the worship leader and the pastor should make every effort to reinforce what the Spirit is saying. Often it is appropriate to draw attention to and reiterate what the Spirit is saying and to elicit a congregational response to that word.

By asking the pastor the subject of his sermon, a worship leader can sometimes gain insight into a good direction for the worship. Usually it is difficult to plan an entire worship time around one specific sermon topic, but perhaps the last song of the worship time could be planned as a springboard for the message. Regardless of the sermon's subject matter, the pastor should be consulted to determine if he has suggestions or preferences for the worship service. Even if the pastor has little input, he will appreciate the willingness of the leader to consult him and honor his wishes.

Many worship services will come and go, though, without any one theme seeming to emerge as the keynote. This is not unusual, and it does not mean that the worship was less meaningful or less than ideal. It simply means that instead of having our minds on a specific subject or idea, we were simply devoting ourselves to loving the Lord and ministering to him. Some folks look so hard for a theme to emerge in a worship service that they miss seeing the Lord! We should not worry about finding a theme for the worship if one has not already been impressed upon our hearts. We should get caught up in the greatness of God, and if he wills to speak to us, that theme will become self-evident. It is nice if our songs can reinforce the pastor's message, but it is more important that they contribute to a release of worship in the people.

VARIETY IN THE SERVICE

Being creative in providing variety in worship is extremely important. If the worship leader becomes too predictable, the people will assume they know what is coming next; their attention will wane, their involvement will be halfhearted, and as a result they will gain little, if anything, from the service.

There are almost as many different forms of worship throughout the body of Christ as there are churches. Regardless of which form our church chooses to adopt, we all fight the tendency to turn our form into a "rut." Those with "free" churches accuse liturgical churches of not only being in a worship rut but even of condoning the rut. The liturgical brethren counter that most "free" churches have their own particular liturgy — it simply is not written out for each service. Whether or not we favor a liturgical worship service, we must all grapple with the problem of ruts in worship.

Ruts cause us to "coast" right through our worship services, and they do not demand that we remain alert contributors to the service. Here are ten "rut-detector" questions — checkpoints to help us diagnose a persistent rut problem.

1. During times of worship, have I become too conscious of things around me? We cannot and should not shut ourselves off from what is happening around us, and yet it is possible to be so involved with horizontal things that we become distracted from the true goal of our worship: the Lord. The primary focus of worship must always be God himself.

2. Does God rarely catch me by surprise while I am worshiping? God is full of surprises, but ruts are comfortably predictable. Nothing unexpected happens in a rut.

3. Is my repertoire of worship becoming stale? Can I sing the songs without thinking? If so, such songs have become the victims of "overkill" or "overfamiliarity." They may need to be placed on the shelf temporarily. Then when they are brought out again, their reintroduction can place fresh emphasis on the messages they carry.

4. Does my mind wander more than it should? Ruts do not require much mental concentration. The key problem in much of our worship is a lack of mental application. Many of us like that "oozy-woozy" feeling of worshiping in spirit, but Jesus also told us to worship in truth, and to worship in truth requires an exertion of the mind. The more actively we involve our minds in our worship, the more meaningful our worship will become.

5. Does worship at church bore me? Or when I look across the congregation, do others seem to be uninvolved or bored with the time of worship? If we are no longer challenged by the worship in our church, perhaps we need help out of a rut.

6. Do I boast of my ability to predict accurately what will happen next in the worship service? When worship becomes predictable, it is not because we have learned to "flow in the Spirit" but because we have found ourselves outside the genuine flow of the Spirit.

7. Are our services too smooth? Ruts are smooth. Someone has said that smooth services are usually the deepest spiritually. But what if we are in a rut? Most worship leaders and pastors are threatened by anything but "smooth" services, but many churches are smoothly coasting right past the Holy Spirit! Something dramatic and jarring must usually take place to help us wake up to the realities of our rut. And who likes to be jarred awake on Sunday morning?

8. Do I become unsettled by new approaches to wor-

ship? If a change in style of worship seems threatening, it may be that we are clinging to familiar patterns — we are dwelling in a rut and we need to climb out.

9. Is the time allotted to worship getting shorter and shorter? This is a deadly syndrome: less and less God-directed time to allow for more and more man-directed time, until God is finally squeezed out of the services conducted in his name. We might rationalize this syndrome by claiming that we are exerting better stewardship in the use of our service time, when in reality we are trying to minimize the amount of time wasted on what has become a meaningless activity. If we are in a rut, no one seems to feel deprived if the worship is cut short.

10. Do visitors have difficulty relating to the way our church worships? Ruts tend to become individualistic and ingrown — "our way of doing things" — and thus of little interest to outsiders. It is imperative that our worship patterns gain the interest of visitors if we are to remain an evangelistic community.

With some creative planning, we can provide variety in our services that will keep the people alert and their worship fresh. Here are some ideas which can be used as springboards for individual innovations:

1. Plan a unique opening for the worship service. Have everyone stand and shake hands with others. Read a Scripture. Begin with a prayer. Do not begin with a prayer. Suggest a theme for the worship. The opening portion of the service can make or break everything thereafter. Have you ever been in a worship service that got off to a bad start, and you knew it was going to be a long service? It is crucial that we give prayerful and careful thought to our opening. As a worship leader, I avoid being predictable. I will attempt to have a slightly different approach each time so that people will have to be attentive in order to follow.

2. Occasionally have the congregation sing without musical accompaniment.

3. Upon a preset cue, have the musicians raise the key

a half step or whole step for a certain verse or chorus. A higher pitch makes it easier for the people to sing the song with more volume, which brings the effect of added enthusiasm and energy.

4. Have half the congregation sing to the other half.

5. Ask the congregation to hum the tune while the musicians softly play through the song.

6. Provide a variety of positions: standing, kneeling, joining hands, and so forth.

7. Vary or even reverse the order of the service. One Sunday, start with the sermon and end with worship. That way we can respond in worship to the message with which God has challenged us from his word.

8. Lead worship from a different location. If worship is customarily led from behind the pulpit, consider changing that for a while. Perhaps the leader may want to move over by the pianist and lead worship while standing next to the piano. I once visited a church in New York City in which no one was visible on the platform at the beginning of the service except the pianist and organist. Suddenly from out of nowhere came the pastor's voice singing "He is all I need." His voice carried well over the P.A. system, and the congregation easily followed. I scanned the building where seventeen hundred people had gathered for the midweek prayer service, and I finally found the pastor standing in the front row, facing the platform and leading worship with a microphone in his hand. I knew nobody was watching him or paying any attention to him, because the people's hands and faces were raised and their hearts were centered totally on the Lord. Without standing before the people, and even without being on the platform, the pastor was able to effectively lead the people into worship in a way that gave glory to God.

9. Plan a complete worship service without any songs. The leader could encourage spontaneous singing, "free praise," times of quiet worship and meditation, or prayer. Who says we have to sing songs in order to worship?

10. Use songs with a variety of styles, rhythms, and moods. Occasionally add the spice of a song in the minor mode. Solomon once wrote, "If you find honey, eat just enough — too much of it, and you will vomit" (Proverbs 25:16). Have you ever heard someone describe a church's worship as "sweet"? "Sweet worship" is very nice, but we can get too much of anything sweet. There is room for much diversity in worship — from warfare to waiting, from shouting to silence, from exultation to exaltation.

The Lord's Supper is an essential part of our corporate worship, and leaders should not overlook the many creative ways it can be administered. The people can come forward and receive the body and blood of our Lord individually; they can be served in their seats; they can serve one another; special times of body ministry can be planned around the Eucharist. And the themes that can surround the breaking of bread are infinite. The Lord's Supper can be used to enhance and reinforce virtually any and every Christian theme with some creative application.

We can increase the significance of the breaking of bread by positioning its occurrence properly in the service. An entire worship service can be planned around the Communion table, with the Lord's Supper being the central focus of the worship. On some occasions the pastor and worship leader can flow together as a team, with the pastor overseeing the distribution of the elements and the worship leader guiding the singing. On other occasions, the timing and distribution of the Lord's Supper can come completely under the worship leader's direction and can be incorporated into the worship service when the time seems fitting.

Another area in which we can be very innovative is the singing of "spiritual songs" *(see* Ephesians 5:19; Colossians 3:16). Spiritual songs are spontaneous expressions of our spirit that are improvised in an unrehearsed, unpremeditated, "off the cuff" manner; they can be sung in a known or unknown tongue. While most churches enjoy a healthy diet of psalms and hymns, many of them seem reticent to venture into forms of spiritual songs. And yet this can be the most exciting of all three categories and can be explored almost endlessly if we will dare to be creative.

Spiritual songs can be incorporated during times of "free praise" (in typical charismatic style, this is sung to one sustained chord). We can direct the people to sing a *current* expression of their praise to God — that is, rather than just singing cliches such as "Praise the Lord" or "Glory to God," we could praise God because of what he has done for us this week, or worship him for that aspect of his character that is especially meaningful to us today. Our praise could thus sound like this: "Lord, I thank you for keeping me in good health this week when others on the job were sick" or "Father, I am awed today by your faithfulness, as I realize how your guiding hand was upon me yesterday in the car. . . ."

Since some people have difficulty being creative in worship or thinking of new things to say to the Lord, we can help them in that. One way to do so is to direct them to open their Bibles to a favorite psalm or other Scripture, and then throughout the worship service they can use that passage as a springboard for creative worship unto the Lord. This can be done in a similar way by using a hymnal rather than a Bible.

It is important that all of us become creatively personal in our worship. Suppose I were to come home to my wife every evening and begin pouring forth prosaic quotes from Shakespeare. She would probably soon stop me and say, "That's very nice of you, dear, to say those sweet things to me — but now, tell me how *you* feel about me!" To sing psalms and hymns unto God is good and right, but is it possible that sometimes God thinks we are merely reflecting "canned" expressions unto him? Perhaps God would sometimes say to us, "I'm so glad you feel that way about me, but I've been hearing those words a lot, ever since Charles Wesley wrote them. Now tell me — what do *you* think about me?" At such times it is fitting to offer up a spiritual song, a song directly from my heart, in my language, expressed in my own unique way unto the Lord.

Worship, in essence, is simply communing with God. These suggestions to become more creative in worship are not intended to encumber that simplicity. But too often we do not enter into the fullness of worship because we have become the victims of spiritual ruts and stale rituals. When we initiate a new style or approach or even sing a new song, it is not that the new style or approach or song is superior to the previous ones. It is simply that we are lazy creatures who must continually be stirred by something new, or else we settle down into easy chairs of complacency and comfort. Through creativity, we can kindle afresh our minds and hearts and find a new dynamic in our worship.

SING A NEW SONG!

We are given the repeated injunction in Scripture to "sing a new song to the Lord" *(see* Psalms 33:3; 40:3; 96:1; 98:1; 144:9; 149:1). By prompting us to sing a new song unto him, God has placed no limit on the creativity and innovation that we are free to apply to our approaches and expressions of worship.

However, we are not urged to sing a new song simply for the sake of novelty. New songs are beneficial because they keep us out of those ever-threatening ruts. When we are supplied with new words and a new tune to sing, there comes a sense of freshness and new enthusiasm. New songs can stoke an old fire, reviving the vitality of our worship.

New songs force us to think. They bring us to an awakened awareness in worship. The more mentally alert we are, the fuller our worship will be as a result.

New songs also expand our vocabulary of worship. They equip us with a wider variety of worshipful expressions. It is good to learn new songs with a different or unique theme. The ideas of a new song may be similar to ones we already know — in fact, sometimes a new song may be taken from exactly the same verse as a familiar one — and yet because of the different tune, we find a new spark igniting in our hearts. At other times a worship leader may become aware of the need to incorporate a song along a certain specific theme, and a search may ensue to find the right song. New songs help us address a wider sphere of themes in worship.

A final reason for singing new songs can be found in asking whether God has been speaking something new or specific to the church recently. If so, write a new song about it! This will be highly meaningful to the people as they respond in song to that which has been the focal point of recent gatherings, and that truth will be impressed more profoundly in their minds and hearts as they repeat it in song.

Worship leaders should be continually on the lookout for new songs that will be strong additions to their repertoire of worship tunes. Many churches and organizations are producing worship cassettes that contain a wealth of new material. (Appendix 1 contains a list of the addresses of many organizations and churches that have produced praise and worship cassettes.)

WRITING NEW SONGS

The first question many musical people ask is how they might begin to write new choruses of praise and worship to be used by their own church. An increasing number of individuals are stepping out in this dimension of songwriting, and many churches have incorporated these songs into their repertoire. If people in our congregations are able to write new choruses, such songs will genuinely reflect the uniqueness of our particular church and the freshness of what God has been saying to our church body. Furthermore, the congregation will find great meaning in personally knowing the authors of many of the songs they enjoy.

Since many church musicians have a desire to write worship songs, the following comments are directed to potential songwriters who are looking for some helpful tips.

There are four general steps in the creative process: preparation, incubation, illumination, and verification.

At the *preparation* stage of songwriting, a person enthusiastically collects ideas and materials. Songwriters must search for good song materials even as preachers continually stay on the alert for good sermon topics or illustrations. A songwriter will glean ideas from any number of sources: a Scripture, a sermon, a book, the newspaper, a TV commercial, a conversation or comment, and many other places. Once something comes to mind that sounds like a good idea for a song, *write it down!* Maybe it is just a phrase or even a single word, but make a permanent note of it. Maintain a songwriting folder in which are kept all such thoughts and inspirations. This could even include some melodic ideas that have come to mind but which as yet have no accompanying words. Most of the things collected in this manner will never be used again, but the entire process becomes worth the effort if just one idea explodes into a success.

During the *incubation* time, there is a shift from the conscious to the unconscious. An idea may have come, but during this time it is almost forgotten as one becomes involved in the other matters of life. This is considered to be the most important phase in the songwriting process because the original idea is given time to incubate or "gel."

When *illumination* comes, suddenly something "clicks." Inspiration flows. Words and music quickly come together. A feeling of certainty and joy rises up, for a song is coming alive.

During the final stage of songwriting — *revision and verification* — the original song undergoes critical analysis. Entire phrases may be reworded; chords may be altered and the melody line smoothed out here and there. The final work is put on paper. At this point the author may solicit the opinions of others.

Some songwriters work on inspiration alone, while others find that songwriting is a discipline of mind. Sammy Cahn, one of America's great pop-song writers, says it is not inspiration but pressure which produces "hits." Cahn, with four Oscars, an Emmy, and more than fifty hit classics to his credit, was once asked, "Which comes first, words or music?" He replied, "Neither. It's the phone call from a producer who wants a great song, preferably a hit. It isn't easy."

Although inspiration does play a role in songwriting (and should never be downplayed by those who want to write worship songs), there are many basic concepts and principles that can be applied to the writing of a song. If these concepts are mastered, it is very possible to write a song on willpower alone. The final test of a song, however, is in its reception. If it becomes a "hit," the songwriter feels successful.

Some readers may have a mental block against writing Christian songs of worship that are "hits." But we have many hits in charismatic and pentecostal circles — songs that have gained wide acclaim as being meaningful and enjoyable to sing. Songs do not become hits accidentally. There are many reasons why certain songs become internationally known, while others do not make it out the back door. The following principles are followed 99 percent of the time in the writing of successful songs; a songwriter should analyze his or her songs according to these principles.

Singability: Is the song easy and fun to sing? The rhythms should not be too difficult — avoid intricate syncopation. The melody should be comprised mainly of small intervals between successive notes, and it should flow smoothly.

Melodic character: Is the melody not only easy to sing, but is there something attractive and catchy about it? Is the melody one that sticks in a person's mind throughout the day? Play the melody for other people to see if they like it. Does the melody interact smoothly with the chords? Are the chord changes smooth and stimulating? Is there a sense of finality at the end of the song?

Message: Does the song have something to say? And does the music have content as well — that is, is the music meaningful, or is it trite? We must ask if the words and music have content apart from each other, but then we must analyze how the words and music flow together to communicate one message. Strive for a "marriage" between words and music so that the mood of the music matches the temperament of the words. Generally, low points in the melody should coincide with the least important words and phrases, whereas high notes in the melody should be used to reinforce those words and phrases that warrant emphasis. Special care should be given to the highest note of the song. The highest note in the melody should coincide with the word or phrase that is most critical to the song. Furthermore, there is a certain songwriting principle that must be obeyed if a song is to be successful: say only one thing. A good song will have a single concept. Most hits can be summarized in one word or one key phrase. And the main theme of a good song is not hard to spot! If the song covers everything from the cross to the second coming of Christ, it will never be effective. The song should be confined to one specific theme, which is then reinforced over and over in the lyrics.

Words: Use familiar phrases, expressions, and terms, but not hackneyed cliches. Select stimulating words that evoke strong mental images. If two words can be used to say the same thing, choose the more colorful word.

Repetition: A good song will incorporate a lot of repetition in both the words and the music. Most songs have what has been termed a "hook" — a short phrase that catches the listener's attention, around which the entire song is built. Sometimes the hook is the first idea to come to a songwriter. Once the hook is established, the heart and life of a song are present; all that remains is to add flesh to the bones. A melody line should contain a good deal of repetition. Certain "melodic figures" can be repeated over and over at varying pitches. And there should be a good deal of repetition in the chordal structure of the song. A good chord progression should be used again and again. Some songwriters, trying to be overly creative, introduce too many musical ideas into a song. Keep the song simple, while repeating many of the words, melodies, and chords that are the most attractive.

Rhythm: The words must line up with the meter of a song. The emphasized syllables of a word always occur on a strong beat ("downbeat"). Key words should also occur on strong beats. With a 4/4 time signature, the strong beats are beats one and three, with the first beat being the strongest. With a 3/4 time signature, the first beat is strong and the other two beats are weak. In the following example, the italicized words should coincide with the strong beats if this were in a song: "the *name* of the *Lord* is to be *praised*."

One must determine the key in which a song should be sung. Some churches pitch their choruses low because people find it easier to sing lower in their ranges. However, when a song is pitched toward the higher end of the average person's range, people are able to sing out more loudly and thereby feel as if they are putting their hearts more fully into the song. For that reason, I prefer to put most songs in the higher spectrum of the voice range, using the following guidelines: the lowest note in the melody should not go below a C and never below a B-flat. The highest note of the song should not go above an E-flat and never above an F. Generally, find a key that places the major portion of the song halfway between these two extremes, where the highest note of the song is close to a D or an E-flat. Following these guidelines will place most songs in a range where most people can sing them with enthusiasm and energy and without straining. There are two exceptions to these guidelines: songs that are prayerful and contemplative maintain a sense of serenity or sobriety when pitched a little lower than normal; also, when I am leading an early morning time of worship, I will drop the key of each song a step or two, to allow for the fact that people's voices are still a bit groggy.

As a point of information, a songwriter deciding to copyright a song should write to United States Copyright Office, Library of Congress, Washington, D.C. 20559, and ask for "Form PA." The songwriter should complete the form, enclose a copy of the song (either on paper or recorded on cassette), include ten dollars, and send everything to the copyright office. Though procuring a copyright is of very little value to a beginning songwriter, the value of holding a copyright on a song is basically twofold: the song is protected from being slightly altered by others because there is proof of authorship of the original version; second, the songwriter has the legal right to receive royalties for any duplication of the song by other parties.

TEACHING NEW SONGS

By frequently teaching new songs to a congregation, a worship leader can help the people to become excited about learning new songs. But as a rule, people do not enjoy learning new songs. This process requires energy and thought, and it is generally assumed that church is the place to conserve on these commodities. Leadership must be careful not to cater to such tendencies. Some initial resistance is to be expected when a new song is taught, but sticking with it will produce some very positive results.

Here are some suggestions for teaching new songs:

1. Use visual aids to teach new choruses — an overhead projector, or a bulletin insert containing the words, or some other method. (An exception might be a song with very simple words — for example, "Alleluia" — for printed words could then actually serve as a hindrance to the learning of the song.)

2. Be sure that those teaching the song and the instrumentalists accompanying it thoroughly know the song in advance.

3. The choir might learn the song first and in turn teach it to the congregation. The song might be sung first as a call to worship and then subsequently taught to everyone.

4. Have a definite plan for learning new hymns and choruses. Some churches teach a "hymn of the month."

5. Do not spend too much time on a new song during its first learning — that may kill interest in it. Go over the song a few times and then move on. Come back to the song the following week and continue to reinforce it periodically until it is quite familiar. And do not be discouraged if a new song does not "take" the first time. Some songs will need to be repeated a few times before the people really catch on to them. But once they have a song, they will not let go.

6. On the other hand, be willing to drop a new song if it is obviously not going anywhere. Not every song will be meaningful or suitable for every congregation.

7. Be very careful about timing when teaching new songs. If introduced at the wrong time in the service, the song can appear to puncture a hole in what seemed to be a good service. When a new song is first introduced, people have to take their hearts off the Lord and place their concentration on the process of learning a new tune. While working on the mechanics of memorizing a new melody line, the people can easily feel as though the spiritual intensity of the service has suddenly disintegrated, and the new song becomes suspect. My suggestion: introduce a new song early in the service and plan to follow it with a well-known song that will get the service off the ground. In this way, the new song will not acquire the association of being a "loser."

8. If the leader's goal is to teach new hymns, a careful look through the hymnal will usually reveal some good hymns that are unknown to his or her particular church. If not, maybe it is time to purchase a new set of hymnals and

donate the old ones to a pioneer church or a mission.

9. Do not try to teach more than two or three new choruses per month, on the average, or the people will not get a good grip on any of them. Furthermore, they will quickly tire of learning new songs if that is all they seem to be doing.

ENHANCING ELEMENTS

By this point we've covered a lot of ground, and the typical worship leader may be groaning to himself, "What next?! There are so many elements in a worship service — how can I possibly get everything to go smoothly?" We already know that when the Spirit is in charge, things do go smoothly; we also know that sometimes God deliberately lets things be "rough." But apart from that, there are some things — we could even call them "mechanical" elements — that a worship leader can use to help smooth out some of the little bumps and keep small problems from becoming big ones. We think of them as "natural," but they do provide spiritual enhancement because they facilitate the flow of the service.

One of these elements is *visual contact* between the worship leader and the key musicians. Visual contact ensures musical unity and so is critical at the following points:

1. After the introduction (if one is played), when the song is about to begin. The worship leader may initiate a tempo different from the one started by the musicians.

2. At the end of each chorus. The worship leader may want to pause and say something, or he may want to go right on into the next verse with no interruption.

3. At frequent points throughout the song. It can be very frustrating if the worship leader is trying to communicate something to a group of musicians whose heads are buried in their music, whose eyes are closed, or whose attention is totally taken up in the playing of their instruments. Musicians should not become oblivious to the rest of the world while playing; they must remain highly aware of everything around them.

4. At the end of the song. The worship leader may want to repeat the song, move directly into another song, change keys, stop singing altogether, or incorporate a slow finish. Visual contact with the worship leader is very crucial at this point, for it is here that the musicians can most easily miss some nuance of change in the leader's direction.

In conjunction with this visual contact, a *set of signals* for leader/musician communication is another key element. When mastered and used well, these signals contribute greatly to the flow of music and worship. Some signals that are very helpful are used to indicate the following:

1. The desired key for the song (the number of flats or sharps). The leader simply holds out the appropriate number of fingers. Usually, fingers pointing up indicate sharps; fingers pointing down indicate flats. (Curving thumb and forefinger into a C shape obviously means "key of C.") To illustrate, the worship leader can inconspicuously show the pianist two fingers pointing upward, meaning "Give me the key of two sharps." The pianist then hits a D chord, and the worship leader can start a totally new song in an entirely different key without saying a word.

2. Raising the key of the song. Often it is desirable to raise the key a half or a whole step before the chorus is repeated, as the higher key brings a sense of greater vitality to the singing. A simple "thumbs up" could suffice for this sign. This may need to be rehearsed with the musicians so that the transition is not jerky.

3. A change in volume (louder or softer). A palm up or down could communicate the leader's desire for the choir to sing more loudly, or the musicians to play more quietly, and so on.

The matter of volume is a very important one. It is an area in which the instrumentalists, especially, must be keenly aware of the tenor of the service and the desires of the worship leader and watch for the leader's signals. All of the instruments have the potential for "standing out" or being distracting at certain points during the worship service. Each instrumentalist must exert sensitivity to support and encourage the flow of worship, rather than demonstrate his or her musical prowess at the expense of worship. Drummers, as a rule, need to be very sensitive in their playing. Many elderly (and not-so-elderly) folks will be quickly turned off by drumming that is too flamboyant or too dominating. Certain majestic hymns, for example, can be ruined by the drummer who must always play. With certain other songs, however, a skillful drummer can contribute a unique, lively touch. Horn players, because of the resonance of their instruments, also have the potential to stand out or be distracting. But given the right context, they can sound forth brilliantly to augment the glorious praises on the heights of Zion. Those instruments whose sounds carry the most loudly (like trumpets, saxophones, and tambourines) must be especially careful not to be overbearing or distracting. This is frequently difficult for the individual musician to discern, so a discreet signal from the worship leader can be an enormous help in keeping the music in balance.

4. A cessation in the music. Sometimes the leader will want the musicians to stop playing altogether, and a sideways motion of the hands can convey this to them.

5. A repetition of the chorus. The leader can show this by simply rotating his pointing finger. This signal can prevent some rather awkward situations. The worship leader can be frustrated when he wants to repeat the chorus at the same tempo, but the pianist thinks he wants to stop and plays a ritard that brings the song to a grinding halt. There stands the leader, mouth open, ready to sing the song again, but the music has stopped! A simple signal with the finger could have told the pianist to keep the music going.

6. A change in tempo (speed up or slow down). This is probably the trickiest of all, for though it may be easy to give a recognizable signal to speed up or slow down the tempo, it is quite another thing to actually do it. How much faster or slower should the tempo be? Which instrument will lead out with the new tempo? Changing the tempo in

the middle of a song is like a large ship trying to make a U-turn midstream. It is often easier to stop the song in its tracks and start anew at a different tempo. But sometimes a series of "quick" or "slow" hand movements will let the musicians know that the change is desired, and sometimes a song lends itself to such a change.

Among themselves, musicians can also use a set of signals to indicate which chords are being played as a song progresses. (These chordal hand signs are discussed in Appendix 2.)

Some churches use a *prelude* and *postlude* to enhance their worship services. Many have found a prelude — a variety of musical selections played by appointed musicians immediately before the service begins — to be effective in preparing people's hearts and minds for worship. The musicians should be sensitive to play music in keeping with the mood of the occasion. Oftentimes happy, up-tempo music is appropriate, and at other times soothing and melodious music should be played while people enter the sanctuary. The prelude often sets the tone for the remainder of the service.

A postlude fulfills a function similar to that of a prelude, except that it is played at the close of the service while the people exit the building. The postlude attempts to cover the disturbance of those leaving and provides an atmosphere conducive to meditation, prayer, and seeking God. Contemplative, worshipful, commitment-oriented songs are in order. This is not the time to display improvisational finesse. The style should be transparent, not drawing undue attention to the instrumentalist. Musical sloppiness can be avoided by having only one instrumentalist playing. In many altar call contexts, it is desirable to have an instrumentalist playing as long as people are still gathered in prayer. If one musician must leave, perhaps another could take over. Playing during altar services is not simply a matter of providing background music; it is in fact a meaningful form of ministry to those praying, and often it is not given enough consideration by musicians and leaders.

A genuinely "mechanical" element which also aids musical worship is an *overhead projector*. Many charismatic and pentecostal churches facilitate worship by projecting the lyrics of the songs they sing onto a large screen near the front of the auditorium (or onto a front wall). This system has worked so well for so many that most churches using contemporary choruses employ this method to reproduce the words of the songs for their people.

Some of the benefits of using an overhead projector during worship are that it keeps people's heads out of a songbook; it frees people from having to pick up and put down a hymnal; it keeps all eyes forward, toward the leader, so leading is facilitated; it makes choruses much more meaningful to visitors when the words are there in front of them. The use of overhead projectors in worship has contributed greatly to liberating people in praise, because instead of looking down into a book, they are looking up at the words, automatically providing them with a posture of openness. The projectors have also greatly enhanced the teaching of new choruses.

The use of a projector, however, is not without drawbacks. One major problem with the use of an overhead projector is its potential to be a distraction to worship. An "overhead syndrome" has developed in charismatic circles wherein our people will gaze faithfully at the projected words long after they have learned the song. They are distracted from worship because their attention is on the screen, not on the Lord. Thus the thing that was intended to be an aid to worship has in fact become counterproductive to its own purpose.

I am not suggesting that we discard our overhead projectors! Instead, we can talk to our people about this tendency and warn them against it. Second, we can instruct our projectionist to notice when the people are looking at the words merely out of habit and to turn off the projector at that point. The timing of when to turn the projector off would vary depending upon how well the people know the song and how many visitors may be present. Also, placing the screen off to one side may help keep it from being the center of focus.

Some churches have handled this problem by using a superior (though more expensive) method. Rather than using an overhead projector, a number of churches are now using a slide projector with a zoom lens that allows the projector to be placed at the rear of the sanctuary or in the front row of the balcony. The song lyrics are typed on white paper and then photographed with a good camera, using a special film; the image is inverted so that the slides have white lettering on a black background. The screen thus remains darkened except for the white lettering that is projected. This makes the projected image far less imposing and reduces the problem of the projection being a visual distraction. I know of one church that has a computerized system that automatically turns the slide carousel to the correct slide simply at the push of the right buttons. In another church, the projector is operated via a remote control unit at the fingertips of the pianist. This remote unit has controls that enables the pianist/worship leader to select any slide, and the projector at the back of the building automatically displays the desired slide. The major difficulty with this type of system is the additional cost of the equipment, but for many churches the advantages have made it a feasible purchase.

As we've pointed out, any of these external elements can help or hinder — or perhaps even help *and* hinder! Anything in the service is a potential distraction or hindrance, but it need not materialize into a problem. Our attitude toward the purpose and use of such elements will keep them in their proper role as tools to further the ministry of the Spirit in our midst. After all, that's what practical application of concepts is all about.

WITH A LOOK TO THE FUTURE . . .

Now that we've "walked the land" and seen the fruit — and the giants — it's time to put everything into perspective. Where do we go from here? How do we start? What should be our priorities as pastors and worship leaders? Answers to such questions must be determined in our own hearts by the Spirit of God in the light of his call upon us and what he has quickened to us.

Changes begin with leadership and filter through to the people. The principles in this book should be allowed to challenge our personal lives. God wants to start by turning church leaders into worshipers. When we as leaders begin to live the life of worship, our people will follow.

We must also give immediate attention to the relationship between pastor and worship leader. So long as differences in values or philosophy exist between these two, or an impasse in communication presides, congregational worship will continue to be hampered by frustration and stagnation. A team spirit must begin with the pastor and worship leader. When that relationship is in order, it is vital to impart a team mentality to the musicians and/or singers presently functioning. To the best of our ability we must build a team from the potential at our disposal, sharing the ministry of worship among a group of dedicated worshipers.

Once a worship team begins to function, we must meet with the team regularly for prayer and the sharing of our spiritual vision. We can begin to talk about our goals for the worship services. Specific services can be discussed, with united prayer offered for a fuller release in the people. Ideas stimulated from the Scriptures and cassettes or books on worship should be explored, with specific ideas of implementation examined. We will profit greatly from the strength of a nucleus that is committed to seeing God's will fulfilled in our corporate worship.

Our constant pursuit of God and his purposes should ever cause us to ask for divine guidance and wisdom to know how and where to lead the people with whom he has entrusted us. Thus we can embark on the glorious and exciting adventure of exploring the uncharted territories of praise and worship that God intends to reveal to his church in the momentous days just ahead.

SOURCES FOR NEW CHORUSES

Cassettes of Worship Choruses

Hosanna! Music
Integrity Communications
P.O. Box Z
Mobile, AL 36616

> *As of this writing, this organization is producing a new worship tape every two months. Both the selection of songs and the musical quality are very good, and each tape includes a printed insert with the words of the songs. These tapes have received rave reviews.*

Starpraise Ministries
Bible Temple
7600 N.E. Glisan St.
Portland, OR 97213
1-800-237-8707

> *Starpraise offers legal use of overhead transparencies and slides, sends out new songs on a quarterly basis, and provides a vehicle for members to introduce their original songs to other members.*

"Music Resource Packet"
The Church on the Way
14300 Sherman Way
Van Nuys, CA 91405-2499

> *This ministry has initiated a program of sending out a music resource packet on a periodic basis. Each packet*

includes a cassette with seven to ten new choruses, one to three hymns, and an occasional band or choral arrangement.

Maranatha! Music
P.O. Box 1396
Costa Mesa, CA 92626
1-800-245-SONG

The praise music produced by this organization has literally circled the globe. Maranatha! also sells overhead transparencies of many songs for which they own copyrights.

"Sounds of Zion"
Zion Evangelistic Temple
700 E. Elmwood
Clawson, MI 48017

As of this writing, this church has produced three very enjoyable recordings of worship choruses. Most of the songs have been written by church members; the main contributor is Daniel Gardner, the minister of music.

Christ for the Nations Tapes
P.O. Box 24910
Dallas, TX 75224

CFN has produced many chorus tapes in recent years, averaging about one new tape per year. This has been a favorite source of new choruses for many churches.

ZionSong Ministries
P.O. Box 2388
Melbourne, FL 32902
(305) 676-3681

This ministry is seeking to circulate new worship choruses throughout the body of Christ as new songs sur-

> *face. With the subscription fee, members receive period-
> ic packets with a cassette and written music, together
> with permission to make overhead transparencies of all
> the songs they produce.*

The following churches and organizations have produced
chorus tapes which are available to the public:

Grace Fellowship
9610 Garnett St.
Tulsa, OK 74012

Lakewood Church
Liberty Rd.
Houston, TX 77029

Evangel Temple
610 Rhode Island Ave., N.E.
Washington, DC 20002

Harvester Booksellers
P.O. Box 371284
Decatur, GA 30037
     ("Kingdom Choruses I-IV")

Grace World Outreach Center
2695 Creve Coeur Mill Rd.
Maryland Heights, MO 63043

People of Destiny International
P.O. Box 2335
Wheaton, MD 20902

Tape Dept.
Elim Bible Institute
7245 College St.
Lima, NY 14485

Vineyard Ministries International
P.O. Box 1359
Placentia, CA 92670
1-800-824-6547

Victory Christian Center
P.O. Box 470016
Tulsa, OK 74147-0016

Mel Bay Publications, Inc.
#4 Industrial Dr.
Pacific, MO 63069-0066
1-800-325-9518

St. Luke Tapes
3636 Yellow Creek Rd.
Akron, OH 44313

Master Song Music
Shady Grove Church
1829 W. Shady Grove Rd.
Grand Prairie, TX 75050

Campus Crusade/International School of Theology
2045 S. Harbor
Anaheim, CA 92802

Tribute Productions
YWAM Hong Kong
10 Barrett Road
Hong Kong, ASIA

Songbooks

Praise Chorus Book
Maranatha! Music
P.O. Box 1396
Costa Mesa, CA 92626

The Fisherfolk Series
Mel Bay Publications, Inc
P.O. Box 66, #4 Industrial Dr.
Pacific, MO 63069-0066

Songs of Praise
Servant Publications
P.O. Box 8617
Ann Arbor, MI 48107

Songs and Creations
P.O. Box 6018
Evanston, IL 60204

Scripture in Song
P.O. Box 525
Lewiston, NY 14092
1-800-263-7296

> *Scripture in Song also features "Overhead Transparency Masters," which give the purchaser permission to make transparencies of the songs they represent.*

ZionSong Ministries
P.O. Box 2388
Melbourne, FL 32902

Melody Music
Gospel Publishing House
1445 Boonville Avenue
Springfield, MO 65802

Music Service — MSN-138
127 9th Ave. North
Nashville, TN 37234
1-800-368-7421

Other Aids

Transparencies for some hymns can be purchased from:

Lillenas Publishing Co.
Box 527
Kansas City, MO 64141

Chorus transparencies are also available through:

Hawks Nest
503 Verwood Ct.
Indianapolis, IN 46234
(317) 271-1484

> *Hawks Nest produces worship choruses on slides or
> overhead transparencies. Chorus books and cassettes
> are also available, as well as orchestral arrangements
> for many choruses.*

Phil Barfoot Music Company
P.O. Box 5867
Pasadena, CA 91107

> *This company produces worship choruses on color
> slides with picturesque backdrops.*

Resource Christian Music
2265 Westwood Blvd. No. 135
Los Angeles, CA 90064
(213) 838-4276

Since ready-made transparencies are not abundant, and
since most churches obviously make their own transparencies (using as sources various tapes, songbooks, and so on,
such as those listed here), we need to consider the copyright
ramifications involved. The controversy over how the current copyright laws affect church worship continues strongly as of this writing. There is no question that it is illegal to
photocopy copyrighted music without the consent of the
copyright holder. But this has not been the controversial
subject. The problem has surrounded the use of overhead
transparencies. Many churches no longer use hymnals but
use an overhead projector to display all their songs on a
screen or wall at the front of the sanctuary. As new choruses are learned, the words are handwritten or sometimes
photocopied on a transparency sheet, which is kept on file
for future use. Depending on one's interpretation of the
copyright laws, this practice can be considered illegal. The

projecting of the words in a public place is not a violation of law, but the violation allegedly takes place at the actual writing (or copying) of the words onto the transparency. The poetic order of the words is what has been copyrighted, and to reproduce those words in any fashion without proper permission is considered a violation of copyright law.

Christian publishing companies are desperately trying to convince churches to seek written permission before making up overhead transparencies. They are pushing this so strongly because they usually charge from fifteen to twenty-five dollars per song, per transparency, and sometimes this is an annual fee. Because of their desire to make a living, publishing companies have often been tagged the "bad guys." I once saw a cartoon that pictured these sentiments; it showed a young man about to sing a song in church, and the caption read, "I'd like to share a song with you that the Lord gave me a year ago . . . and even though he did give it to me, any reproduction of this song in any form without my written consent will constitute infringement of copyright laws, which grants me the right to sue the pants off you . . . praise God. . . ." But remember that these publishing companies formerly made their money by incorporating the royalties for songs into the cost of hymnals. Few charismatic churches are currently purchasing hymnals, and the publishing companies are feeling the pinch. By making transparencies, churches are able to circumvent totally the paying of royalties to those who own legal rights over the choruses and songs.

Churches, on the other hand, are extremely reticent to pay publishers a royalty charge for making up transparencies, and usually for good reasons. Rarely is it that churches are stingy or unwilling to do right by those owning the copyrights. But the process of finding the publishers who own rights to the choruses each church sings is tedious and in many cases virtually impossible. It is insufficient simply to notify publishers in writing of the song titles sung in the church, because there are many duplicate titles. Publishers need the transcribed melody and words of a song in order to identify the song as theirs. Even if a church manages to contact the publisher of a certain song, the paperwork can take weeks to complete, and the church is frustrated over its inability to make a transparency for that song in the interim. The cost of postage, the photocopying of letters and forms, the extensive secretarial time required, and then the payment of the royalty fees, all add up to a mouthful too big for most churches to chew.

What is the answer? In my opinion, the publishing companies and churches must take a step toward each other. The publishing companies can do this by marketing preprinted transparencies of those songs for which they own copyrights. Some publishers are beginning to do this *(see* "Sing a Song in Harmony With Copyright," by Robert A. Johnson, *Ministries Today* Magazine, Nov./Dec. 1986, p. 35). Churches can help publishing companies by willingly buying preprinted transparencies when available. Churches can also show their integrity by donating money to those publishing companies they have knowingly slighted in the past or whose materials they have been privileged to use without acknowledgement in the form of remunerative thanks.

Publishing companies deserve their royalties. Not only are they legally entitled to them; they need those monies in order to survive. And their survival is a blessing to the church. Without these companies, our sources of new songs of praise and worship would be significantly reduced. We have benefited from these publishing companies for so many years, and we would do them and ourselves a big favor by doing our utmost to support them continually with our finances.

For a better understanding of the ramifications of this copyright dilemma, I suggest the following material:

"Copyright: The United States Copyright Law, A Guide for Church Musicians." This pamphlet is available from Church Music Publishers Association, Box 4329, Washington, DC 20012.

"Circular R1: Copyright Basics," is available from the Copyright Office, Library of Congress, Washington, DC 20559.

"Hitting Sour Notes: The Clash." This article, a very provocative and educational discussion of the issues involved, appeared in the September 16, 1983 issue of *Christianity Today*.

CHORD PROGRESSIONS IN WORSHIP

As we discussed the prophetic song and the singing of "spiritual songs" unto the Lord, we noted that the customary charismatic form is to sing to one sustained chord. However, there is another musical form that easily lends itself to this singing of one's own song unto the Lord; it involves the use of chord progressions that are repeated by the musicians, while the congregation sings simultaneously. In this musical form, a short, simple chord progression is played on the instruments, and the congregation can sing along with the chord progression, improvising their own tune and words unto the Lord. Once a set chord progression is initiated, it is not changed midstream but is continued unchanged so that all the musicians and singers can be sure of what will continue to happen.

This is just one musical step beyond the common charismatic practice of singing to one sustained chord. This approach incorporates two new musical ideas: chord changes and rhythm. The potential for variety in singing to chord progressions is much greater than in singing simply to one sustained chord. And when there are greater possibilities of musical variety, there is usually more potential for variety and creativity in our expressions of worship.

Chord progressions readily enhance the flow of prophetic song, for they provide a chordal base from which a prophetic song can spring. When no music is being played, or when just one chord is being sustained, prophetic songs can sound drab or weak. But when sung in conjunction with a chord progression, a prophetic or spiritual song comes alive. The musical and rhythmic variety of the chord progression allows the singer to improvise a melody that can be created extemporaneously to fit the mood and content of the prophetic song.

The beauty of this musical form cannot be appreciated simply by reading about it; it must be experienced first-hand. Many charismatic and pentecostal churches are now incorporating the use of chord progressions into their worship.

Here is an illustration of how a chord progression could feasibly be introduced in a worship service. Suppose the musicians have been playing in the key of C. As the people wait upon the Lord in worship, the pianist feels prompted to begin a chord progression. He or she might play a progression something like this: C→A minor→D minor 7→G7. There are four chords in this progression, and each chord can be given four beats. The entire progression would thus take sixteen beats, or four measures, and then would repeat over and over. Try playing this progression on a piano or guitar to see how it sounds. Then try improvising your own tune and words to this progression, and you will begin to understand how this works.

As the congregation begins to move in this expression, each individual will sing his own unique melody, but since his melody will be in keeping with the chords being played, all the melodies will join together to sound like one mass choir with eight or more different parts being sung. Imagine what a beautiful sound an average congregation can produce with this method!

Let us review the four major types of chord progressions that occur most frequently in all styles of music.

The first, and most common, type of chord progression follows the "circle of keys" or "circle of fifths." (If you are unfamiliar with this "circle," buy a music theory book and study this concept, as it is foundational to an understanding of chord progressions.) Essentially, this "circle" concept means that each chord resolves into another chord until all the chords have been played, and one has circled back to the in-

itial chord. From a C chord, the progression goes as follows:
$C \rightarrow F \rightarrow B^b \rightarrow E^b \rightarrow A^b \rightarrow D^b \rightarrow G^b/F^\# \rightarrow B \rightarrow E \rightarrow A \rightarrow D \rightarrow G \rightarrow C$.
The circle is drawn as follows:

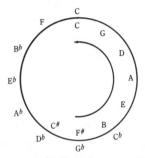

Notice that the arrow, pointing in a counterclockwise direction, indicates the direction of resolution from one chord to the next.

Let us look again at the chord progression given as an illustration and see how it follows this "circle." The progression was C→A minor→D minor 7→G7. When the progression went from the C chord to the A minor chord, from the A minor onward the progression resolved back to the C chord via the circle. Look at the circle: An A chord will resolve to a D chord; a D chord will resolve to a G chord; a G chord will resolve to a C chord. In the progression from one chord to the next, each successive chord could conceivably occur in any number of configurations — as a major chord, a minor chord, a seventh chord, and so on.

A second type of chord progression moves in the opposite direction of the circle of keys. For example, in the key of C, the progression is C→B^b→F→C. Notice that when we move from B^b to F and then from F to C, we are moving in a direction opposite from the circle of keys. C normally resolves to F, and F normally resolves to B^b. This type of chord progression can be used very effectively from time to time, although it is almost always limited to the example just given. In music theory terms, this is equivalent to the "I chord" resolving to the "flatted VII chord," to the

"IV chord," and finally back to the "I chord."

A third type of chord progression has been given names such as "pedal point" and "pedal tones." In this progression, one sustained note in the bass (or organ pedal) continues throughout the progression, and the chords on top change. Here is an example, with a C being maintained in the bass, and chord changes occurring above the C bass:

$$\frac{C \rightarrow G \rightarrow F \rightarrow G}{C}$$

This sequence of four chords could be repeated with each chord getting four beats. As a general rule of thumb, almost all chord progressions like this will repeat every two, four, or eight measures, regardless of the type of chord progression used.

A fourth type of chord progression involves the idea of stepwise motion in the bass. In the key of C, the notes in the bass (or pedal) might move like this: C,B,A,G,F,E,D,G,C. Notice that the first seven notes in the bass are moving stepwise in a descending motion. If the bass notes were moving like that, the progression could sound like this:

$$C \rightarrow \frac{G}{B} \rightarrow \frac{F}{A} \rightarrow \frac{C7}{G} \rightarrow \frac{F}{F} \rightarrow \frac{C}{E} \rightarrow \frac{D \min 7}{D} \rightarrow \frac{G7}{G} \rightarrow C.$$

This type of chord progression uses chords in *inversion.* That simply means that when a C chord is being played, the bass note could be any of the notes in a C chord — a C or an E or a G. For example, the symbol C over G means that a C chord is in effect, with a G being played in the bass.

This last form of chord progression is probably the most difficult to master, but it contains the most potential for variety. The use of stepwise motion in the bass together with chord inversions will add an exciting dimension to any form of music, whether in chord progressions or regular songs. Music theory books or classes can be of great help to a musician in mastering these concepts. For some suggested music theory texts, see the suggested reading materials at the back of this book.

A given chord progression will not necessarily adhere to just one of these four types of progressions. For instance, it is possible for a chord progression to follow the circle of keys while at the same time incorporating some pedal point. As these four types of progressions are studied, it quickly becomes apparent that the potential for variety in chord progressions is virtually endless, particularly when it is remembered that the rhythmic patterns can also vary considerably with each progression.

CHORDAL HAND SIGNS

Hand signs can be used to communicate what chords to play within a given key. Such signs are especially helpful when an orchestra is improvisationally playing chord progressions in worship. This technique can also be used to indicate the chords being played when a new song is unexpectedly taught. Not all musicians have developed the ability to hear chord changes and play improvisationally in conjunction with changing chords. If a chief musician is able to recognize a chord progression in effect, then he or she can communicate the chords to the orchestra with hand signs so that the musicians can adjust their playing accordingly.

Usually when we try to indicate what chord to play, we call out chord names — C, F, or whatever. But hand signs do not indicate chord *names;* they show chordal *relationships.* If a sign for the "I chord" is formed, the musicians must think *relationship* — they must translate that into the key in which they are playing.

The "I chord" (notice the Roman numeral rather than an Arabic number) is a reference to the chord that is built on the first note of the scale. In the key of C, the "I chord" would be a C chord; in the key of A^b, the "I chord" would be an A^b chord; and so on. So if the orchestra is playing in the key of D, and the leader gives the chordal sign for the "I chord," everyone in the orchestra would play a note in the

D chord.

This system of Roman numeral labeling is a foundational concept in music theory. Each chord that can be played in a given key is assigned a Roman numeral, based upon the root note of that particular chord. For example, in the key of C, the note G is the fifth note in the C scale. So a G chord would be known as the "V chord" in the key of C. If the leader gives the sign for the "V chord," all the musicians would know they should play a G chord or a note that is in the G chord.

The "II chord" is built on the second note of the scale, so in the key of C, the "II chord" would be a D chord. In the key of A^b, the "II chord" would be a B^b chord. Similarly, the "III chord" would be the chord built on the third note of the scale, so in the key of C, the "III chord" would be an E chord. That same principles applies to all six of the chords in any given key.

Here is a simple chart for the keys of C and B^b.

Key of C

	Chord Name	Notes in Chord
I chord =	C	C,E,G
II chord =	D	D Major: D,F$^\#$,A; D minor: D,F,A
III chord =	E	E Major: E,G$^\#$,B; E minor E,G,B
IV chord =	F	F,A,C
V chord =	G	G,B,D
VI chord =	A	A Major: A,C$^\#$E; A minor: A,C,E

Key of B^b

	Chord Name	Notes in Chord
I chord =	B^b	B^b,D,F
II chord =	C	C Major: C,E,G; C minor: C,E^b,G
III chord =	D	D Major: D,F$^\#$,A; D minor: D,F,A
IV chord =	E^b	E^b,G,B^b
V chord =	F	F,A,C
VI chord =	G	G Major: G,B,D; G minor: G,B^b,D

No matter what key is being played, the relationships of the Roman numeral system always apply. The II chord will always be based upon the second note of the scale of the key at hand. This system is very versatile, as it can be used regardless of the key in which the musicians might be playing.

In regard to hand signs for designating these chord progressions, one uncommon approach is the "Curwen Hand Signs." In this system, signs are made with the entire hand and arm. A certain arm position is assigned to each chord — the I chord, II chord, etc. More frequently, the leader will use fingers to designate chords: one finger held up means that the musicians should play the I chord; five fingers denote the V chord; and so on. However, if musicians adopt finger signals for indicating the key signature (described in chapter 10), there will be a problem determining whether the leader is calling for a chord or a key. If he holds up two fingers, for example, does he want a II chord or the key of two sharps? Some definite distinctions will have to be made to avoid confusion of this type. Whatever signals are used, they should communicate clearly and be easy to use while being as inconspicuous as possible.

In order for such a system of signals to be workable, there must be some sort of differentiation between the major and minor modes. For example, suppose the leader holds up three fingers to indicate that the III chord should be played. In the key of C, that would be an E chord. But are the musicians to play an E major or an E minor? There should be some way to communicate to the musicians not only that a III chord is to be played but that it is to be a major (or minor) chord. One way to do that would be to predetermine that a hand sign given at eye level designates a major chord, and a hand sign given at waist level indicates a minor chord.

Let's put these signs in the context of a worship service. Suppose the pianist has initiated a new chord progression, the people are worshiping, and the orchestra wants to join the pianist in the chord progression. The pianist is playing the following progression in the key of C:

$$C \rightarrow \underset{B}{\underline{G}} \rightarrow \underset{A}{\underline{F}} \rightarrow \underset{G}{\underline{C}} \rightarrow F \rightarrow D \text{ min } 7 \rightarrow G7 \rightarrow C.$$

A chordal analysis of this progression (without worrying about the inversions the pianist is playing) is:

$$I \rightarrow V \rightarrow IV \rightarrow I \rightarrow IV \rightarrow ii7 \rightarrow V7 \rightarrow I$$

(Lower case Roman numerals indicate a minor chord.)

The orchestra conductor or chief musician would need to think in terms of chordal analysis, according to the Roman numerals. As the I chord is played, the leader would hold up his hand and give the designated sign for the I chord (at eye level, since it is a major chord). When the progression changes to the V chord, IV chord, and so on, the leader would change the hand signs (and hand position) accordingly.

Most musicians will need extensive training and practice before they will be able to move comfortably in this system. They will have to understand some rudimentary principles of music theory so that when the leader indicates which chord is to be played, each orchestra member will know what notes are in that chord of the key in effect at the time.

A MASTER SONG LIST

One of the basic tools and continual standbys of the worship leader is a master list of all the songs the church sings. This list is invaluable in preparing for the worship service, and it is also very helpful in the middle of a worship service. If the leader feels prompted to take a direction different from his preparation, he can glance at the master list and immediately have some possibilities before him.

Although there are different approaches to compiling a master list of songs, I will describe the system that I have found to be the most helpful for me.

I divide my master song list into two categories — fast songs and slow songs. I find this to be the easiest distinction because the mood of most services can blend into one of these two categories. I then divide the "fast songs" category into two major subdivisions. One is a listing of all the songs according to the individual key in which each is sung. The other subdivision is called "songs in the same tempo." It can be helpful to be able to move from one song to the next not simply by remaining in the same key but also by remaining in the same tempo, so this subdivision provides a grouping of songs which can be sung to the same (fast) tempo. Of course, these songs are all found in the first subdivision, but their placement in the second simply means that they can be sung to the same tempo.

In the list which follows, there are twenty songs in the key of F which can be sung at the same tempo. When I am leading one of those songs, I have nineteen other songs at my disposal to which I can move with relative ease, because there is no change in key or tempo.

The other category is for "slow songs." I divide this category into two major subdivisions also. Again, I group the songs together according to the keys in which they are sung. The second subdivision is a grouping of songs according to topic. Since there is always a need for songs during Communion, I have quite a few listed under that theme. Also, it is good to have a listing of songs suitable for altar calls, as a worship leader can be asked at a moment's notice to lead a song during an altar call. Other themes can be listed as desired or as space permits.

Some songs are easily sung in more than one key, so those are listed under each key; for example, the chorus "Alleluia" is listed under the keys of F, G, and A^b because it can be sung in any of those keys. Also, some songs are adaptable to being sung either fast or slow, and so they appear on both lists — for example, the chorus "Hallelujah, for [the Lord Our God, the Almighty, Reigns]."

This matter of key choice must be determined by the individual worship leader when compiling his list, for different leaders, musicians, and congregations have varying preferences. As a pianist, I frequently use the keys of E^b, A^b, and B^b. But a guitar player would probably prefer keys such as A, E, or B. If a pianist is able to play in most or all keys and a guitar player is not, the pianist will probably adapt to the keys in which the guitar player is comfortable; if the guitar player is able to adapt to the pianist's selection of keys, then that gives added flexibility in key choices. Of course, the keys must be suitable for the average voice range of the congregation.

When I actually put these lists on paper, I type them on standard-size sheets (8-1/2 x 11 inches). I leave small gaps after each key so that there is room to make additions as new songs are learned. When there are too many additions, I revamp and update the entire sheet.

I place these sheets back to back so that "fast songs" are on one side and "slow songs" are on the other. That way I have merely to flip the sheet to have all the songs together. I also cover them with plastic to protect them from rain or spilled coffee and to make them stand upright on the music stand of the piano. They can be covered with the self-stick plastic which is available in standard-size sheets; I also have used overhead transparency sheets, cutting them to fit and fastening them together all around the edges with Scotch tape.

Space is often a problem when assembling a list like this. There may not be enough room on one sheet of paper to list all the songs that the leader would like to include. One solution would be to have two separate lists — one for fast songs and one for slow songs. These could still be put together back to back, but the leader would simply have to handle two separate sheets instead of one. Another solution would be to have a "working list" of the songs that are used most frequently. Still another possibility would be to type the songs on a long sheet of paper and reduce it on a photocopier that has a reduction mode. (Incidentally, I do this with my master list so that I have a complete list on a sheet that will fit inside the cover of my Bible.)

Following are copies of song lists which I prepared some time ago according to the system I have just described.

(over)

FAST SONGS

Key of C
All over the world
Arise, O God
Break forth into
From glory to glory
Horse and rider
I'll never be the
If the same Spirit
Let everything that
Let God arise
Not by might
O Zion, O Zion
Some trust in chariots
They rush on the
We are all rocks
Whoso offereth praise

Key of D
Ah, Lord God
Arise, shine
Clap your hands
I will call upon
I will sing of the

Key of E^b
But as truly as I
City, O city
Come and let us go
Give unto the Lord
Hallelujah, for
Let the people rejoice
My soul escaped
O bless ye the Lord
Sing unto God
The joy of the Lord
We will rejoice in

Key of F
Abiding in the vine
Blessing and honor
Come bless the Lord
From the rising of
God's got an army
God's not dead
He didn't bring (Fm)
He is the King of
I am a part of the
I go to the rock
I hear the sound
I'm confident of
I've got a river of
Lift Jesus higher
Make mention that
Making melody in my

Rejoice in the Lord
The weapons of our
This is my commandment
This is the day
Victory in Jesus
We bring the sacrifice
What a mighty God
Wherever I am

Key of G
Arise and sing
Behold the tabernacle
Let God be magnified
The name of the Lord
The victory is ours

Key of A^b
I'm so glad Jesus
The Lord reigneth
The Lord thy God

Key of B^b
Therefore the redeemed
Thou hast turned my
Unto him be glory

Key of E minor
Awake, O Israel
Every place on which
He is the lion of
In the presence of
Jehovah Jireh
King of kings and Lord
The zeal of God
They rush on the city
You shall go out with

I will call upon
I will sing of the mercies

Key of E^b
But as truly as I live
Give unto the Lord
My soul escaped
Sing unto God
The joy of the Lord

Key of F
Blessing and honor
God's got an army
God's not dead
He is the King of kings
I have put on the garment
I will arise
I've got a river of life
Lift your vision high
Lift Jesus higher
Make mention that his
Making melody in my
The weapons of our warfare
There's therefore now
This is my commandment
This is the day
Victory in Jesus
We bring the sacrifice
What a mighty God we
Wherever I am

Keys of G,A^{b}B^b
Arise and sing
Let God be magnified
Lift up your heads, O
I'm so glad Jesus lifted
The Lord reigneth
Unto him be glory in the

SONGS IN SAME TEMPO

Key of C
Break forth into joy
Horse and rider
If the same Spirit
Let God arise
They rush on the city (Cm)

Key of D
Ah, Lord God
Clap your hands

SLOW SONGS

Key of C
Commune with me
Emmanuel, Emmanuel
Father, I love you
Glory to the Lamb
Jesus Christ
My soul followeth
Worthy is the Lamb

Key of D
I will bless
Let us adore (Dm)
Surely goodness
When I look into

Key of E^b
Deep in my heart
Hallelujah, for
I will sing unto
Let the words of
Let there be glory
Open my eyes, Lord
Praise the name of
Prepare ye the way
Worthy, oh, worthy

Key of F
Alleluia
All hail King Jesus
Bind us together
Bless the Lord, O
Cause me to come
Draw me
Father, I adore you
God is so good
Great is the Lord
He is our peace
He is Lord
Here comes Jesus
His banner over me
His name is wonderful
Humble thyself (Fm)
I exalt thee
I love you, Lord
In my life, Lord
They that wait upon
Thy lovingkindness
The steadfast love
Unto thee, O Lord
We have come into
With my hands lifted

Key of G
Alleluia
Amazing grace
Ascribe greatness
Create in me a clean
From the rising of
He is Lord
Majesty
My soul doth magnify

Key of A^b
Alleluia
Because he lives
He is Lord
Lift up your heads, O
How lovely are thy
We worship and adore

Key of B^b
And I beheld and I
Emmanuel, O Emmanuel
How lovely on
How great thou art
I will give thanks
Lord I love you
Thou art worthy

LOVE
Behold what manner (F)
Bind us together
Father, I adore you
His banner over me
I keep falling in
I love you, Lord
I'm so glad I'm a
Oh, how I love Jesus
This is my commandment
Thy lovingkindness
Lord, I love you (B^b)
Oh, how He loves you and

COMMUNION
Commune with me (C)
Jesus Christ
Worthy is the Lamb
Glory to the Lamb
Holy, Holy
I will praise Him (D)
Worthy, oh, worthy are
At the cross (F)
Bind us together
Draw me nearer
For God so loved the world

He is our peace
He touched me
He's the Savior of my
Jesus Christ is made to
Oh, how marvelous
Search me, O God
There is a river
Alleluia (G)
Amazing grace
Create in me a clean
I am so glad that our Father
When I survey the wondrous
Oh, how he loves you and (B^b)
There is power in the blood
Thou art worthy
And I beheld and I heard
Emmanuel, Emmanuel

ALTAR CALL
He is all I need (C)
I have decided to follow
I surrender all
Cause me to come (E^b)
Just as I am
Father, I adore you (F)
Jesus, be the Lord of
Seek ye first
The greatest thing
He is Lord

MISSIONS
All over the world (C)
Father, I love you
Let God arise
But as truly as I (E^b)
God's got an army (F)
Lift your vision high
How lovely on (B^b)
The Lord reigneth
Unto him be glory

REFERENCES
AND RESOURCES

Ades, Hawley. *Choral Arranging.* Delaware Water Gap, PA: Shawnee Press, Inc., 1966.

Alford, Delton L. *Music in the Pentecostal Church.* Cleveland, TN: Pathway Press, 1967.

Appleby, David P. *History of Church Music.* Chicago: Moody Press, 1965.

Argue, Pat. *Creative Music Ministry.* Minneapolis, MN: Alpha Editions, a Division of Burgess Publishing Company, 1982.

Ashton, Joseph N. *Music in Worship.* Boston: Pilgrim, 1943.

Bailey, Albert E. *The Gospel in Hymns.* New York: Charles Scribner's Sons, 1951.

Baker, E. Charlotte. *On Eagle's Wings.* Seattle, WA: The King's Temple, 1979.

Baker, Paul. *Why Should the Devil Have All the Good Music?* Waco, TX: Word Books, 1979.

Barth, Karl. *Worship: Its Theology and Practice.* London: Lutterworth, 1965.

Bay, William. *The Beauty of Worship.* Pacific, MO: Mel Bay Publications, Inc.

Benson, Dennis C. *Creative Worship in Youth Ministry.* Loveland, CO: Group Books, 1985.

Boschman, LaMar. *The Prophetic Song.* Bedford, TX: Revival Press, 1986.

—————— . *The Rebirth of Music.* Little Rock, AR: Revival Press, 1980.

Breed, David R. *The History and Use of Hymns and Hymn-Tunes.* New York: AMS Press, 1975.

Cornill, Carl Heinrich. *Music in the Old Testament.* Chicago: The Open Court Publishing Company, 1909.

Cornwall, Judson. *Elements of Worship.* South Plainfield, NJ: Bridge Publishing, Inc., 1985.

_____. *Let Us Draw Near.* South Plainfield, NJ: Logos International, 1977.

_____. *Let Us Praise.* Plainfield, NJ: Logos International, 1973.

_____. *Let Us Worship.* South Plainfield, NJ: Bridge Publishing, Inc., 1983.

_____. *Meeting God.* Altamonte Springs, FL: Strang Communications, 1987.

Crouch, Andre. *Through It All.* Waco, TX: Word Books, 1974.

Darrand, Tom Craig, and Shupe, Anson. "Metaphors of Social Control in a Pentecostal Sect." *Studies in Religion and Society,* Volume Six. New York: The Edwin Mellen Press.

Delamont, Vic. *The Ministry of Music in the Church.* Chicago: Moody Press, 1980.

Ellsworth, Donald P. *Christian Music in Contemporary Witness.* Grand Rapids, MI: Baker Book House, 1979.

Flynn, Leslie B. *Worship: Together We Celebrate.* Wheaton, IL: Victor Books, 1983.

Gaglardi, B. Maureen. *The Key of David.* Vancouver, British Columbia: Mission Press, 1966.

Green, Joseph F. *Biblical Foundations for Church Music.* Nashville, TN: Convention Press, 1967.

Grout, Donald Jay. *A History of Western Music.* New York: W.W. Norton and Company, Inc., 1960.

Halter, Carl. *God and Man in Music.* St. Louis, MO: Concordia Publishing House, 1963.

_____. *The Practice of Sacred Music.* St. Louis, MO: Concordia Publishing House, 1955.

Hardin, H. Grady; Quillian, Joseph D.; and White, James F. *The Celebration of the Gospel.* Nashville, TN: Abingdon Press, 1964.

Hibbert, Mike, and Hibbert, Vivian. *Music Ministry.* Christchurch, New Zealand, 1982.

Hilson, Stephen E. *What Do You Say to a Naked Spotlight?* Leawood, KS: Sound III, Inc., 1972.

Hinnebusch, Paul. *Praise: A Way of Life.* Ann Arbor, MI: Servant Books, 1976.

Hoon, Paul Waitman. *The Integrity of Worship.* Nashville, TN: Abingdon Press, 1971.

Hustad, Donald P. *Jubilate! Church Music in the Evangelical Tradition.* Carol Stream, IL: Hope Publishing Company, 1981.

Johnson, Charles. *One Hundred and One Famous Hymns.* Delavan, WI: Charles Hallberg & Company, Inc., 1982.

Jones, Judie. *Succeeding as a Woman in Music Leadership.* Soquel, CA: Creative Arts Development, 1983.

Julian, John. *Dictionary of Hymnology,* Volumes I & II. Grand Rapids, MI: Kregel Publications, 1985.

Keith, Edmond D. *Christian Hymnody.* Nashville, TN: Convention Press, 1956.

Kendrick, Graham. *Learning to Worship as a Way of Life.* Minneapolis, MN: Bethany House Publishers, 1984.

Kerr, Phil. *Music in Evangelism.* Glendale, CA: Gospel Music Publishers, 1959.

Lang, Paul Henry. *Music in Western Civilization.* New York: W.W. Norton and Company, 1941.

Larson, Bob. *Rock.* Wheaton, IL: Tyndale House, 1980.

_____. *Rock and the Church.* Carol Stream, IL: Creation House, 1971.

Law, Terry. *The Power of Praise and Worship.* Tulsa, OK: Victory House Publishers, 1985.

Lawhead, Steve. *Rock Reconsidered.* Downers Grove, IL: InterVarsity Press, 1981.

Lovelace, Austin C., and Rice, William C. *Music and Worship in the Church.* Nashville, TN: Abingdon Press, 1960.

Lunde, Alfred E. *Christian Education Through Music.* Wheaton, IL: Evangelical Teacher Training Association, 1978.

Madge, Wallace. *Bible Music and Its Development.* London: Chester House Publications, 1977.

Marsh, Don J. *Music Is a Ministry.* Scottsdale, AZ: Kaydon Publications.

Martin, Ralph P. *The Worship of God.* Grand Rapids, MI: William B. Eerdmans Publishing Company, 1982.

_____ . *Worship in the Early Church.* Grand Rapids, MI: William B. Eerdmans Publishing Company, 1964.

McLuhan, Marshall. *The Medium Is the Message.* New York: Bantam Books, 1967.

Meyer, Leonard B. *Emotion and Meaning in Music.* Chicago: University of Chicago Press, 1956.

Miller, Andrea Wells. *A Choir Director's Handbook.* Waco, TX: Word Books, 1981.

Mitchell, Robert H. *Ministry and Music.* Philadelphia: The Westminster Press, 1978.

Mowinckel, Sigmund. *The Psalms in Israel's Worship.* Nashville, TN: Abingdon Press, 1962.

Murchison, Anne. *Praise and Worship: In Earth As It Is in Heaven.* Waco, TX: Word Books, 1981.

Nicholls, William. *Jacob's Ladder: The Meaning of Worship.* Richmond, VA: John Knox Press, 1958.

Nininger, Ruth. *Growing a Musical Church.* Nashville, TN: Convention Press, 1969.

Ortlund, Anne. *Up With Worship.* Glendale, CA: Regal Book Division, Gospel Light Publications, 1975.

Osbeck, Kenneth W. *The Ministry of Music.* Grand Rapids, MI: Kregel Publications, 1971.

Reynolds, I.E. *Music and the Scriptures.* Nashville, TN: Broadman Press, 1942.

Reynolds, William Jensen. *A Survey of Christian Hymnody.* New York: Holt, Rhinehart and Winston, 1963.

Roberts, Debby. *Rejoice: A Biblical Study of the Dance.* Little Rock, AR: Revival Press, 1982.

Rookmaaker, H.R. *Modern Art and the Death of a Culture.* London: InterVarsity Press, 1970.

Routley, Erik. *Music Leadership in the Church.* Nashville, TN: Abingdon Press, 1967.

_____. *Twentieth Century Church Music.* New York: Oxford University Press, 1964.

Rowley, H.H. *Worship in Ancient Israel.* Southampton, England: The Camelot Press Ltd., 1974.

Rudolph, Otto. *The Idea of the Holy.* London: Oxford University Press, 1923, 1925.

Sankey, Ira D. *My Life and the Story of the Gospel Hymns.* New York: Harper and Brothers Publishers, 1907.

Segler, Franklin M. *Christian Worship: Its Theology and Practice.* Nashville, TN: Broadman Press, 1967.

Sendrey, Alfred. *Music in Ancient Israel.* London: Vision Press Limited, 1969.

Skoglund, John E. *Worship in the Free Churches.* Valley Forge, PA: The Judson Press, 1965.

Sorge, Sheldon. *Improvisation for the Church Pianist.* Lima, NY: Elim Bible Institute, 1979.

Steere, Dwight. *Music in Protestant Worship.* Richmond, VA: John Knox Press, 1960.

Stevens, John Robert. *Worship.* North Hollywood, CA: Living Word Publications.

Stevenson, Robert. *Protestant Church Music in America.* New York: W.W. Norton and Company, Inc., 1966.

Sydnor, James Rawlings. *Hymns and Their Uses.* Carol Stream, IL: Agape, 1982.

Taylor, Jack R. *The Hallelujah Factor.* Nashville, TN: Broadman Press, 1983.

Terry, Lindsey. *How to Build an Evangelistic Church Music Program.* Nashville, TN: Thomas Nelson Publishers, Inc., 1974.

Thayer, Lynn W. *The Church Music Handbook.* Grand Rapids, MI: Zondervan Publishing House, 1971.

Thomas, Edith Lovell. *Music in Christian Education.* New York: Abingdon Press, 1953.

Topp, Dale. *Music in the Christian Community.* Grand Rapids, MI: William B. Eerdmans Publishing Company, 1976.

Trombley, Charles. *Praise: Faith in Action.* Indianola, IA: Fountain Press, Inc., 1978.

Truscott, Graham. *Every Christian's Ministry.* Calgary, Alberta: Gordon Donaldson Missionary Foundation, 1977.

_____ . *The Power of His Presence.* San Diego, CA: Restoration Temple, 1969.

Urang, Gunnar. *Church Music for the Glory of God.* Moline, IL: Christian Service Foundation, 1956.

Wainwright, Geoffrey. *Doxology — The Praise of God in Worship, Doctrine, and Life.* New York: Oxford University Press, 1980.

Wayland, John T. *Planning Congregational Worship Services.* Nashville, TN: Broadman Press, 1971.

White, James F. *Christian Worship in Transition.* Nashville, TN: Abingdon Press, 1976.

_____ . *Introduction to Christian Worship.* Nashville, TN: Abingdon Press, 1980.

Whittlesey, Federal Lee. *A Comprehensive Program of Church Music.* Philadelphia: The Westminster Press, 1957.

Wienandt, Elwyn. *Opinions on Church Music.* Waco: TX: Baylor University Press, 1974.

Willis, Wendell. *Worship.* Austin, TX: Sweet Publishing Company, 1973.

Wilson, John F. *An Introduction to Church Music.* Chicago: Moody Press, 1979.

Wohlgemuth, Paul W. *Rethinking Church Music.* Chicago: Moody Press, 1973.

MUSIC THEORY TEXTS

Clough, John. *Scales, Intervals, Keys, and Triads.* New York: W.W. Norton and Co., Inc., 1964.

> I recommend this text as an excellent self-study guide for the beginning theory student.

Lee, William F. *Music Theory Dictionary.* Miami Beach, FL: Hansen House, 1965.

Ottman, Robert W. *Elementary Harmony.* Englewood Cliffs, NJ: Prentice-Hall, Inc., 1970.

Piston, Walter. *Harmony.* New York: W.W. Norton and Company, 1978.